Pick for Humans:
made plain

Pick for Humans:
A powerful business system made plain

James Binney and Mark Newman

McGRAW-HILL BOOK COMPANY

London · New York · St Louis · San Francisco · Auckland
Bogotá · Caracas · Hamburg · Lisbon · Madrid · Mexico
Milan · Montreal · New Delhi · Panama · Paris · San Juan
São Paulo · Singapore · Sydney · Tokyo · Toronto

Published by

McGRAW-HILL Book Company (UK) Limited

SHOPPENHANGERS ROAD · MAIDENHEAD · BERKSHIRE · ENGLAND

TEL: 0628-23432; FAX: 0628-770224

British Library Cataloguing in Publication Data

Binney, James
  Pick for humans: a powerful business system made plain.
  1. Business firms. Applications of computer systems.
  Operating systems: Pick
  I. Title II. Newman, Mark
  658.0543

  ISBN 0-07-707243-X

Library of Congress Cataloging-in-Publication Data

Binney, James
  Pick for humans: a powerful business system made plain /
    James Binney and Mark Newman.
  p.   cm.
  Includes index.
  ISBN 0-07-707243-X
  1. PICK (Computer operation system) 2. Business–Data processing.
  I. Newman, Mark. II. Title.
  HF5548.4.P53B56 1991
  650'.0285'5446–dc20   90–41738

1234 M&AT 9321

Typeset by James Binney and Mark Newman at the University of London Computer Centre and printed and bound in Great Britain by M & A Thomson Litho Ltd, East Kilbride, Scotland.

Contents

PART TWO   PICK FOR PROGRAMMERS AND SYSTEM MANAGERS

8   Pick BASIC

About this book

From now into the foreseeable future *everybody* in the business world must be enough of a computer buff to be able to get good work out of a desktop machine. But although machines of great power are now commonplace, people who know how to get even adequate results out of these devices are woefully scarce. We believe an important contributor to this scarcity is the incomprehensibility to ordinary people of the bulk of computer literature. All too often companies market products that represent tens of thousands of hours of work by brilliant engineers, with incomprehensible manuals, tattily produced and often not even written in any recognizable dialect of English.

We have found this problem particularly acute in the case of the Pick operating system, all the books on which appear to have been written by experts for experts rather than by humans for humans. What Pick needs is a decent guide that explains things clearly at the level of ordinary business people. This book represents our attempt to meet this need.

The book is divided into two parts. Part One explains the basic things that every user of a Pick machine needs to know, starting from the beginning with what a computer *is* and what makes a Pick computer special. We then cover in turn how data are stored on a Pick machine, how you can search through them for the information you need, and how you can get them printed out. In Part Two we discuss things that you'll need to know only if you have to manage or program a Pick machine: how to edit files; how to keep the disk tidy and secure against hackers; how to write programs in Pick's programming languages, Pick BASIC and PROC. At the end of the book you will find various useful lists and the source code of diverse utilities, including a screen editor.

We include many sample dialogues with the computer. The user's contributions are printed in green to distinguish them from the computer's, which are in black.

James Binney
Mark Newman
Oxford, 1990

Trademark acknowledgments

Apple, Mac and Macintosh are trademarks of Apple Computer Inc.
Centronics is a trademark of the Centronics Data Computer Corp.
dBASE is a trademark of Ashton-Tate.
DEC, VAX and VT are trademarks of the Digital Equipment Corp.
DOS and OS/2 are trademarks of International Business Machines Corp. and the Microsoft Corp.
Epson is a trademark of the Seiko Epson Corp.
IBM, PC and AT are trademarks of International Business Machines Corp.
Intel and 386 are trademarks of the Intel Corp.
Motorola is a trademark of Motorola Inc.
Pick, Advanced Pick and R83 are trademarks of Pick Systems Inc.
Reality is a trademark of McDonnel Douglas Computer Systems.
Revelation is a trademark of Cosmos Inc.
UNIX is a trademark of AT&T.
Word is a trademark of the Microsoft Corp.
WordPerfect is a trademark of the WordPerfect Corp.

Part One

Basic Pick

1   What is a computer?

Though this book is specifically about Pick computers, it is well worth while taking a few pages here at the beginning to draw a rough outline of what a computer is and how it works. If you have not used a computer before, or if you are not very clear why computers behave the way they do, you will probably find it useful to read this chapter. It can be very helpful, even in ordinary day-to-day work with a computer, to have some idea of what goes on inside one. And surprisingly, it's not very hard to understand.

Computers have actually been around for a long time—much longer than many people suppose. The first true computers were mechanical, and date from the first half of the nineteenth century. The reason for the sudden up-surge in their popularity in the last decades was the invention of *electronic* computers, which are far easier to manufacture and operate than their me-chanical counterparts, and in particular *micro-electronic* computers, a tech-nological offshoot of the American space programme, which are very cheap as well.

Computers were originally created to perform arithmetic calculations quickly and accurately, and to save their makers from the tedium of long division and logarithms. But any pocket calculator will do sums—today's computers offer far more than this. In the modern world a computer has two important jobs to do:

(i) the storage and retrieval of large quantities of information (or 'data') in the form of words or numbers;

(ii) the manipulation of these data.

Long before the technology to build computers existed, it was realized that it should be possible to create machines to take these jobs out of the hands of humans, and in 1937 the English mathematician Alan Turing described how he thought such a machine would work. His idea was that a computer would consist broadly of two parts: the first, the **processor**, would undertake all the tasks involved in manipulating data, while the second, the **memory**, would store the data. Remarkably, all modern computers are constructed in exactly the way Turing described, though he himself died in 1954 when effective computers were still figments of fertile imaginations. Let us now examine in more detail the rôles of the processor and the memory in a modern computer.

The processor, or **CPU** (which stands for "central processing unit"), is the brains of a computer. In the simplest of computers the CPU consists of just one silicon chip, about the size of your thumbnail, called a **microprocessor**, but in most business machines it is made up of several chips which share the job of data manipulation, so that tasks are completed more quickly. The CPU contains millions of specialized circuits for performing all kinds of tasks: it has circuits designed to do arithmetic at enormous speed, circuits for making simple decisions, and circuits for moving data from one bit of the memory to another.

The memory is essentially a vast array of identical boxes in which the processor can store data. Each box can hold one **byte** of data (also known as a **character**), which means one letter, digit, space or punctuation mark. A single word in a document stored on a computer will occupy as many boxes as it has letters, and a book the size of this one maybe a million boxes. The boxes are numbered like the houses in a street to distinguish them from one another, and a typical computer's memory might consist of a hundred million of them—a hundred million bytes, a hundred million letters.

Essentially what the computer does is this: it has a numbered list of instructions, a **program**,[1] written in a special form that it understands, and it works through these instructions in order, performing one task according to what each instruction says, and then moving on to the next. This process is called **running**, or sometimes **executing**, the program. The instructions are in fact just numbers, and they are stored in the memory in exactly the same way as all the other data. A typical instruction tells the machine to fetch a byte from box number such-and-such, put one away there, perform a calculation with a couple of numbers, or to make a 'jump' (i.e., to go to instruction number such-and-such, and to continue obeying instructions from there). A more cunning possibility, is that of a 'conditional jump', whereby the computer is instructed to consider such-and-such a number, and to make a jump to some other part of the program only if that number is less than ten, or greater than twenty, or equal to 3.14159 or whatever.

With a little forethought, lists of instructions, programs, can be constructed to perform the most complex manipulations on data stored within the computer's memory.

However, to be of interest to humans the results of the CPU's manipulations must somehow be communicated to the computer's operator. To achieve this, computers are equipped with 'ports'—sockets into which one can plug

---

[1] In Britain this word would normally be spelt 'programme' but it has become accepted practice to spell it without the final 'me' when one is referring to a *computer* program, so as to distinguish it from the other, more ancient kind of programme.

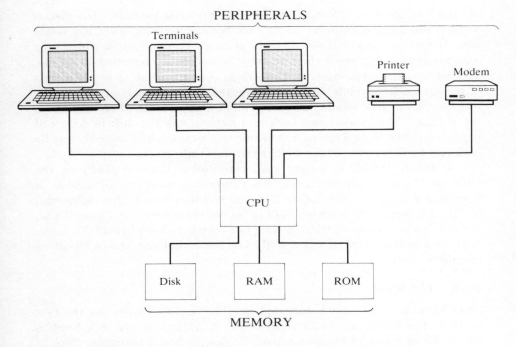

Figure 1.1 Schematic diagram of the main components of a computer

various pieces of hardware like 'terminals' and 'printers' (collectively known as 'peripherals'). The computer then communicates with the world at large by sending data from the memory out of these ports down the wires, so that they appear on screens, or get printed on pieces of paper, according to the instructions in the programs. We explain about ports and peripherals in §1.2.

This then is, in essence, all there is to a computer: a processor to move and manipulate data, a memory to hold data and instructions for the processor, and peripherals plugged into ports so that the machine can communicate with its operators.

1.1   The memory

From the point of view of a mathematician such as Turing a computer consists of just a CPU and memory. But in practice things are more complicated than this because the memory is actually composed of three distinct blocks.

1.1.1   The disk

The **disk** (often called a 'hard disk' to distinguish it from the 'floppy disks' used by microcomputers, sometimes called a 'disk drive' by people with lots of breath to spare) is the computer's main storehouse for data. The disk *is* actually disk shaped, though you can't tell because it comes sealed in a metal box. In fact it consists of several disks of magnetic material on which your data are recorded in much the same way as sounds are recorded on a tape. When the computer is running, these disks spin round at many thousands of revolutions per minute and data is written on them, or read off, by tiny magnets called **disk heads**, skimming about a thousandth of an inch above the surface. The heads move back and forth across the disk in search of requested pieces of data in much the same way as you might move the needle back and forth across a record to find your favourite track.

A disk is capable of storing vast quantities of data—typically on the order of a hundred million bytes. When discussing such large quantities of information there are two technical terms you may find useful: **kilobyte**, or "K" for short, which means 1024 bytes (or characters); and **megabyte**, or "meg", which means 1,048,576 (i.e., just over a million) bytes.[2] Thus one might well hear our typical disk described by the computer-wise as a "hundred megabyte" one.

1.1.2   The RAM

Disks have one rather grave disadvantage. They cannot be read by the CPU anything like as fast as the CPU can think. It might take the disk heads a hundredth of a second to move across the disk to find a particular piece of information, and in the worst case it could be a tenth of a second before the CPU got the data it needed. If you wanted thousands of pieces of data from all over the disk the tenths of a second would quickly mount up and you could be waiting minutes, hours or even days for the machine to find them all for you. Fortunately, there is an alternative to the hard disk: the Random Access Memory or **RAM**, a special kind of silicon chip which performs exactly the same job as the disk, but does it *much* faster. Typically it takes about a hundred millionth of a second to find a specified piece of data 'in RAM'.

So why don't we forget about the disk altogether and just stick with RAM? Two reasons:

(i) RAM is very expensive, byte for byte, compared to a disk, and a computer with 100 megabytes of RAM would be well out of most people's price range.

(ii) The data stored in the RAM are lost when the computer is turned off, whereas those stored on a disk are not. It would clearly render your computer useless if you had to enter all your data over again every time you turned the computer on. Even if you were to leave the computer on

---

[2] The reason for choosing these slightly awkward numbers rather than nice round ones, lies in the 'binary' arithmetic system employed by computers; one kilobyte is actually 2^{10} bytes and one megabyte is 2^{20} bytes. Luckily, however, there is no need to memorize the exact figures. Remember only that they are about one thousand and one million respectively.

all the time, there would inevitably be a power failure someday, and then you would be in deep trouble.

So the accepted strategy is to compromise and build computers with both disks *and* RAM. The typical Pick machine has between one and ten megabytes of RAM as well as a hundred megabytes or so of disk space. When a program requires a piece of data that is stored on the disk, the computer locates that piece of data, and copies it from the disk into RAM. Now if you ask for the same piece of data again the computer doesn't have to fetch it from the disk—it can get it out of the RAM, which is much quicker. If you decide you wish to change this bit of data, you only have to change the copy in RAM and not the one on the disk, and so you save time again. When you have finally finished with your piece of data, you can instruct the computer to copy it back onto the disk again, so that any changes you may have made will be preserved there, even after the machine is turned off. Thus, during the execution of a program, every piece of data that the program needs has, in theory, only to be retrieved from the disk once, and copied back onto the disk once, no matter how many times you look at it or change it.

While the CPU is perfectly happy to read data requested by your program from either the RAM or the disk in this way, it is completely unable to take its next *instruction* from the disk—it simply will not wait the age required to do this. So when you tell your computer to run a program, the first thing it does is to copy the instructions that make up that program from the disk where they are normally stored, into RAM. Only when it has done this does the computer start to execute the program. The inability of computers to run programs until they have been copied into RAM does not usually affect the user much—it takes only a second or so for the machine to make a copy of even the largest of programs. However, for the builder of computers it does pose a couple of technical problems.

The first concerns the running of very large programs. You will sometimes come across a program so large that it won't fit into your computer's RAM. Many machines cannot run such programs, but more sophisticated ones, including all Pick computers, can, by copying blocks of instructions into RAM in such a way that the next instruction is always waiting there ready when the CPU needs it. Machines that can accomplish this trick are called **virtual memory** machines.

The second problem brings us on to the last type of memory found in modern computers—the ROM.

1.1.3   The ROM

If the CPU will only take instructions from RAM and the contents of the RAM are erased every time the machine is switched off, where does the computer get its instructions from when it is first switched on? The answer is that it gets them from a "read-only memory chip", or **ROM**. This is a special type of memory chip which is as fast as RAM, but whose contents never change, either when the computer is running or when it is turned off. The name "ROM" derives from this property that it can be read by the CPU but not written in.[3] The CPU is quite happy to take its instructions from ROM in exactly the way it takes them from RAM.

So the idea is this. We put a little bit of ROM containing a simple program into the computer, and when the computer is first turned on the CPU looks for instructions in this ROM. Having found the simple program it starts to execute it. Under the direction of this program, the CPU copies other, larger programs from the disk into RAM, and then these other programs start running and take over control of the computer and we have business as usual. Way back in the dark ages, some anonymous electrical engineer dubbed this process **bootstrapping** because it seemed logically equivalent to picking yourself up by your own bootstraps and flying away. And from the same root the verb 'to boot' (a computer) has entered the language, meaning to start (the computer) up.

1.2 Peripherals

Once you understand roughly the rôles taken by CPU, disk, RAM and ROM in running a computer, you understand more about how the machine works than most people. These four components together perform all the complicated tasks one takes for granted of a computer. However, to be useful the computer must also be equipped with mechanisms by which data can be fed into it, and answers got out. These jobs are undertaken by the class of devices known as **peripherals**—'terminals', 'printers' and 'modems'. In this section we explain briefly what these devices do.

The peripherals we shall discuss are usually not housed in the same box that houses the computer's main components—the CPU, the disk drive, and so on—they are connected to it by cables. The cables have plugs on the end, and are plugged into sockets on the main box. These sockets are called **ports**. When the computer wants to communicate with the outside world it sends data out through its ports. Ports are discussed in more detail in §§4.2.3, 7.10 and Appendix 1.

1.2.1 Terminals

By far the most important type of peripheral on a Pick computer system is the **terminal**. A terminal is the familiar public face of a computer—the thing with the computer screen on top and the keyboard in front. It is used for

---

[3] "How then", we hear you ask, "do a ROM's contents come to be in it in the first place?" Well the chip is manufactured with them already in there—the contents of a read-only memory are built into it in the factory.

feeding instructions and data into the computer (through the keyboard) and for getting replies out (on the screen). Many computers have lots of terminals connected to them so that lots of people may use the computer at once. Given long enough cables you can scatter your terminals over many widely separated locations so that there will be one near you wherever you are. (It is perfectly possible for someone in Britain to connect his or her terminal to a computer in America. In fact it's frequently done.)

A terminal is a very simple beast, with very little more to it than the screen and keyboard. This makes terminals cheap to buy—much cheaper than buying a separate computer for each person who has cause to use one. On the other hand, many businesses already own a small fleet of personal computers like IBMs or Macintoshes for word processing. And, seeing as these computers are also equipped with a screen and a keyboard, it seems a bit of a waste of money to go buying terminals when you have almost everything you need right in front of you. Mindful of this, enterprising computer programmers have written programs for micro-computers that will fool a bigger computer into thinking there is one of these simple-minded terminals on the line, when actually it's your IBM PC. Such a program is called a **terminal emulator**. There are terminal emulators available for most common micros. (If you wish to connect your micro to your Pick computer in this way you will also need a cable to plug the micro into the port on the main computer case. Getting hold of the right cable can often be just as difficult as getting hold of the terminal emulator program.)

1.2.2 Printers

There are times when merely seeing information on the screen of a terminal is not enough, you want to have it printed on a real piece of paper—you want 'hard copy'. If you need to print invoices, or receipts, or pay-slips, or the totals of the accounts, or anything like that, then you want hard copy. A **printer** is the machine to do this for you. A printer is connected to a cable plugged into one of the ports on the computer in exactly the same way as terminals are.

There are a number of different types of printer. These days the two most common are 'laser printers', which are quick, quiet and produce very neat results on paper but which are expensive to buy and maintain, and 'dot matrix' printers, which are cheap to buy and run, but produce a lower quality of print. Disappearing fast, but still available from a few manufacturers, are the 'daisy wheel' and 'golf ball' varieties of printer, which produce print of a quality somewhere in between the other two, but which are rather slow in their work and noisy with it.

1.2.3   Modems

It is worth just mentioning one other type of peripheral. A **modem** is a device with two cables coming out of it, one of which is plugged into a port on your computer and the other into a normal telephone line. The modem translates the data it receives from the computer into sounds and sends them off down the telephone wires. It also translates the sounds it hears on the phone line into data again and communicates them to the computer. Thus two computers with modems connected can 'talk' to one another over the phone—they can swap data. On occasions this can be very useful.

1.3   The operating system

After reading the preceding sections of this chapter you will appreciate that your computer is a complicated animal, comprising many different lesser machines, each important, each doing its own bit. It is one of the jobs of the CPU to keep the whole thing together and coordinate efforts so that the job gets done. There is a vast, sprawling program—the **operating system**—which steers it through this job; in many ways the operating system is the most important program on the computer. It is their operating systems that distinguish computers from one another. A computer can be no better than its operating system. Pick computers use the operating system known as **Pick**. On the whole Pick is a good operating system.

The jobs of the operating system are:

(i) To manage the computer's memories—the disk and the RAM. It is the operating system that pins down exactly where the data you want are on the disk and gets them for you. It is the operating system that keeps track of which bits of data have copies in the RAM and which don't.

(ii) To handle the computer's peripherals. It is the operating system that decides which data should be sent to which terminal, so that things don't get muddled up when several people use the computer at once. It is the operating system that watches your keyboard and notes everything you type. It is the operating system that takes care of printers and modems.

Pick, however, does much more for you than this. In the next chapter we discuss some of the other things Pick will do.

2   What can pick do for you?

Running any kind of organization involves collecting, keeping up to date and referencing a considerable body of data. For example, the administrators of a club must keep an accurate record of each member—his or her name, address, year of election to the club and so on—as well as a similar record of each of the club's employees, records of stock, sales, taxes, debts, investments, etc. Traditionally these records have been kept on index cards or in ledgers. But over the last decade, as computer hardware has become ever cheaper, more and more clubs, partnerships and small businesses have taken to keeping their records on some kind of computer, because such records can be interrogated much more rapidly than traditionally held records and are in principle easier to keep up to date. These are very substantial advantages; they allow the organization to make its decisions on the basis of accurate and up to date information, and to explore the likely consequences of alternative policies in moments. And yet the world is filled with horror stories of organizations thrown into pandemonium by attempts to computerize their affairs. In these circumstances it is not surprising that many club treasurers, senior partners and proprietors of small businesses respond with dread and anxiety to suggestions that their organization computerize its records.

The aim of this chapter is to explore what is involved in the computerization of a small- to medium-sized organization and to explain how the Pick computer operating system can contribute towards the successful attainment of this goal. Our discussion will be highly condensed so don't panic if we seem to go too fast. Most of the topics we touch on are covered in greater detail later in the book, especially in Chapters 3 and 4.

2.1   Divide and rule

The first step in ordering any body of data is to group it under headings, and within each heading to group under sub-headings and so on until the individual units become small enough to be easily managed. For example, the material of this book is divided into chapters, each chapter into sections, most sections into sub-sections and a few sub-sections are further divided into topics. Similarly, many businesses group their data under headings such as Stocks, Finance, Marketing and Personnel. Then within each area there are further sub-divisions. For example, under the heading "Personnel" you might keep personal data on employees, records of pay and tax records. A satisfactory computer operating system must also divide an organization's data into units and sub-units to reflect this structure. Let's see how Pick divides a body of data, which taken as a whole we shall refer to as a **database**.

We start at the top, with the largest unit of information recognized by Pick. This is the 'Account'; in our example Stocks, Finance, Marketing and Personnel would all have their own account. So you might start building your database by creating an account called "PERSONNEL" which is to contain all information pertaining to employees. Figure 2.1 illustrates this situation.

The data held within each account are divided into 'files'. So within the account "PERSONNEL" you create a file called "STAFF" to hold the personal details of employees and one called "PAY" to hold details of rates and amounts of pay and deductions.

Pick divides the data held in any file into 'items'. Thus within the files "STAFF" and "PAY" we might allocate each employee one item for the storage of his or her personal details. For example, J. J. Newman's items in each file might be called "NEWMAN-J-J". Within the item "NEWMAN-J-J" of the file "STAFF" you would store details of full names, date of birth, address, date of appointment, etc., and within the item "NEWMAN-J-J" of the file "PAY" you would store Newman's basic and overtime rates of pay, monthly totals of gross and net pay, taxes deducted, and so on.

Within an item Pick divides data into 'attributes'. So the first attribute of the item "NEWMAN-J-J" in the file "STAFF" might contain his surname "Newman", the second attribute his initials "J. J.", the third attribute his title "Mr" and so forth.

Pick allows you to divide each attribute into further sub-units called 'values' and 'sub-values'. Thus the fourth attribute of the item "NEWMAN-J-J" in the file "STAFF" might contain Newman's forenames "James Jeffrey", each name being a separate value.

We see then that Pick enables you successively to divide your data into accounts, files, items, attributes, values and sub-values; a total of six levels of structure. This is more than adequate for the overwhelming majority of administrative applications.

2.2   To name is to rule

Of course dividing your data into manageable sub-units is only the first step in the creation of a useful database. Having divided up the data neatly you need

Figure 2.1   The structure of a Pick database. An 'account' such as PERSONNEL may be
thought of as a filing cabinet. An individual 'file' within an account may be compared with
one of the filing cabinet's drawers. An 'item' within a file is like a folder within the drawer.
An 'attribute' within an item is like a piece of paper within the folder. Attributes may be
divided into values and sub-values in the same way that a page of text can be divided into
lines and words. See Chapter 3 for a detailed explanation of these divisions of the database.

to be able to enquire after any given bit of information in a simple fashion. For example, you need to be able to ask the computer "what's Newman's first forename?" and get a speedy reply.

2.2.1   Dictionaries

Suppose you have set things up so that each employee's forenames are held as values in the fourth attribute of his or her item in the file "STAFF" under the account "PERSONNEL" (see Figure 2.2). Then from the computer's point of view it would be handiest if you asked 'what do you have stored in the first value of the fourth attribute of the item "NEWMAN-J-J" in the file "STAFF" under the account "PERSONNEL"?' But computers exist to serve users, not users to serve computers, and it is unacceptable to be expected to remember exactly where you placed your data; in a good system the computer remembers where you have put things as well as what you have put there. So the computer needs to understand what you mean by Newman's "first forename" and be able to locate it without further ado. Pick is very unusual amongst computer operating systems in providing such a facility.

The way Pick enables you to ask for a "first forename" is as follows (see §3.5 for details). Each Pick file is accompanied by a list of the words you can use when asking questions about the contents of that file—this list is called the file's 'dictionary'. When you set up the database and the location of each piece of information is still fresh in your mind, you define a word, say "FIRST.FORENAME", to mean "the contents of the first value of the fourth attribute". Once you have defined the word in this way, you can forget exactly where you are storing forenames and concentrate on more interesting questions, since it will henceforth be possible to ask simply for the FIRST.FORENAME of NEWMAN-J-J or any employee in the database.

2.2.2   Gluing data together

We shall see in §3.5.1 that Pick's dictionary facility is a very powerful one, because the words in a dictionary can point to a grouping of several different pieces of information rather than to just a single data item such as a forename. For example, when printing labels for pay packets, you might want the machine to write "Mr J. J. Newman". This line contains information held on three different attributes of the item "NEWMAN-J-J": you put "Newman" into the first attribute, "J. J." into the second attribute and the title "Mr" into the third attribute (see Figure 2.2). Hence we are in danger of having to tell the machine to print on the first line of each label TITLE, INITIALS and SURNAME. This would be tedious, so Pick allows us to define a word, "NAME", which refers to these three pieces of information at once. Then when we tell the machine to print NEWMAN-J-J's NAME, it prints "Mr J. J. Newman" as required.

NEWMAN-J-J

Surname:	NEWMAN . . . .
Initials:	J·J· . . . .
Title:	MR . . . .
Forenames:	JAMES JEFFREY . . . .
Address:	14, HOME AVE, WOKING, SURREY . .
Telephone:	(0345) 314159 . . . .
Appointed:	1 APRIL 1990 . . . .

Figure 2.2 The structure of records in the file "STAFF".

2.2.3 Cross-references

Your records are much more likely to be accurate and up to date if each piece of information is the responsibility of only one member of staff and is kept in just one place. Indeed, is often helpful to make one person responsible for all the information kept in a given file. For example, the personnel director's assistant might be responsible for ensuring that personal details of staff members are accurately entered into the file "STAFF". The problem with this scheme is that the same piece of information will often be wanted by people who work in different departments and are responsible for different files. For example, the pay clerk might need to know each employee's home address, and might find it handy to be able to list these alongside data such as tax deducted that are stored in the file "PAY". Unfortunately, these data are stored within "STAFF", and though this information *could* be copied across from "STAFF" to "PAY" this would be unwise since there would be no way of ensuring that both copies were kept up to date and agreed at all times. There would be a danger of confusion as a result of certain employees having different addresses recorded in the files "STAFF" and "PAY". Pick resolves the conflict by letting you define a word, say "HOME.ADDRESS", that appears to refer to data held in the file "PAY" but actually refers to the address stored in the file "STAFF". Once this word has been defined, both the personnel director and the pay clerk can behave as though home addresses were stored in their own file without the least danger of conflict.

Databases within which it is possible to establish this kind of connection between different blocks of data are called **relational databases** and are considered superior to other types of database.[1]

2.2.4   Searching the database

Sometimes you don't so much want to know specific facts about, say, clients, as want to know which clients satisfy certain criteria. For example, you might need to discover which clients are located in London, or which clients in London have outstanding accounts in excess of £10,000. Pick provides an (almost) natural language for asking such questions. In §4.3 we shall see that Pick's "ACCESS" enquiry language enables you to ask these questions by typing at a terminal

```
SORT CLIENTS WITH AREA.CODE "Ø1"
```

or

```
SORT CLIENTS WITH AREA.CODE "Ø1" AND WITH DUE > 1ØØØØ
```

You can tell the machine to print the answers to these questions on the screen or on paper, ordered alphabetically, by magnitude of indebtedness or according to any other convenient scheme. If all you want to know is *how many* clients have large outstanding accounts, you can simply tell the machine to

```
COUNT CLIENTS WITH DUE > 1ØØØØ
```

and the machine will report the number of heavily indebted clients. The ability to extract information from the database in this common-sense way is an important feature of the Pick system.

2.3   Simplifying the daily routine

Most of the time business computers are used to perform routine tasks, such as enquiring how many parts of a particular type are in stock, filing orders or recording the hours of overtime worked by employees during the last month. Since the machine must be used by staff who are unlikely to be computer freaks, it must help them as much as possible by asking the right questions, checking the consistency of the answers it is given and by explaining clearly what information it is printing out on the screen or on paper. One teaches the machine to do this by writing a program.

---

[1] More precisely, a relational database is one in which (i) all data appear to be stored in tables made up of rows (items or 'tuples') and columns (attributes), and (ii) a language is provided for the construction of new tables from old. The defining reference is *Database Language NDL*, American National Standards Institute, New York, 1986.

Writing computer programs can be a time-consuming and costly business. Luckily, if all you require is a program to accomplish some mundane task, such as working out monthly pay slips, which tens of thousands of other businesses have to do, you will find that there are plenty of software suppliers keen to sell you one. And since they will have spent a great deal of time and money to ensure that theirs is the best possible program for the given task, it obviously makes sense to take them up on their offer and save yourself the trouble of writing your own program. Pick Systems[2] and ALLM Systems and Marketing[3] publish directories, *Pick Hits* and *Pick Resources Guide International*, containing descriptions of several thousand programs that will run on almost any Pick machine. You may find the programs you need listed there, or you may get them from one of the software consultants who are also listed in these directories. (These often specialize in programs for one particular line of business, such as automobile repairs or restaurants.)

Unfortunately, you are unlikely to be able to buy in ready-made all the programs you need for your business. Programs are useful precisely because they focus the machine on one particular job; in order to be useful they have to be highly specific. But your business is unique and its requirements are unlikely to be exactly the same as those of any other. So you will not be able to get by with ready-made programs unless you are prepared either to adapt the programs to your business or your business to the programs. Off-the-shelf programs can usually be 'configured' to suit the need of a particular installation, but there is a limit to what can be achieved in this line without the configuration process becoming a programming exercise in itself. So it is likely that for some jobs you will rely on ready-made programs and for others you will need to write your own.

Unfortunately, it is not yet possible to write programs in plain English—computers are too stupid to understand you when you address them as you would an adult or even a six-year-old. You have to be *very* clear and explicit when giving a computer instructions, which in practice means giving your instructions in the computer's own **programming language**. Fortunately, Pick provides an excellent programming language, **Pick BASIC**.

As programming languages go, Pick BASIC is easy to learn. In fact, if you have ever programmed a toy computer in ordinary BASIC, you will be able to do simple things in Pick BASIC immediately and you will undoubtedly find this facility invaluable. On the other hand, Pick BASIC is a powerful language that makes it easy to write comprehensible programs that accomplish complex tasks.

---

2 1691 Browning, Irvine, CA 92714, U.S.A., tel. (714) 261 7425.

3 21 Beechcroft Road, Bushey, Herts WD2 2JU, U.K., tel. (0923) 30150.

2.4   Moving up with your system

Times change, organizations grow, machines become obsolete and must be discarded. Sooner rather than later you will be obliged to replace whatever computer you have installed now with another machine. It is vitally important that when you install a new machine you can carry over to it whatever software you already have. Not only will this software represent an enormous investment of labour and experience, but your organization will be totally dependent upon the continuous flow of information which it provides, and may be severely damaged by even a brief hiatus while a new machine is installed.

In the bad old days when computer hardware was vastly expensive, the general rule was "one computer, one operating system". When a new computer was put on the market, its manufacturer provided a brand new operating system tailored to its specific hardware requirements. This was tremendously inconvenient for computer users since their software had to be extensively rewritten every time they bought a new machine. But it was good for computer companies, who by offering a limited degree of compatibility between their old and new models were able to lock customers into purchasing only their brand of machines. And it was good for the machines too since they could achieve top performance under tailor-made operating systems.

Over the last decade all this has changed. Now there are a few standard operating systems that run on most widely purchased machines. Consequently, if you invest your time and money in software that runs under one of these standard operating systems, your software will run on a great many machines, and you may be reasonably sure that it will also run on the machines that manufacturers will be bringing out five or ten years from now. In the jargon of the trade, your software will be **portable**.

What are these standard operating systems? At the bottom end of the market there is **DOS**, the system under which the vast majority of IBM-compatible personal computers run. This is now a rather old-fashioned system (introduced in 1981), and IBM is endeavouring to replace it with **OS2**. OS2 is designed to run all software written for DOS as well as more powerful programs that will not run under DOS. However, many people think OS2 was overtaken by technological change before it could become a true standard and it is still unclear what will replace DOS as the dominant operating system for desk-top computers if OS2 fails to become the market leader.

A desk-top computer usually interacts with only one user at a time. Operating systems such as DOS that are designed to give exclusive control of the machine to one user are called **single-user operating systems**. Traditionally, however, computers divided their efforts between tasks imposed by several users. Each user would have his own terminal connected to the computer and would issue his own instructions to it. It is clearly a special computer that can keep track of several users' needs simultaneously, and to do it a computer must be running a **multi-user operating system**. It is helpful to divide operating systems into these two broad categories—single- and multi-user systems—since multi-user systems are much more complex, bulky and expensive than single-user systems. A key decision when purchasing a computer system is whether one should go for a single-user or a multi-user system.

The clear market leader among multi-user operating systems is the original portable operating system, **Unix**. Since Unix was created at Bell Laboratories in the late 1960s, it has gradually become the operating system of choice for medium-sized computers, and has been spreading more slowly upwards to super-computers and downwards to desk-top computers.

Pick is in some ways in competition with Unix. Like Unix it is for computers that must interact with several users simultaneously, and like Unix it is available for machines that range from the more expensive desk-top computers up to middle-range mainframe computers. In other respects it differs greatly from Unix, which offers the business user a smaller range of facilities. In particular, Unix provides neither a dictionary facility analogous to Pick's (see §3.5), nor an analogue of the ACCESS enquiry language described in §4.3. Nor does it provide a programming language with all the features of Pick BASIC. Unix users who want facilities of this sort must purchase extra software packages that make them available on a Unix computer. Such software is likely to prove expensive and may contain more 'bugs' than a tried and tested operating system such as Pick. So if you are a business user interested in purchasing as a single package most of what you will need for your organization, Pick may be the operating system for you.

However, before you commit yourself to Pick, you should consider carefully whether your requirements could not be more cheaply and conveniently satisfied by software written to run under DOS or OS2. In the next section we explain the advantages and disadvantages of these single-user systems as compared with multi-user systems such as Pick and Unix.

2.5   Multi-user machine or networked single-user machines?

We have seen that Pick offers businessmen and administrators a number of remarkable database facilities. But similar facilities are available on any IBM-compatible personal computer by purchasing a good database package such as the current version of dBASE. Is it better to buy a Pick system or to install a package such as dBASE on a garden-variety PC that runs DOS or OS2?

Operating systems for personal computers such as DOS and OS2 are relatively simple things. Their simplicity is a twofold advantage: they are cheap to buy and easy to install and manage. Also they are sold in immense numbers, so expertise in their management and good, cheap programs for use with them are widespread. Hence if your job is simple enough to be accomplished effectively by a software package that runs under such an operating system, this may be the way to go. But the operating system's simplicity can be a disadvantage as well. There are three significant ways in which it may be restrictive:

(i) Since the system is designed to give a single user complete control of the machine, a separate computer has to be purchased for every user.

(ii) If these users are all to have access to a common database, an expensive and non-standard 'local area network' has to be purchased.

(iii) The operating system has to work within the confines of the computer's random-access memory (RAM—see §1.1.2), which is usually very much smaller than the memory available on disk.

More sophisticated operating systems such as Pick and Unix allow you to escape from all of these restrictions: the operating system is designed to interact simultaneously with several users and it allows the computer to use memory on disk essentially interchangeably with more expensive RAM (see §1.1.2). So if your organization does require several users to interact with the database simultaneously, you should probably be considering a multi-user operating system such as Pick rather than a single-user system such as DOS.

To clarify what is involved here, consider two strategies for setting up a three-user system based on IBM-compatible equipment. In each case we buy a machine with a hard disk to hold the database. We shall refer to this as the "main machine". This might be a computer of the **AT-compatible** class, that is a computer based on the Intel 80286 microprocessor, or it might be one of the more powerful **386 machines**, that is a computer based on Intel's 80386 microprocessor. The cost of this hardware would lie in the range £900–£4,000 ($1,200–$6,000, say). To get a three-user system running either under Pick or DOS would involve the following additional expenditures:

Pick system
- Pick operating system for three users, say   £700   ($800)
- Additional 1 Mbyte or RAM, say   £500   ($750)
- Two dumb terminals at, say, £250 ($400)   £500   ($800)
  Total cost (less main machine):   £1,450   ($1,950)

DOS-based system
- Two basic PCs at, say, £600 ($800)   £1,200   ($1,600)
- Three copies of DOS at, say, £50 ($70)   £150   ($210)
- Networking hard- and soft-ware, say   £750 ($1,000)
- Database software, say   £400   ($600)
  Total cost (less main machine):   £2,500   ($3,410)

From these figures for setting up equivalent Pick- and DOS-based three-user systems, it is clear that Pick enjoys a cost advantage even though a single copy of Pick costs around £700 compared to about £50 for DOS. There are two reasons for Pick's cost advantage:

(i) With Pick one is buying not only a conventional operating system, but also database software that one must otherwise buy separately.

(ii) Since DOS is a single-user operating system, one is compelled to buy an additional computer for each person who needs his or her own screen and keyboard, and a **local area network**[4] to connect them together.

A local area network works on a fundamentally different principle from a multi-user operating system and it is perhaps worth explaining the pros and cons of such systems. If we set up our three-user system under Pick, the main machine is the only computer that will do any real thinking. Thus the other two screens can be basic 'dumb terminals' that simply send to the main machine what is typed on a keyboard, and display on their screens what the main machine sends back. By contrast, if we set up our system under DOS, each keyboard and screen must be served by its own computer, so we will have to buy as many independent computers as we have keyboards and screens. Networking hardware and software is then required if these computers are to read and write the hard-disk on the main machine. (In effect the network enables all three machines to share the same hard disk.)

The advantage of using a network is that the load on the main machine's processor is much less than it would be under Pick since it does not have to keep track of what every user is up to. Hence with a DOS-based network the speed with which the system responds to requests is likely to be faster for a given specification of the main machine than under Pick. The more users there are on a system the more pronounced this effect will be. To speed Pick along a little in our three-user system, we have included in the budget above an additional megabyte of RAM on the main machine—this will reduce delays while Pick looks for data on the hard disk. It is probably also a good idea to make the main machine one of the 386 class rather than an AT-compatible. Thus with a Pick-based system some of what one saves through not needing several independent computers and a network should be spent on boosting the performance of the main machine. At the end of the day, however, Pick must be judged a very cost-effective way of setting up a small business system.

2.6 Pick dialects

We have hitherto spoken simply of 'Pick' and 'Unix' as though they were single operating systems. Would that they were. In reality there are several dialects of both Pick and Unix, so that an instruction that works on one Pick machine cannot be *guaranteed* to work on another machine that also runs under Pick, and the same is true of instructions to different Unix machines.

This diversity amongst machines that ostensibly use the same operating system is much to be regretted, but is the price we have to pay for the

---

[4] Often abbreviated to 'LAN'.

amazing speed with which computer systems have evolved in the two decades since Pick and Unix were first conceived. Indeed, this rapid development has been achieved through many different institutions and manufacturers working independently to perfect hard- and soft-ware. Inevitably different people come up with slightly different solutions to similar problems, with the result that differences develop between versions of an operating system that evolve independently in different places.

Dick Pick, the originator of the Pick operating system, developed the prototype Pick system around 1969 under contract to the US Defense Department. Subsequent development of this system was done by several corporations that were eventually absorbed by McDonnell Douglas Computer Systems, which currently markets a derivative of Pick as **Reality**. Dick Pick later founded his own organization, "Pick and Associates", but in 1984 he abandoned it to set up another, which he called "Pick Systems". The legacy of these three periods in Dick Pick's career is that three corporations now have rights to versions of Pick: McDonnell Douglas Computer Systems, Pick and Associates, or the Ultimate Corporation as it is now known, and Pick Systems.

The spread of Pick gathered speed in the early 1980s in the wake of the introduction by IBM and other vendors of a range of cheap but powerful microcomputers. In 1981 IBM established a widely accepted hardware standard for microcomputers—that of the IBM PC, a machine based on the Intel 8088 microprocessor—and a standard operating system for these machines, DOS. In 1984 IBM followed this by introducing the 'AT', a computer also intended to run under DOS but based on Intel's considerably more powerful 80286 microprocessor. Around this time Motorola introduced the first of its 68000 series microprocessors and these chips, like the Intel 8088 and 80286 chips, were soon being used by a host of manufacturers as the CPUs of microcomputers.

The rapid spread of computers based on the Intel and Motorola microprocessors soon led to the introduction of cheap implementations of Pick on them. Cosmos Inc. led the field by marketing **Revelation**, a Pick look-alike designed to run under DOS on IBM-compatible micros. A little later Pick Systems brought out a full Pick implementation for IBM-compatibles, the current version of which is **R83**, and at the same time licensed numerous implementations of Pick on 68000-based machines. Meanwhile vendors such as System Management Inc. and the Ultimate Corp. implemented Pick on larger machines such as DEC's VAX and IBM's 43xx and 30xx series of machines.

Prior to 1990 all Pick implementations licensed by Pick Systems, rather than by McDonnell Douglas or the Ultimate Corp, were almost identical. In 1989 however, Pick Systems released a preliminary version of a new operating system, **Advanced Pick**, for AT-compatibles and machines based on Intel's 80386 microprocessor. This product is intended to eventually supersede the **R83** version of Pick. In many respects it is a simple extension of **R83**, so that much software written for *R83* will run with minimal modification under *Advanced Pick*. But *Advanced Pick* does differ from *R83* in many minor details and in some major functions. So in this book we confine discussion to *R83*, which has been characterized as 'generic Pick'. If you have a Pick system purchased before 1991, it probably runs either *R83* or a very similar Pick implementation and this is the book for you. A companion volume *Advanced Pick for Humans* is planned for users of *Advanced Pick*.

3   How the disk is organized

Though no two disks will ever contain exactly the same data, the general pattern on which they are organized is common to all Pick computer systems. It is vital to understand the pattern if you want to run your computer efficiently. To this end we now devote a chapter to a detailed explanation of how a Pick disk is organized.

3.1   Data files

A Pick disk's millions of bytes are regimented in **frames**. On most systems the size of a frame is 512 bytes (half a kilobyte, see §1.1.1), but on some it may be 1024 or 2048 bytes (one or two kilobytes). Just like the houses in a street, each frame has a unique number. We will refer to these numbers as the **addresses** of the frames. The addresses start at zero rather than one so that the highest address is one less than the total number of frames on the disk. You can pin down any byte out of the whole vast array by giving the address of the frame in which it lies and saying where it occurs in the frame; for example the 314th byte of frame 159. Usually there will be some frames that are not in use, because you don't need every one of your enormous number of bytes all the time. Frames that are not in use just contain random letters and numbers. In each frame that is in use, 500 of the bytes are given over to storing your data and the remaining 12 are used by the operating system to store various pieces of information for its own purposes. As well as customer records and ledger entries and so forth, the data stored in the frames on the disk include programs. Programs, like your records, are simply rows of letters and numbers, so you don't need anywhere special to store them. They can just go on the disk with everything else. A particular example of this is the operating system, Pick, which is itself a program. The whole of the first 400 frames of the disk are given over to storing this important program. In Pick jargon these frames are referred to as the **ABS frames**.

To help you keep track of what you have on the disk, your data are divided into **files**. A file is a collection of related data; names and addresses, orders and invoices. Whatever. Each file on the disk has a name and when you feed new data into the machine you must give the name of the file in which you want it put. Thus *all* data are in one file or another. Usually all the data of one type are put together in one file, which is given a name to remind you what you have put there. For example you might keep all your employee records in a file called "STAFF" (like the one we introduced in §2.1), or your customer accounts in a file called "CUSTOMERS".

Physically a file is a collection of frames on the disk. The number of files you can have on your disk is limited only by the number of frames you have (or, if you like, the number of bytes). Certainly the number could run into hundreds of files. In the next chapter we will explain how to create new files and how to destroy old ones (see §4.2.6).

To take up the example of the STAFF file, it is clear that if we wish to store all our personnel records in the one file we need to have some method of distinguishing between different people's records. To this end every file is divided into **items**. An item is merely a smaller collection of data within the bigger collection, the file.[1] An item too has a name, usually referred to as its **ID**.

Because you will probably want to store many different pieces of information about each of your personnel—name, position, home address and so on—the items are further split into **attributes**. An attribute is a small piece of data; like a name or an address. Unlike files and items, the attributes in an item do not necessarily have names—they are numbered, starting with one. We will explain in §3.5 how you can give an attribute a name, but since this is optional we postpone its discussion until the end of the chapter. There can be as many attributes as you like in an item, and different items in a file may contain different numbers of attributes.

Thus, when you feed a piece of data into the computer, you actually have to specify not only the name of the file in which you would like it put, but also the ID of an item in that file, and the number of an attribute within that item.

Undoubtedly this is all a bit complicated and hard to assimilate in one go. In fact, no matter how long you have been using a Pick computer, it is still possible to confuse all these various divisions and sub-divisions of data and the various words that describe them. We have found it very helpful in reducing these confusions to have a picture of how our data are arranged. For example we would draw the item called "BLOGGS-J" in the file "STAFF" like this:

---

[1] Some authors refer to items as 'records'. We shall not use the term record in this way.

```
        File: STAFF   Item: BLOGGS-J
Attribute
  Number    Contents of Attribute
       1    Bloggs
       2    Joe
       3    14 Home Ave
       4    Woking
       5    Surrey
       6    14576
```

That is, we write the name of the item and the name of the file that contains it at the top, and underneath we put the contents of each of the attributes on a separate line, numbered down the left for convenience. There will be many such diagrams in the remainder of this book.

In this example we have supposed that successive attributes of our file contain, in order, the surname and first name of the relevant member of staff, three lines of his or her address, and a telephone number. We imagine that the file contains many such items, one for each staff member. Generally it is good practice to give each item an identical form, with the same attributes always storing the same data, because it makes it simpler to track down a particular piece of data amongst hoards of similar ones. If, for example, we want to find someone's telephone number and we know that it is stored in the sixth attribute of his item in STAFF, then it is a simple task to retrieve it quickly. For the same reason it is very desirable to name all the items in a file in a methodical way so that we can work out what the ID of the item containing a person's record must be quickly, without having to go through the whole list looking for likely candidates. In the example above we have supposed that each person's data have been fed into an item in STAFF whose ID consists of their surname in capitals, followed by a hyphen, followed by all of their initials separated by further hyphens. This is a decent system. We use it for some of the files on our own computer. It only breaks down in the unlikely event that two people come along with the same surname and initials, in which case one of them might gain a number as an initial or something like that, so as to create a unique item ID for that person.

We ought to point out that there are one or two very minor restrictions on your choice of names for files and items. First bear in mind that no two of your files can have the same name. Otherwise there would be no way to tell the two apart. Similarly two items in the same file cannot have the same ID. However, there is no reason why two items in different files should not have the same ID since to specify an item you have to say *both* what the name of the item is *and* in which file it resides. More subtly, filenames must not start with a number and they must not contain any commas or semi-colons. So, while "STOCK-RECORD" and "STOCK.RECORD" are lawful filenames, "STOCK,RECORD" and "STOCK;RECORD" are not. Names containing spaces, for example "BAD IDEA", are lawful, but will in practice lead to all kinds of complications and should be avoided.

3.2   Master dictionaries

If, like most people, you consider the construction and maintenance of computers to be a form of black magic, then it probably does not surprise you to learn that you have merely to mention the name of a file to your computer and the machine will immediately know where to look on the disk for your data. But, as we have said, in reality the computer regards the disk as being a numbered collection of frames, and so it needs a way to work out which frame to look at when you ask for data from a certain file. This information is stored on the disk as well. It is stored in special files called **master dictionaries** or **MDs** for short. There are many MDs on a Pick computer. Each user may have his own, or several users may share one.

Despite its special status, a user can treat his MD like any other file and refer to it by the file name "MD". Even though different users may have different MDs, each calls his own MD "MD" and the computer always knows that he is referring to his *own* MD and to no one else's. This is a special case of a more general principle that we will see in action later on (§3.2.2) whereby different users may refer to the same file by different names, or to different files by the same name.

Like other files, MDs are made up of items, each item consisting of several attributes. Some of these items contain information about 'verbs', but we postpone description of these until we have explained what a 'verb' is. Others contain information the computer needs to locate a file on the disk. These divide into two types: 'Q-pointers', which are discussed in §3.2.2, and **file-defining items**.

3.2.1   File-defining items

The item in our MD that describes the file "STAFF" would look something like this:

File: MD	Item: STAFF

```
Attribute
   Number    Contents of Attribute

      1      D                        (File type)
      2      27182                    (Base frame address)
      3      7                        (Modulo)
      4      1                        (Separation)
      5                               (Retrieval lock)
      6                               (Update lock)
      7
      8
      9      L                        (Justification of item IDs)
     1Ø      15                       (Width reserved for item IDs)
```

What do the numbers and letters mean in a file-defining item such as the item "STAFF" shown above? You will need to create or alter items like these from time to time if you want to keep your computer on its feet, so it is well worth our while explaining in detail what they mean.

Attribute 1: The file type.   The first attribute tells the computer what type of file STAFF is. In this case it is a D-type file. This means that it is an ordinary data file, containing ordinary data. The other main type of file is the DC-type file, which means a file containing Pick BASIC programs (see the introduction to Chapter 8).

Attribute 2: The base frame.   This attribute contains the address of the first frame on the disk used to store the file.[2] Typically this is a five figure number. Many files will occupy more than one frame on the disk, but once the computer has the address of the first frame of a file it can find all the others belonging to the same file, even though they do not necessarily come one after another.

Attributes 3 & 4: Modulo and separation.   These two numbers tell the computer how much space to reserve for the file on the disk and how that space is to be divided up. They are familiarly referred to as **mod** and **sep**.

The frames used to store the data in a file are divided into **groups**. The **modulo** tells us how many groups are used to store the data in the file, and the **separation** tell us how many frames are reserved for each group. Hence if we multiply the modulo by the separation we get the total number of frames reserved for the file. Thus, in the example above, the mod is 7 and the sep is 1, which means that the file consists of seven groups, for each of which Pick initially reserves one frame—a total of seven frames for the entire file.

You may well ask why we should bother to divide the file into groups of frames at all. The answer is that it speeds up the retrieval of a piece of data from the file. When you feed new data into a file, Pick doesn't just take the frames designated for that file, and fill them up starting at the beginning. It splits the frames up into groups and puts different items into different groups, and it does this on the basis of the item IDs. For example, we might have a system under which an item called "AAAA" is put in the first group, one called "AAAB" is put in the second and so on in alphabetical order. So on being fed an item called "AAAE" the computer would say to itself, "Hmmm. This item is called 'AAAE'. Therefore it clearly belongs in the fifth group." And into the fifth group it would go—even if this is the first item to be put into the file. It makes no difference what data are already in the file. The choice of where to put a new item is made entirely on the strength of its name. A typical file might contain about ten groups of frames, so often many different items

---

[2] The base frame address, and all other addresses stored on Pick machines, are in decimal (base ten) notation, rather than the hexadecimal (base sixteen) notation used on most other computers.

have to be stuffed together into each group. For example, in our system if the mod were eleven, an item called "**AAAK**" would be put into the eleventh group, but "**AAAL**" would go in the first, along with any other items, such as "**AAAA**", already stored there.

The truth is that the system Pick actually uses to decide into which group an item should be placed is much more complicated than this simple alphabetical example, and its choices of location would appear completely random to a human being. Nonetheless there is a system there. We don't need to know what it is, only that it exists. The operating system is capable of working out very quickly in which group an item should be stored. It is this that speeds the retrieval of your data because when you ask for a particular piece of data by name, the computer works out in a flash in which group it is stored and goes straight there. There may be many items stored in that group, and they will not be in any particular order so the computer will have to check each one in turn until it finds the right one. But even so this is much quicker than putting all the items of a file together in a single giant group, and then searching through the whole lot to find the item you want.

The amount of data you can store in a file is not limited by the number of frames reserved for that file. If the computer needs to put a new item into a group that has already eaten up all the frames originally reserved for it, then it finds an empty frame somewhere on the disk and designates it an extension or **overflow frame** of this group. Any further items added to the group are stored here. If the overflow frame overflows, another empty frame is located and filled with the new data. So there is almost no limit to the amount of disk space that any given group can take up. However, allowing groups to overflow is likely to slow retrieval because the overflow frames may be almost anywhere on the disk. In particular, they are probably nowhere near the frames containing the bulk of the file, so the disk heads (see §1.1.1) may have to move a long way to reach them. It is perfectly normal to have some of the groups in a file overflowing, but if too many do, data retrieval will become slow. This is a situation you should try to avoid.

In the next chapter we will discuss the choosing of mod and sep for a file in some detail (§4.2.6). For the moment we merely state the method:

1. Work out approximately how much data the file will hold when it is full by estimating the average length in bytes (characters) of each item and multiplying it by your estimate of the number of items there will be in the file.

2. Divide this total by the number of bytes of data to a frame on your computer (which is probably 500, but could be 1000 or 2000) to get the number of frames the data in the file will occupy when it has all been typed in.

3. The modulo of the new file should be the next number bigger than this in Table 4.3, and the separation should be 1.

Attributes 5 & 6: Security locks. Attributes 5 and 6 of a file-defining item are to do with the security of your data. In §7.8.2 we explain how they can be used to limit the number of users on the computer who can read or write the file. For the moment we note only that the computer will function perfectly well if these attributes are left blank, and that you would be unwise to put anything in them unless you know exactly what you are doing.

Attributes 7 & 8: Not used. These attributes do not have a use and to avoid confusion it is as well to leave them blank.

Attributes 9 & 10: Justification and width of ID. In the next chapter (§4.3.1) we will explain how to get the data in a file displayed on the screen. We can ask the computer to display the item IDs along with the data if we like, so that we can see at a glance in which item each piece of data belongs. When you produce such a list the number in attribute 10 tells Pick how much space to allow on the screen for the display of the ID. For example, we will shortly see how to produce a list of data from the file "STAFF", like this:

```
STAFF.......... FORENAME....... SURNAME........ TELEPHONE..

BINNEY-J-J      James           Binney              314159
BLOGGS-J        Joe             Bloggs              141421
NEWMAN-M-E-J    Mark            Newman              271828
OTHER-A-N       Annabel         Other                57721
```

The IDs are listed in the leftmost column, which is fifteen characters wide (including spaces). This reflects the fact that attribute 10 of the item "STAFF" in our MD has the value 15. None of the IDs in our example is that long, so Pick has put blanks to the right of every ID. This ensures that the beginnings of all the forenames line up one above the other. (Notice that the beginnings of the surnames are all neatly lined up as well, so clearly Pick also knows how much space it is to leave for the forenames. In §3.5 we will see how it comes to know this too.)

Attribute 9 of a file-defining item can contain the letters L or R, which stand for left and right. This attribute tells the computer whether to put the IDs in the above list on the left or the right of the gap we have asked it to leave for them. This is called left or right **justification**. In the above example the IDs are left justified because we said "L". If we had said "R" we would have got a list looking like this:

```
STAFF.......... FORENAME....... SURNAME........ TELEPHONE..

    BINNEY-J-J James           Binney              314159
      BLOGGS-J Joe             Bloggs              141421
  NEWMAN-M-E-J Mark             Newman              271828
     OTHER-A-N Annabel          Other                57721
```

We feel this is not as clear as the other way so we always put "L" in attribute 9 on our computer, but the choice is completely up to you.

Attributes 11 & 12: Not used.   These attributes do not have a use and to avoid confusion it is as well to leave them blank.

Attribute 13: Resizing attribute.   By placing appropriate numbers in this attribute you can make Pick change the mod and sep of the file the next time you perform a 'full file restore'. The use of this attribute is explained in §7.5.2.

3.2.2   Q-pointers

For each file on the computer there can be *only one* file-defining item. It is forbidden for there to be two items defining the same file in two different MDs. And yet different users, not necessarily sharing the same MD, will often want to examine the same data. So Pick provides a device called a **Q-pointer** by which this can be achieved. You can put an item in your MD which appears to behave like an ordinary file-defining item, but which does not in fact contain all the important information (base frame, mod, sep, etc.) which such items must hold. Instead it contains the name of a user in whose MD that information *can* be found and the name of the item in that MD which contains it.

Suppose, for example, that you are anxious to retrieve some data from the file "STAFF". STAFF 'belongs' to Joe Bloggs; i.e., there is a file-defining item in his MD with the ID "STAFF". When you ask for data from the file "STAFF", Pick will go to *your* MD and look for an item called "STAFF". Finding no such item it will say

    [1Ø] File name missing

which is not very helpful. The solution is to put an item in your own MD which looks like this:

File: MD	Item: STAFF

Attribute Number	Contents of Attribute
1	Q
2	BLOGGS
3	STAFF

This is a **Q-pointer**. The first attribute is Q to mark it as such. The second is the name of a user. The third is the ID of an item in that user's MD. Now when you ask for data from the file "STAFF", Pick goes to your MD and finds this item. On seeing the "Q" in the first attribute it realizes that you are talking about a file somewhere else, so it picks up the user name and the item name from the other two attributes and goes off to inspect the item "STAFF" in the BLOGGS' MD. There it finds the base frame, mod and sep of the file "STAFF" and uses these to fetch the data you requested. Thus with an appropriate selection of Q-pointers any user can gain access to any data on the computer.

This is only the simplest use of a Q-pointer. On most Pick systems it is also possible for a Q-pointer to point to an item in another MD which is itself

a Q-pointer. And that Q-pointer could point to another Q-pointer, and so
on. The computer will patiently follow the trail until it finds the item that
contains the real hard facts about the file's location. However it is not a good
idea to make trails like this too long. One can become confused over where
the real file-defining item is if there are more than three steps in the chain.

A Q-pointer's item ID defines the name by which you will refer to the
file it points to. The ID does not have to be the same as the original name
of the file. So for example you could put the Q-pointer above in the item
"EMPLOYEES" in your MD:

```
          ┌─────────┬──────────────────┐
          │ File: MD │ Item: EMPLOYEES │
          └─────────┴──────────────────┘
Attribute
   Number      Contents of Attribute

      1      Q
      2      BLOGGS
      3      STAFF
```

And henceforth, whenever you ask for data from the file "EMPLOYEES", you
will get data from Bloggs' STAFF file.

A Q-pointer need not point to a file belonging to somebody else. You
can put a pointer in your MD that points to another item in that same MD,
thus allowing you to refer to the same file by two different names. So if you
are Joe Bloggs, and you have an item "EMPLOYEES" like the one above in your
MD, then you will be able to ask for that file by the name "STAFF" *or* by
the name "EMPLOYEES". In fact if a Q-pointer is to point to one of your own
files then you don't have to give the user name at all—you can just leave the
second attribute blank and the computer assumes you to mean that the item
that really defines this file is to be found in your own MD. So Bloggs could
have a Q-pointer like this

```
          ┌─────────┬──────────────────┐
          │ File: MD │ Item: EMPLOYEES │
          └─────────┴──────────────────┘
Attribute
   Number      Contents of Attribute

      1      Q
      2
      3      STAFF
```

in his MD and it would serve this exact same purpose of allowing him to refer
to the STAFF file by the name "EMPLOYEES".

You can also make Q-pointers that point to MDs themselves, which after
all are only files too. Indeed these are very important Q-pointers because
your MD is one file you definitely *will* need to look at, whatever else you do
or don't do with your computer. If your user name is JACK you could make a
Q-pointer to your MD like this:

```
┌─────────┬──────────────────┐
│ File: MD │ Item: JACKSMD   │
└─────────┴──────────────────┘
Attribute
    Number    Contents of Attribute
         1    Q
         2    JACK
         3
```

The blank third attribute means that you want the MD. For any other file you have to give the full name in the third attribute, but for MDs you just leave it blank. In fact, in the light of the previous example you could cut out the "JACK" in the second attribute as well:

```
┌─────────┬──────────────────┐
│ File: MD │ Item: JACKSMD   │
└─────────┴──────────────────┘
Attribute
    Number    Contents of Attribute
         1    Q
         2
         3
```

knowing that the computer will interpret this to mean you want your own MD. Actually this is a pretty silly example, because if you don't already have a pointer to your own MD then you have no way to refer to it, and you can't tell the computer where you want this new Q-pointer put. For this reason no one has to create a Q-pointer to their MD. Everyone is given one automatically when they start out. Irrespective of the user name of your MD this Q-pointer is always called "MD", so you refer to your MD by the file name "MD", as explained in §3.2.

A more sensible example would be this:

```
┌─────────┬──────────────────┐
│ File: MD │ Item: BLOGGSMD  │
└─────────┴──────────────────┘
Attribute
    Number    Contents of Attribute
         1    Q
         2    BLOGGS
         3
```

If JACK had this item in his MD then he would be able to examine or change the contents of Bloggs' MD by referring to it by the file name "BLOGGSMD".

3.3 The system dictionary

Master dictionaries enable the computer to retrieve data from a file when all you give is the name of the file and the name of the item you want from it. The computer takes a look at the file name you've handed it, goes to your master dictionary and looks for the item which has this same name. Then, assuming this is a file-defining item, it looks down the list of attributes in that item and picks out the second one. This tells it the address of the first frame in the file. It also picks out the mod and sep of the file from the third and fourth attributes and then it is all set to track down whatever item it was that you asked for, using the quick and clever grouping method described in §3.2.1.

But when you think about it we still have a problem because, as we said earlier, your MD is just another file like other files—stored in frames on the disk, made up of items and attributes—and before we can get all this important information about base frames and mods and seps from it we need to know where *it* is. So we need an 'MD of MDs' to tell us where to find the MD! And in fact there is just such a file—a directory in which all the master dictionaries are listed. It is called the **system dictionary**, and there is *only one* on each Pick computer. "But wait!" you say, quick as a flash. "This is silly, because now we are going to need a dictionary to point to *this* dictionary, and so on for ever, and we are never going to solve the problem once and for all." Actually this is not such a problem because there is only the one system dictionary on the disk. Pick has a few bytes somewhere in its portion of the disk (the ABS frames, see §3.1) which permanently contain the system dictionary's mod and sep and the address of its first frame, so locating the system dictionary is never a problem.

If *you* need to refer to items in the system dictionary, then you will need a Q-pointer to it in your MD. There is a special form of Q-pointer for this purpose. It looks like this:

| File: **MD** | Item: SYSTEM |

```
Attribute
   Number      Contents of Attribute
        1      Q
        2      SYSTEM
        3      SYSTEM
```

This will allow you to refer to the system dictionary by the filename "SYSTEM". The name SYSTEM is standard in this application, and such is the importance of the system dictionary that it would be imprudent to call a Q-pointer to it by any other name, or to give the name SYSTEM to any other item in your MD. Changing the contents of the system dictionary is a hazardous thing to do at the best of times and changing them by mistake would be suicidal.

The items in the system dictionary are very similar to the items in any other dictionary except that they are describing MDs and not ordinary data files. In particular they fall into two classes—Q-pointers which are explained in §3.2.2, and **account-defining items**.

3.3.1   Account-defining items

Each account-defining item in the system dictionary has its own unique name, called an **account name**. It does two things:
(i) It contains the mod, sep and base frame address of an MD.

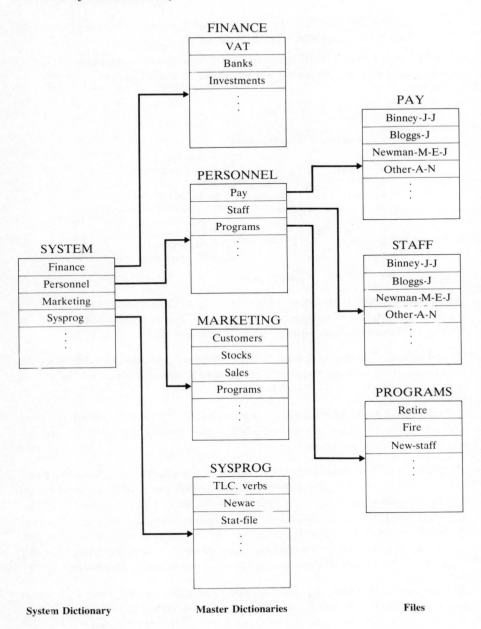

Figure 3.1 The structure of a Pick database. Data are stored as items like BINNEY-J-J, in files such as STAFF. Details of files are held in master dictionaries (MDs), such as PERSONNEL or MARKETING. Details of master dictionaries are held in the system dictionary "SYSTEM".

(ii) It contains the password and other security information associated with the user whose user name is the account name.

To take an example, Bloggs' MD might have the account name "BLOGGS" and be defined by the following item in the system dictionary:

```
          ┌──────────────────┬─────────────────┐
          │ File: SYSTEM     │ Item: BLOGGS    │
          └──────────────────┴─────────────────┘
Attribute
   Number      Contents of Attribute
        1      D                    (Account type)
        2      31415                (Base frame address)
        3      29                   (Modulo)
        4      1                    (Separation)
        5                           (Retrieval lock and keys)
        6                           (Update lock and keys)
        7      C3347E02             (Encoded password)
        8      SYS2                 (System privileges)
        9      U                    (Logon accounting and TCL access)
```

The attributes in this item are, in order:

Attribute 1: Account type.   Usually this attribute contains just the letter D meaning that this describes an ordinary MD. You may also run into DX- or DY-type dictionaries from time to time. These are explained in §7.5.2.

Attribute 2: The base frame.   This attribute contains the address of the first frame used to store the MD. This allows the computer to find the MD on the disk.

Attributes 3 & 4: Modulo and separation.   These two contain the mod and sep of the MD. Modulo and separation play exactly the same rôle in MDs as they do in data files (see §3.2.1).

Attributes 5 & 6: Security keys/locks.   These attributes have two functions: they allow you to stipulate to which files the user is to be granted access by the computer and they also function as 'security locks' on the MD in the same way as the corresponding attributes in file-defining items. Their use is described in detail in §7.8.2. In the mean time, unless you are sure of what you are doing, it is as well to leave them blank because you could cause yourself a lot of trouble if you put the wrong thing in one of these attributes.

Attribute 7: Password.   The seventh attribute contains the user's logon password, encoded so that no one else can find out what it is. When a user logs into the computer the password he types is encoded using the same code, and the result is compared with this attribute of his item in the system dictionary. Only if the two match is he allowed onto the computer.

If the seventh attribute is left blank, no password is needed to log on using this MD's account name.

Attributes 8 & 9: System privileges, logon accounting & TCL access. These attributes tell the computer to which facilities the user is to be allowed access (like the system debugger or the magnetic tape unit). Their use is explained in §§7.8.1, 7.8.3 and 7.9. It would be unwise to toy with these attributes until you feel confident that you understand exactly how they work.

The word **account** is used to refer to an MD and all the files whose defining items it contains. An account is identified by the account name of its MD (which explains the origin of the term "account name"). As explained above, an account name is also the user name of one of the users on the computer. However, by no means all user names are account names. Most users are what are called "synonym users".

3.3.2 Synonym users

It is not always convenient for every user to have his own MD. It often happens that several people—clerks in the pay department, the sales manager and his or her representatives—will need constantly to refer to the same files and use the same programs. Pick makes it possible for several users to share the same MD, so that a file available to one is available to all.

For example, suppose we wish the user JILL to have the same MD as BLOGGS. We achieve this by putting a **user-defining item** in the system dictionary which looks like this:

File: SYSTEM	Item: JILL

```
Attribute
  Number      Contents of Attribute
     1      Q                        (User type)
     2      BLOGGS                   (Account name)
     3
     4
     5                               (Retrieval keys)
     6                               (Update keys)
     7      45EE8211                 (Encoded password)
     8      SYS1                     (System privileges)
     9      U                        (Logon accounting and TCL access)
```

The first three attributes are in the standard form of a Q-pointer to an MD (see §3.2.2); the first attribute is the letter Q, the second is the account name of the MD and the third is blank indicating that we want the MD and not any other file. The fourth attribute is also blank, and the remaining attributes take exactly the same form as in the account-defining item of an MD such as that of BLOGGS' MD shown above.

Now when the computer needs something from JILL's MD, it goes to the item "JILL" in the file "SYSTEM" to find out at what frame her MD starts. But instead of an account-defining item, it finds there a Q-pointer which instructs it to use BLOGGS' MD instead. Thus, BLOGGS' MD is now also JILL's MD, and everything available to one is available to the other.

A user such as JILL, whose item in the system dictionary is a Q-pointer rather than a D-type account-defining item, is called a **synonym user**. There is no limit on the number of synonym users who can share the same MD. In fact, we strongly recommend that you make all the users of your computer synonym users, because it will greatly simplify the organization and maintenance of your system. Accounts should be given names that describe the data held in the files which they contain, like FINANCE, PAY, LEDGERS and so on, and no one should be allowed to log on under these names. Real human beings should log on as synonym users under the account most appropriate to their work. This plan ensures that the structure of the database reflects the structure of your organization, and will save you time by making it easier to remember how things are arranged and easier to decide where new additions should be put.

3.4   Sub-dividing your data

In the first half of this chapter we have seen how Pick stores data in files divided into named items and numbered attributes. In many case, this will be all the sub-division you require, but there will be times when you want to divide your data into even smaller units, and Pick is unusual amongst operating systems in providing for this. It is touches like this that set Pick apart from its competition and make it particularly suitable for people whose main concern is with the storage and retrieval of large quantities of data. In this section we explain these features.

In §3.1 we took the example of Joe Bloggs' personnel record to demonstrate how you could divide up the data on your personnel; giving each person one item, and using the different attributes in that item to store the various pieces of information on them. We suggested that you might arrange Bloggs' item like this:

```
| File: STAFF | Item: BLOGGS-J |
Attribute
   Number      Contents of Attribute
        1      Bloggs
        2      Joe
        3      14 Home Ave
        4      Woking
        5      Surrey
        6      14576
```

This is a perfectly workable system, and some people do store their data in this way. However we can perhaps foresee a problem. We would like to store the same type of information in the same attribute of each item, so that we know on which attribute we can find telephone numbers, for example. So if telephone numbers are to follow immediately after addresses, we must reserve the same number of attributes for each address, irrespective of how many lines it contains. In particular, though Bloggs' address has only three lines, others might have four or five, so we should leave at least two blank attributes at the end of Bloggs' address:

File: STAFF	Item: BLOGGS-J

```
Attribute
   Number    Contents of Attribute
        1    Bloggs
        2    Joe
        3    14 Home Ave
        4    Woking
        5    Surrey
        6
        7
        8    14576
```

But this plan is not ideal either because when you ask for data from a file you have to give the numbers of all the attributes you want displayed, and it's going to be very laborious if you have to ask for attributes 3, 4, 5, 6 and 7 every time you want an address. It would be much better if you could have all the address in one attribute and then just ask for that one. So you might feel that a better solution was to store the complete address on one line like this:

File: STAFF	Item: BLOGGS-J

```
Attribute
   Number    Contents of Attribute
        1    Bloggs
        2    Joe
        3    14 Home Ave, Woking, Surrey.
        4    14576
```

Now you have only to ask for attribute 3 to get a person's address. And it doesn't matter how many lines there are to the address, they will always fit into the one attribute. But this is still less than perfect. It's no use, for example, if you want your computer to print out an address label—then you need all the different bits of the address on different lines again.

Values.   Pick provides the ideal solution to all these problems by letting us further sub-divide the attributes in an item into as many parts as we like. These parts are called **values**. In this case each value would contain one line of the address, but the whole address would still be entirely contained within the third attribute. Then the address can have as many lines as we like, and we can still get the whole thing just by asking for attribute three. But when we need to print a label with Joe's address on it, we can instruct the computer to print out attribute three with each value on a separate line. In our diagrams we will denote the end of one value and the beginning of another by the symbol "]".[3] So the best way to store Bloggs' record would be thus:

| File: STAFF | Item: BLOGGS-J |

```
Attribute
Number      Contents of Attribute
   1        Bloggs
   2        Joe
   3        14 Home Ave]Woking]Surrey
   4        14576
```

As another example we might decide we wanted to store *all* a person's forenames in their personnel record. In Bloggs' case there is no problem because he's only got the one. But other people might have two or three. Rather than make an estimate of the maximum number of forenames a person is likely to have, and then devote one attribute to storing each name, we could put *all* the forenames in attribute 2 as separate values like this:

| File: STAFF | Item: BINNEY-J-J |

```
Attribute
Number      Contents of Attribute
   1        Binney
   2        James]Jeffrey
   3        15 Home Ave]Woking]Surrey
   4        314159
```

or this:

| File: STAFF | Item: NEWMAN-M-E-J |

```
Attribute
Number      Contents of Attribute
   1        Newman
   2        Mark]Edward]John
   3        16 Home Ave]Woking]Surrey
   4        271828
```

Now there is no restriction on the number of forenames we can fit in when the need arises. And we can see them all just by asking for the second attribute of a person's item; there's no need to ask for five different attributes by number, just on the off chance that the person you are interested in has an unusually large number of forenames. On the other hand, if you want only a person's first forename, you can ask simply for the first value in attribute 2.

Sub-values. There is still more to this story of successive division and sub-division. The values themselves can be further sub-divided into **sub-values**. The rules governing sub-values are the same as those governing values; there can be as many sub-values in a value as you like and when you ask to see their contents you can ask either for the whole value at once, or for just one sub-value. You will probably use sub-values much more rarely than values (and it

---

[3] The reason for this apparently random choice is that this is the symbol used by the Pick System Editor to denote the end of a value (see §6.2.1).

certainly wouldn't be helpful to extend the division of data any further) but they do have their uses.[4]

For example, suppose the file "STAFF" is to contain a record of the days each member of staff has taken off since he or she joined the company. Each break will, presumably, have a starting date and a finishing date. We *could* store these like this:

```
┌─────────────────┬──────────────────┐
│ File: STAFF     │ Item: BLOGGS-J   │
└─────────────────┴──────────────────┘
Attribute
  Number    Contents of Attribute
     1      Bloggs
     2      Joe
     3      14 Home Ave]Woking]Surrey
     4      14576
     5      5 Sep 89]2 Jan 90]27 Apr 90
     6      9 Sep 89]6 Jan 90]5 May 90
```

Attribute 5 now contains all the starting dates in separate values, and the corresponding values in attribute 6 contain the finishing dates. So for example Bloggs' most recent holiday was from April 27th, 1990 to May 5th. This is certainly a workable system. It stores all the necessary data in an unambiguous fashion. However, we are unlikely to want to see a departure date without a return date, which means we are forever going to be asking to see both attribute 5 and attribute 6. An alternative and preferable scheme would be to store the two dates for each holiday in two sub-values of the same value. Like this:

```
┌─────────────────┬──────────────────┐
│ File: STAFF     │ Item: BLOGGS-J   │
└─────────────────┴──────────────────┘
Attribute
  Number    Contents of Attribute
     1      Bloggs
     2      Joe
     3      14 Home Ave]Woking]Surrey
     4      14576
     5      5 Sep 89\9 Sep 89]2 Jan 90\6 Jan 90]27 Apr 90\5 May 90
```

The symbol "\"denotes the end of one sub-value and the beginning of another.[5] Now it is clear which dates correspond to which others, and you only have to ask for the one attribute to get all the information you need.

3.5 Dictionaries

There is one respect in which data files differ from all others on a Pick system. They have **dictionaries**. We do not use the word dictionary in the same

---

[4] Unlike values, sub-values can only be retrieved individually by a Pick BASIC program (see Chapter 8), and not by an ACCESS command (see §4.3). So some people avoid using them.

[5] Again the reason for this choice is that this is the symbol used by the Pick system editor to denote the end of an attribute (see §6.2.1).

sense here as it has been used earlier in this chapter—to describe the files containing the information the computer where to find other files. In this context a dictionary is a special file which contains information that helps the computer to search through a data file more easily. These dictionaries are associated exclusively with data files and, as we will see shortly, can simplify the retrieval of data immensely. The origin of the double use of the word dictionary is in certain similarities of structure between these dictionaries belonging to data files and the master dictionaries. But similarities or not, it is a very confusing choice of nomenclature, and it is unfortunate that we are stuck with it. Where it is necessary to distinguish we will refer to these dictionaries as dictionaries belonging to data files, and the others as MDs or the system dictionary.

A dictionary belonging to a data file is a file in its own right. It is made up of items split up into attributes. Any data file may have a dictionary associated with it and most do. In fact one tends to think of a data file and its associated dictionary as together making up the entity we call a 'file'. You will often see books (this one included) refer to a data file and its dictionary as the "data and dictionary *portions* of the file", though each individually has the form of a file on its own.

Dictionaries allow you to refer to attributes in a file by names instead of numbers, which saves you from having to remember which attribute stores which piece of data. For example, if you create a dictionary for the file "STAFF" containing appropriate entries, you will be able to ask for Joe Bloggs' ADDRESS or TELEPHONE number when you want them, rather than having to ask for attribute 3 or 4 of his item in the file. Hence in the long run making dictionaries for each of your data files will save you an enormous amount of time. Here is how you do it.

The filename of a dictionary is the same as the filename of the corresponding data file, except that it is prefixed with the word "DICT". Thus we would refer to the dictionary portion of the file "STAFF" as "DICT STAFF", or the dictionary portion of the file "CUSTOMERS" as "DICT CUSTOMERS". For consistency you are also allowed to refer to the data portion of STAFF as "DATA STAFF" if you want, but if you just say "STAFF" Pick will assume you mean the data portion, so the word "DATA" is redundant.[6]

The individual items in a dictionary define the names by which you can refer to pieces of data in your file. By analogy with real-life dictionaries we will call these names **words**. The words in a dictionary are the IDs of the items it contains, and the contents of the items tell Pick to which data those words apply. Here is an example:

---

[6] This is not completely true. We will see in Chapter 4 that there are some circumstances in which the computer takes you to mean both the data *and* dictionary portions when you talk about "STAFF". For example, we will see that when you ask the computer to delete the file "STAFF" it will assume, unless you tell it otherwise, that you want to delete both the data file and the associated dictionary.

```
┌──────────────────────┬──────────────────┐
│ File: DICT STAFF     │ Item: ADDRESS    │
└──────────────────────┴──────────────────┘
Attribute
   Number     Contents of Attribute
       1      A
       2      3
       3      ADDRESS
       4
       5
       6
       7
       8
       9      T
      10      20
```

This dictionary item is stored in the dictionary portion of the file "STAFF" and its ID is "ADDRESS". The second attribute contains a 3, which tells Pick that the word "ADDRESS" is the name by which you want to refer to the third attribute of each item in the data portion of STAFF. Once you have an item like this in DICT STAFF you can ask for someone's address by calling it an ADDRESS. We will demonstrate this in the next chapter. In the meantime we run through exactly what each of the attributes means in detail.

Attribute 1: Item type. An A in the first attribute tells the computer that this item is a dictionary entry defining a word you want to use. Since dictionary entries are the only things that can legitimately be put in dictionaries (at least in the current version of Pick) *all* the items in a dictionary should have an A in the first attribute.[7]

Attribute 2: Number of attribute in data portion. This tells Pick which attribute in the data portion of the file is to be referred to by the word you are defining. Thus if you want to be able to refer to attribute 1 of any item in STAFF as "SURNAME", you should create an item called SURNAME in DICT STAFF that begins like this:

```
┌──────────────────────┬──────────────────┐
│ File: DICT STAFF     │ Item: SURNAME    │
└──────────────────────┴──────────────────┘
Attribute
   Number     Contents of Attribute
       1      A
       2      1
```

Attribute 3: Column heading. A example was given in §3.2.1 of the kind of list that Pick can produce from the data held in a file. (We will explain how to call up such lists in §4.3.1.) Each column contains the data described by a single dictionary item. In the third attribute of a dictionary item you should put the heading that you want printed at the top of the relevant column in such lists. Though it is common to make the heading the same as the word

---

[7] Well actually you can also put an S there if you like—it means exactly the same thing. The reason for this peculiar redundancy is unclear.

you are defining, it is by no means compulsory. For example you could have
the surname column headed "SURNAME" by doing this:

```
        ┌─────────────────────┬─────────────────┐
        │ File: DICT STAFF    │ Item: SURNAME   │
        └─────────────────────┴─────────────────┘
Attribute
   Number     Contents of Attribute
        1     A
        2     1
        3     SURNAME
```

or we could have it headed "Family name" by doing this:

```
        ┌─────────────────────┬─────────────────┐
        │ File: DICT STAFF    │ Item: SURNAME   │
        └─────────────────────┴─────────────────┘
Attribute
   Number     Contents of Attribute
        1     A
        2     1
        3     Family name
```

Attribute 4: Controlling and dependent value indicator.   This attribute governs the rather esoteric 'dependent value' facility. We have never
seen this facility used, so we leave it to the avid enthusiast to consult the
technical manual on this one. When not in use this attribute should be left
blank.

Attributes 5 & 6: Not used.   These two attributes serve no function,
and for the sake of tidiness should be left blank.

Attribute 7: Conversions.   This attribute may contain one of a set of
codes, 'conversions' for short, which instruct Pick to perform some reorganization of your data before they are displayed to make them easier to read.
The different types of conversion codes are explained in §3.5.2. In the meantime, unless you know exactly what you want to put in this attribute, leave
it blank.

Attribute 8: Correlatives.   This attribute can contain any of the same
codes as attribute 7. However, codes in this attribute are referred to as 'correlatives' rather than conversions. Just like conversions, correlatives instruct
Pick to perform a reorganization of your data. In §§3.5.1–3.5.3 we explain
how conversions and correlatives differ and when you should use one or the
other, and we also give an explanation of the different types of codes that you
can put in these attributes. In the meantime, unless you know exactly what
you want to put in attribute 8, leave it blank.

Attributes 9 & 10: Justification and width.   The contents of the 10th
attribute tell the computer how many columns to allow on the screen or the
printer when printing the data. In our first example, ADDRESS, we said 20
columns.

The 9th attribute specifies how data are to be justified on the screen. It can take the values L, R, T or U. If it takes the value L, the attribute will be left justified on printing, like these forenames:

```
FORENAME.......

James
Joe
Mark
Annabel
```

And if it takes the value R the attribute will be right justified:

```
FORENAME.......

         James
           Joe
          Mark
       Annabel
```

The T and U options are only useful when the contents of an attribute are wider than the space designated for them in attribute 10 of the dictionary item. In this case specifying T (for 'text') will cause the data to be left justified, and the computer will not break up words but will start new lines at the beginnings of words. Thus if attributes 9 and 10 of a dictionary item called JOKE contain "T" and "15" respectively and the data stored in the data portion of the file says "My computer's got no nose. How does it smell? Bloody awful" then when we asked to see that displayed we would get:

```
My computer's
got no nose.
How does it
smell? Bloody
awful.
```

Which is a lot better than what we would get if attribute 9 said L:

```
My computer's g
ot no nose.  Ho
w does it smell
?  Bloody awful
.
```

Only if there were words so long that they would not fit into a space fifteen columns wide, would the computer resort to breaking words in the middle.

The other possibility is that we put U (for unconditional) in attribute 9. This makes the computer spill over the space allotted if the text is too long. This might mess up your printout, but at least you will be able to read it:

```
My computer's got no nose.  How does it smell?  Bloody awful.
```

3.5.1   Conversions and correlatives

As we mentioned briefly in the last section, there exists a selection of codes which, when placed in either attribute 7 or attribute 8 of a dictionary item, instruct the computer to perform some reorganization of your data in between fetching them from the file and printing them out. There are codes which allow you to specify how you want your dates and times displayed and how you want decimal places and negative numbers represented. There are codes that allow you to ask for two pieces of data from different attributes with one word. There are even codes that allow you to ask for a piece of data from a totally different file without having to explicitly ask the computer to look in that file. When placed in attribute 7 these codes are referred to as **conversions**, and when placed in attribute 8, as **correlatives**. The difference between a conversion and a correlative is quite subtle, but it is important if you wish to use the 'ACCESS' commands described in §4.3 to sort through your data. Technically, the difference is that a manipulation specified as a correlative is applied to the data immediately after they are fetched from the file, and before the computer performs any checking or sorting of them, whereas a manipulation specified as a conversion is applied to the data after the checking and sorting, just before the data are printed out. If you want your computer to behave in a sensible fashion, you will have to ensure that you use conversions and correlatives in the right places. Fortunately, that doesn't mean you have to understand the technical gibberish above, because none of the conversion/correlative codes find frequent use *both* as conversions and as correlatives—they are all almost always used only as one or as the other. So, once you have decided which code it is that you want to use in a particular dictionary definition, the choice of whether to put it in attribute 7 or attribute 8 is simply a matter of following convention. Below we give a list of the most useful codes, divided by whether they are usually employed as conversions or as correlatives. It is extremely unlikely that you will ever have to use one of these codes in the way other than the way described here.

3.5.2   Codes commonly used as conversions

The date conversion.   The most commonly used conversion codes are the ones used to display stored dates and times. In §3.4 for example we suggested a way of storing the dates of everyone's holidays in their personnel record. But if we were *actually* going to do this we would not store the dates as shown there.

To make the point let us take a simpler example and suppose we want to add dates of birth to the information stored in our file. Perhaps (having scrapped our plan of keeping track of everyone's holidays) we decide to put this in attribute 5. If we settle on the same notation for the dates as we used before, Joe Bloggs' item might look like this:

```
┌─────────────────────┬──────────────────────┐
│ File: STAFF         │ Item: BLOGGS-J       │
└─────────────────────┴──────────────────────┘
Attribute
  Number      Contents of Attribute
      1       Bloggs
      2       Joe
      3       14 Home Ave]Woking]Surrey
      4       14576
      5       5 NOV 54
```

And then we could define a word "DOB" in the dictionary to refer to it:

```
┌─────────────────────────┬──────────────────┐
│ File: DICT STAFF        │ Item: DOB        │
└─────────────────────────┴──────────────────┘
Attribute
  Number      Contents of Attribute
      1       A
      2       5
      3       DATE OF BIRTH
      4
      5
      6
      7
      8
      9       L
     1∅       9
```

which would allow us to ask for this date as Joe Bloggs' DOB. Many people
do store dates in just this fashion. But in truth it is unsatisfactory because
although this notation for the date is perfectly clear to humans, it is a bit
of a mystery to computers. A Pick computer likes to have dates given as a
single number. Specifically it likes dates in **Pick internal format**, that is, as
the number of days elapsed since December 31st, 1967. Dates before this are
represented by negative numbers. So for example January 1st, 1968 would be
denoted by the number 1 and December 30th, 1967 by the number -1. This
avoids confusions such as the perennial trans-Atlantic bickering over whether
the number of the day or the number of the month should come first, whether
you should use hyphens "-", slashes "/" or dots "." between the numbers
and whether or not you should pad numbers out with leading zeros (05-11-54
or 5-11-54). More to the point, it also makes it much quicker and easier for the
computer to arrange dates in chronological order, because it does not have to
work out what the dates mean. It can just arrange the numbers in numerical
order and have done.

Anyway, let us accept that for various reasons the designers of the Pick
operating system have defined an approved notation for the storage of dates
in data files. So Bloggs' item in STAFF should actually look like this:

```
┌─────────────────────┬──────────────────────┐
│ File: STAFF         │ Item: BLOGGS-J       │
└─────────────────────┴──────────────────────┘
Attribute
  Number      Contents of Attribute
      1       Bloggs
      2       Joe
```

```
3    14 Home Ave]Woking]Surrey
4    14576
5    -48Ø4
```

But this still leaves you with a problem because if all your dates are stored as numbers like 7559 or -12Ø7 then, helpful as it may be for the computer, they are completely meaningless to you, and it's going to take you several minutes with a calculator to work out what they really mean. This is where attribute 7 comes in. If you put a "D" in attribute seven of the dictionary item defining the word "DOB",

File: DICT STAFF	Item: DOB

```
Attribute
  Number      Contents of Attribute
        1    A
        2    5
        3    DATE OF BIRTH
        4
        5
        6
        7    D
        8
        9    L
       1Ø    11
```

then you tell the computer that this particular number, in attribute 5 of each item in STAFF, is a date. So when you ask to see Bloggs' DOB, Pick quickly turns the number back into human-readable form for you before displaying it. It will display it in the form "5 NOV 1954" to prevent any argument about

Table 3.1. Date conversion codes

Conversion code	Effect	Example
D	Full date conversion	Ø5 NOV 1954
D2	Only two digits of the year number	Ø5 NOV 54
D2-	Use numerical form for date	Ø5-11-54
DD	Day of month only	5
DM	Month number only	11
DMA	Month in words	November
DQ	Number of quarter	4
DY	Full year only	1954
D2Y	Last two digits of year only	54
DW	Day number in the week (1 is Monday)	3
DWA	Day of week in words	Friday
DJ	Day number in year	3Ø9

which number represents the month.[8] There are other date conversions you
can ask for in attribute 7. The complete list is given in Table 3.1.

You are allowed to have several words in the dictionary which all refer
to the same attribute. So you can have two identical items called "DOB" and
"BIRTHDATE" which both display the person's date of birth when you ask for
them. But you can also define two words that are nearly the same except that
the conversion code in attribute 7 is different. For example you could have
DOB defined as above, but define YOB thus:

File: DICT STAFF	Item: YOB

Attribute Number	Contents of Attribute
1	A
2	5
3	DATE OF BIRTH
4	
5	
6	
7	DY
8	
9	L
10	4

Both of these words will extract data from the fifth attribute of any item in
the file "STAFF", but the conversion performed in the two cases is different:
if we ask to see someone's DOB we get their complete date of birth in human-
readable form (e.g., 5 NOV 1954), but if we ask to see their YOB we get only
the year (e.g., 1954).

The other types of conversion are:

The time conversion.   Pick's designers also specified an internal format for
the storage of times of day—as the number of seconds elapsed since midnight.
The time conversion allows you to display times stored in this fashion in legible
form.

The output mask.   This allows you to specify various simple rearrange-
ments of the characters in an attribute before printing. For example, you can
have decimal points inserted in appropriate places, or commas between the
thousands, or a particular part of the data extracted and printed, leaving the
rest behind.

Useful as they are, these are features that you will have call to use only
rarely, if at all. So we will say no more about them.

---

[8] This still leaves you with the problem of how to work out what numbers to feed *into*
the computer in the first place when you are putting the data into the file. This is normally
dealt with by a Pick BASIC program, see §8.5.

3.5.3   Codes commonly used as correlatives

The translation correlative.   The **translation correlative** allows you
to treat a piece of data from one file as if it were stored in another file. Let
us illustrate these correlatives with an example.   Suppose you have a file
"SALES" that contains details of your dealings with each of your customers.
Each item contains the date of a transaction, a customer account number,
the relevant stock codes and so on. And suppose you wish it also to contain
the name and address of the customer. You *could* put these in attributes of
the file "SALES". However these data are already stored in another file on the
computer—the file "CUSTOMERS". Items in CUSTOMERS have customer account
numbers for IDs and they contain everything you need to know about your
customers, including names and addresses. It would certainly be possible to
duplicate the relevant parts of this file in SALES. But, while this would save
you switching endlessly back and forth between the files to find names and
addresses, it would not be a good idea. To see this, consider what would
happen when one of your customers changed his address, or his trading title,
or indeed anything stored in the CUSTOMERS file. If you keep a customer's
address in the file "CUSTOMERS" and in every item in SALES that relates to a
transaction with him, then you are going to have an terrible job changing its
every occurrence to keep yourself up to date when he moves premises. And
the chances are that you wouldn't get it right every time either, and some of
the addresses would disagree with some of the other addresses, and confusion
would abound.

Correlatives provide a way to save yourself the trouble of changing all
these identical addresses, and eliminate the possibility of your making any
mistakes when you change them. You can create a word in the dictionary of
the file "SALES"—ADDRESS, say—which instructs the computer to look up the
customer's address in the file "CUSTOMERS". It then appears to the user that
addresses are stored in the file "SALES", although in reality they are stored
in the file "CUSTOMERS", and nowhere else. For example, suppose that items
in SALES are identified by invoice number, and that the first attribute of each
contains the account number of the customer involved. A typical item might
look like this:

File: SALES	Item: CØØ3914

```
Attribute
  Number      Contents of Attribute
      1       89MCPØØ1                    (Customer account number)
      2       7693                        (Date of transaction)
      3       ØØØ6Ø                       (Stock code of item sold)
      4       1999                        (Price in pennies each)
      5       1                           (Quantity of item sold)
      6       JB                          (Initials of salesperson)
              . . . .
```

Now we can create items in DICT SALES that allow us to look up the contents of any one of these attributes in the normal fashion. ACC.NO for example might be the word we define to refer to attribute 1 so that we can ask for account numbers in a simple, mnemonic way. And we might define a word DATE with a D conversion code in attribute 7 so that we could check on the date of a transaction easily. But we could also define the word ADDRESS thus:

| File: DICT SALES | Item: ADDRESS |

Attribute Number	Contents of Attribute
1	A
2	1
3	CUSTOMER ADDRESS
4	
5	
6	
7	
8	TCUSTOMERS;X;;3
9	T
1Ø	3Ø

Attribute 8 is a **translation correlative**. The formula for putting it together is:

1. Start with a T. This says that it's a translation correlative.
2. Give the name of the file containing the information you want, followed by a semi-colon. In this case it is the address of the customer we want, which is in the file "CUSTOMERS".
3. Next you put either an X or a C, followed by a semi-colon. The difference between X and C lies in what the computer does if the requested item in CUSTOMERS does not exist. If you put X and it doesn't find the item in CUSTOMERS, the computer responds with a blank—it gives you nothing. If you put C and it doesn't find the item, it prints the customer's ID, so that at least you have something to go on.
4. The next thing to enter is the "input field", followed by a semi-colon. Having never found any use for one of these, we recommend you always leave this bit blank, and just put in the semi-colon (which *is* important). Hence the two consecutive semi-colons in our example.
5. Finally you add the number of the attribute in the other file (CUSTOMERS in our example) that contains the information you want (e.g., attribute 3, as above). This does not need a semi-colon after it.

And how does the computer know which *item* to look at in the CUSTOMERS file? Clearly it needs to know the item ID, i.e., the customer's account number, so we put the number of the attribute in SALES which contains this information into attribute 2 of our dictionary item. Thus, above, attribute 2 of ADDRESS says "1", meaning that the ID of the item the computer is to look for in CUSTOMERS, is to be found in attribute 1 of the item in SALES.

No doubt you are now thoroughly confused about this whole issue and are considering skipping the rest of the chapter, and going on to something new and (possibly) interesting instead. There is probably much to be said in favour of this, but just in case you are still with us, let's try to clarify the action of the translation correlative by working through what the computer will do when it comes across this one.

So, suppose our SALES file is set up as shown above and that we have a customer—the Miserable Computer Products Company of Great Britain, or MCP for short—entered in our files like this:

File: CUSTOMERS	Item: 89MCP001

```
Attribute
  Number    Contents of Attribute
       1    7689
       2    MCP (UK) Ltd.
       3    74-156 Work Ave]Homing]Surrey
       4    JB
            . . . .
```

89MCP001 is their account number and their address is in attribute 3 of the item. Now you ask the computer for the ADDRESS of the customer at the receiving end of transaction number C003914 in the SALES file. Here is what the computer does:

(i) It goes to the dictionary "DICT SALES" and looks for an item called "ADDRESS". It finds it, and notices that there is something, presumably a correlative, in attribute 8.

(ii) So it checks out this correlative and sees first that it begins with a T, which means that it is a translation correlative, i.e., one which involves looking something up in another file. Next it sees the filename "CUSTOMERS" and the attribute number "3" on the end. Armed with this information it has almost all it needs to find the data you want. The only thing it doesn't know is which item to look at in CUSTOMERS.

(iii) So it goes to attribute 2 of the dictionary definition and sees a "1". This tells it that the ID it needs is to be found in attribute 1 of the item "C003914" in the data portion of the file "SALES".

(iv) So it goes to the item "C003914" and looks up attribute 1, where it finds the customer number "89MCP001".

(v) Now it has everything. It goes to the item "89MCP001" in the file "CUS-TOMERS" and retrieves the contents of attribute 3 and displays them for you, and there you have it—MCP's address:

```
74-156 Work Ave
Homing
Surrey
```

And of course all this is done with lightning speed and accuracy and clearly saves you a whole lot of time making these cross-references yourself. Furthermore, if one of your customers *should* move to new premises, you have only to change their address as held in the file "CUSTOMERS" and you are up to date, because there aren't any other copies of the old address to change.

Extraction of a single value.   There is another, somewhat arcane use for the translation correlative, and that is in defining a word to refer to a particular value within a multi-valued attribute. Taking the example of the CUSTOMERS file again, suppose you want to define a word "ADDR.1" to refer to the first line of the address of one of your customers. This piece of information is stored in the first value of the third attribute of each customer's item in the file. The correct definition of this word is:

File: DICT CUSTOMERS	Item: ADDR.1

Attribute Number	Contents of Attribute
1	A
2	Ø
3	First line of address
4	
5	
6	
7	
8	TCUSTOMERS;X1;;3
9	T
1Ø	3Ø

It is undoubtedly more trouble than it's worth to explain how this correlative works. Just regard it as a formula for making your own. The important points are:

(i) Attribute 2 should contain a zero.

(ii) The correlative points to "it's own file"—that is, it points to the file "CUSTOMERS", even though it's in the CUSTOMERS dictionary.

(iii) The correlative takes exactly the same form as an ordinary translation correlative, except that it has an extra number after the "X" or "C" and before the second semi-colon. This number is the number of the value containing the data you want to extract.

The concatenation correlative.   After translation correlatives probably the most commonly used correlatives are **concatenation correlatives**. Concatenation correlatives allow you to ask for two or more pieces of data from a file using only one word. For example, suppose that you wish to define a word "NAME" in the STAFF file's dictionary, to refer to the full names of the members of staff whose details are stored in the file—you want to be able to ask for BLOGGS-J's NAME and get back "Joe Bloggs". There is no attribute in Bloggs' item in the STAFF file that contains exactly this information, so you want to join together—concatenate—the first and second attributes of

his item. This you can do by putting a concatenation correlative in attribute
8 of the item defining the word "NAME" in DICT STAFF:

File: DICT STAFF	Item: NAME

Attribute Number	Contents of Attribute
1	A
2	
3	NAME
4	
5	
6	
7	
8	C;2 1
9	L
1Ø	25

The correlative consists of the letter C, then a semi-colon ";", then the
numbers of the attributes that you want concatenated. The space between the
2 and the 1 in the example above tells the computer to put a space between
the two names it gets from the attributes, so that you get "Joe Bloggs", not
"JoeBloggs". You could put any other character here (except a digit or a
semicolon) and it would have come out between "Joe" and "Bloggs" in the
same way as this space does. If you put a semicolon between the attribute
numbers then the computer would put nothing at all between the names,
and you *would* get "JoeBloggs". You are also allowed to put a string of
characters, in single or double quotes, in place of any of the attribute numbers
in a concatenation correlative, and that too will get printed out when you ask
for somebody's NAME.

Thus to take a more complicated example, if you defined the word "FULL-
NAME" in DICT STAFF by the item

File: DICT STAFF	Item: FULLNAME

Attribute Number	Contents of Attribute
1	A
2	
3	FULL NAME
4	
5	
6	
7	
8	C;"FULL NAME: ";1,2.
9	L
1Ø	35

then on asking for the FULLNAME of BLOGGS-J you would get:

FULL NAME: Bloggs,Joe.

Notice that, since the attribute numbers of the data to which the words "NAME"
and "FULLNAME" refer are given as part of the correlative, there is no need to
put anything in attribute 2, and you can just leave it blank.

There are several other types of correlative. You may come across the following:

Arithmetic correlatives.   These allow you to specify some arithmetic operation to be performed on the data. For example, you could define a word "TOTAL" which contains a correlative in its defining dictionary item to make the computer multiply the price and the quantity entered on an item in SALES to give you the total value of the transaction.

Extraction correlatives.   These can be used to pick out just one part of an attribute for display.

Pattern matching correlatives.   These cause data to be printed only if it matches a pattern you give in the correlative attribute.

User defined correlatives.   These call on some PROC or Pick BASIC program (see Chapters 8 and 9) to process the data before displaying it.

We will say no more on these advanced forms of correlatives here. They are very useful to have when you need them, but you will need them so rarely that it is probably enough for you to know that they exist and can be looked up in your Pick manual if and when the time comes.

4 Command-line Pick

Computers exist in order to run programs. The disk on your computer probably contains hundreds, maybe even thousands of programs, and it is clearly an important requirement of the operating system that it provide some means by which you can specify which out of all these programs the computer is to run next. In practice this means there has to be a special 'master program' which takes its orders from you, the user, and then sees to it that the computer runs the programs you have asked for. Every operating system provides such a program. On a Pick system it is called the **TCL interpreter**.[1] When the TCL interpreter is running on a machine, we say simply that the machine is "running TCL" or "in TCL". You know when a machine is running TCL because a symbol ">" appears at the left-hand edge of the screen with the cursor flashing next to it.

The TCL interpreter ensures that the computer is at all times alert, ready for your instructions and able to understand and act upon a wide range of commands. Furthermore, it is capable of running *any* program on the entire disk. In this respect it is unusual. If you buy software packages from specialist software vendors you will rarely find them so flexible. One program from a suite may be willing to surrender control of the computer to another, but very rarely will it be willing to surrender control to a program from outside the suite.

Often this restriction of the programs you can run to the members of a suite of, say, accounting programs is just what you want. If the total number of programs in the suite is not very large, convenient menus can be provided on which all the available programs are listed. This makes it easy to choose the next program to be run. Also it prevents you running programs that might erase or otherwise damage valuable data. But restricting a user to a menu is analogous to restricting a toddler to a play-pen; it may be acceptable for the odd afternoon, but in the long run it won't do. Children *must* open

---

[1] The letters TCL stand for "Terminal Control Language". Actually, the TCL interpreter is not really a program in its own right, just a part of the operating system program, see §1.3.

all the cupboards, run up and down the stairs, race on their bikes around the neighbourhood. They have to learn to explore and be free. If you are to feel confident and in control of your computer you too must explore and be free, and the key to freedom is the TCL interpreter.

If you buy an absolutely basic Pick computer that comes with no additional software, your machine will run TCL whenever you log on. However, if you have additional programs for your machine, it is likely that one of these programs starts running automatically when you log on,[2] so we next explain how you can break out of one of these self-starting programs and get the TCL interpreter to run.

4.1 Getting to TCL

If you have a completely menu-driven system like the one described above, then before you can try out any of the examples in this chapter you need to know how to get out of the closed world of your menus. You may find an item on one of the menus saying "Go to TCL" or just "TCL" or maybe you need to type "T" or "TCL" at one of the menus. Perhaps there is some cryptic paragraph in a manual somewhere explaining how to "access TCL". If all else fails you can try pressing the BREAK key.[3] That should produce either an exclamation mark or an asterisk on the screen, to which you should reply END in capitals and then press the RETURN key. If all is well, you will have the attention of the TCL interpreter. You will know when you have reached TCL because a symbol ">" will appear at the left-hand edge of the screen with the cursor flashing next to it. If it doesn't then somebody is conspiring against you and you should seek the assistance of one of the conspirators—probably your suppliers.

The character ">" is called a **prompt**. It indicates that you are in charge. The computer is waiting for you to tell it what to do next. If you know what to type you can make it do almost anything. In general you must type a line of text (a **command**). It will appear on the screen as you type it, and when you have finished you press the big key on the right marked RETURN or maybe ENTER. Always press this RETURN key when you have typed in the last bit of the line, to let the computer know you are done—we won't keep reminding you.

4.1.1 Examples of things to type

First of all you may be worried that you don't know how to get yourself out of this mess we've persuaded you to get yourself into. (Far more likely you've

---

[2] We explain in §9.1 how to make a program start running automatically when you log on.

[3] If your keyboard hasn't a BRK key, hold down the CONTROL or CTRL key and press C. We shall denote this operation 'Ctrl-C'.

not tried anything at the computer at all yet because you're reading this at home and the wretched thing is miles away. But just in case...) The simplest way is to type "OFF" at the symbol ">" (and then press RETURN/ENTER) and the computer will then log you off. You could also type "off" in small letters. When you're using TCL you can do either.[4]There may be other ways back to the menus. For example on our machine you type "MENU" and you get back to the menu you came from. But this is not true on all machines and this may be another case for referring to the manual. ("What manual?", you say.) Anyway, just for practice you might do worse than to type "OFF" at the machine just to check that it really works, and then log on again and find your way back to TCL and the prompt ">".

Next try typing "WHO" (followed by RETURN of course). The computer will reply by displaying a number followed by your user name—the name by which you identify yourself when you log on—like this:

```
>WHO
11 JACK
```

The word "WHO" is a TCL command that tells the computer to run a simple program that looks up the name you gave when you logged on and prints it on the screen. You see? By giving commands in TCL you are running programs. Every time you ask the computer to do a thing you are really running a program, even if it is a very simple one like this. You don't need to know how the programs work to use them. In fact a lot of the time you don't even need to know that you are running a program. You can just think of things like WHO as being orders. The computer knows what they mean and responds appropriately. Even experienced computer users tend to think of TCL commands this way although they know that what they are really doing is telling the computer to run a program. Incidentally the number that WHO displays in front of your user name is your 'line number', which indicates which terminal you are using. More on this in §4.2.4.

Another useful command is LISTU. If you type this after the TCL prompt ">" you will see something like this:

```
>LISTU
CH# PCBF NAME......... TIME.. DATE.......

00 02C0 KING          15:48  29 OCT 1990
08 0320 BINNEY        09:45  29 OCT 1990
11 0340 JACK          11:14  29 OCT 1990
18 0400 NEWMAN        13:03  29 OCT 1990
22 0410 JILL          12:27  29 OCT 1990
```

---

[4] There are other times when this is not true, for example when typing END to get to TCL as above. If you can't remember these subtle and rather poorly thought out distinctions then it might be as well to stick to capitals all the time.

This is very similar to the WHO command, except that it lists all the people using the computer at the moment, not just yourself. As well as the names and line numbers of all the users (the third and first columns respectively), LISTU tells you the time and date when they logged on (which might be useful) and the "primary control block frame" or PCBF (which certainly won't be, so there's no need to worry about what it is). Thus, for example if you want to know whether your friend Jack is at work on the computer or has gone off to the pub to get some lunch, you could type a quick LISTU at your terminal and discover that he has been logged on on line 11 for the last two hours. So it would definitely be worth your while to pop round to his office and look for him before you disappear off down the pub yourself.

There are of course much more complex programs that you can run by typing a TCL command, many of which will perform useful tasks on your database. Really specialist jobs like running off the customer invoices are best left to your professionally written, menu-driven software. But simpler jobs like listing all the customers in the database can be done using TCL commands rather more easily than with many proprietary software packages. Here is a quick example of this which also serves to show that a command can consist of more than one word. To get a list of all the items in our file "STAFF" we would type

```
>SORT STAFF

STAFF.........

BINNEY-J-J
BLOGGS-J
NEWMAN-M-E-J
OTHER-A-N
    ....
```

The explanation of this command comes later in the chapter, but it might be worth trying it out on your computer now, just to prove to yourself that it works. You will have to substitute the name of one of your own files for STAFF and it will be the item IDs of your data that will be printed in the list, but apart from that things should look exactly as above. It is worth noting that none of the commands shown in this section ever *changes* anything in the files so you can do absolutely no harm by experimenting with them. There are only a few TCL commands that are capable of deleting or altering items in your files and we will warn you about these. So there is little chance of your doing any damage by experimenting with TCL.

4.2   TCL verbs

In Pick jargon one refers to the first word in a command (LISTU, SORT, and so on) as the **verb** in the command, because that is the word which specifies

what the computer is to do. The other words in the command (if there are
any) specify which data the computer is to do it with. Generic types of
commands are distinguished by giving their verbs, so that one may talk of a
"LISTU command" or a "SORT command" meaning one which starts with the
verb "LISTU" or the verb "SORT". We now begin a run-down of the commands
available in TCL, classified by the verb they start with. It is not an exhaustive
list because the list of verbs is not immutable; verbs can be added by your
software suppliers, or by you if you know how (see §§7.2.1 and 9.1, and the
introduction to Chapter 8). So your machine's list of verbs will undoubtedly
be different from that on every other machine in the land. What's more, the
list of verbs that you can use is stored in your MD, so it is even possible for
different users on the same computer to have different lists because they have
different MDs. And quite apart from anything else there are an awful lot of
verbs and most of them are useless, so we only mention the most important.

We begin by listing some of the simpler verbs such as OFF and WHO, which
do not read any data from your files, or write any in them.

4.2.1 OFF

Typing "OFF" logs you off the computer. When you use it the computer will
display a message on the screen telling you how long you have been logged on
for and other miscellaneous information, like this:

```
>OFF
<   CONNECT TIME 94 MINS.; CPU 3 UNITS; LPTR PAGES 0   >
<   LOGGED OFF AT 16:08:00 ON 29 OCT 1990               >
```

On many Pick computers this information, while in theory a Good Thing, is
next to useless because the machine immediately erases it to make way for
the message that tells the next user to log on.

4.2.2 LISTFILES & LISTVERBS

LISTFILES lists all your files (or to be precise all those for which there are
file-defining items or Q-pointers in your MD):

```
>LISTFILES

Page    1   Files within: MD                10:35:26  30 Oct 1990

MD.................... Code F/BASE........ F/MOD......... F/SEP...

PAY                    D    20854         3                      1
STAFF                  D    27182         7                      1

                       ***

PROGRAMS               DC   31415         13                     1

                       ***

ACC                    Q    ACC           ACC
```

```
CONFIG                    Q   SYSTEM     CONFIG
ERRMSG                    Q   LIBRARY    ERRMSG
MD                        Q
QFILE                     Q   FINANCE
SYSPROG.VERBS             Q   SYSPROG    SYSPROG.VERBS
SYSTEM                    Q   SYSTEM     SYSTEM
TCL.HELP                  Q   LIBRARY    TCL.HELP
TCL.VERBS                 Q   LIBRARY    TCL.VERBS
TERMINAL.DRIVERS          Q   LIBRARY    TERMINAL.DRIVERS

                              ***

***

14 Items listed
>
```

As you can see it lists data (D-type) files first, followed by program (DC-type) files (see Chapter 8), followed by Q-pointers to files belonging to other people. For D- and DC-type files the columns give, in order, the name, type, base-frame, modulo and separation of the file. In the case of a Q-pointer the fourth column gives the name of the file to which the Q-pointer points, while the third column gives the account name of the MD in which that file is defined.

To most people it is only the filenames, and possibly the file types (D, DC, Q and so on) that matter, so you can usually ignore most of the stuff LISTFILES produces. On your computer the list of files may be rather large—much more than one screen-full of text (24 lines). In this case the computer will only display the first screen-full. When you have finished scrutinizing this you must press the RETURN (or ENTER) key to get the next page. If you have found what you were looking for in the list and you don't want to go through ten more pages of boring file-names you can, alternatively, type Ctrl-X which[5] will finish the list there and then and return you to the prompt ">". These conventions regarding the use of RETURN and Ctrl-X are common to many TCL commands.

You can also type "LISTVERBS" to get a list of all the verbs that are defined in your MD. This is a less common thing to want to do and you may not use this verb very often. The tricks of pressing RETURN to get the next page and Ctrl-X to finish the list prematurely work here as well.

4.2.3   WHO & LISTU

Examples of these simple, but useful verbs are given above (§4.1.1). The only thing that is perhaps worth explaining in a little more detail is the idea of a line number. A Pick computer may have many terminals connected to it by cables which plug into the ports on the back of the computer (see §1.2). Each

---

[5] Recall that this means holding down the key marked CONTROL or CTRL and pressing the X key.

port has a number which is fixed by the way the computer is wired and is probably printed next to the port. Your **line number** is the number of the port to which your terminal is connected, and it is the users' line numbers which are given in the displays produced by WHO and LISTU. So you can see that as long as no one plays about with the plugs and sockets at the back of your computer, the line numbers tell you which terminal someone is using. If you feel inclined, a little experimentation with the verb "LISTU" will rapidly reveal which numbers correspond to which terminals and so you will be able to tell where people are working from the list produced when you type LISTU.

4.2.4   MESSAGE

Having established by typing "LISTU" that someone, Jack say, is using the computer on another terminal, you can use the verb "MESSAGE" to make a short message appear on his screen. This could be useful if Jack's terminal is some distance away, and there is no handy telephone. You type MESSAGE followed by the user name of the user you would like to contact—JACK—and the message you would like passed to him—"Time for tea?", perhaps—and magically it will appear on Jack's terminal. To you it would look like this:

```
>MESSAGE JACK TIME FOR TEA?
```

and to Jack it would look like this:

```
>
16:34:45  29 OCT 1990  From JILL:
TIME FOR TEA?
>
```

Even if the user on the receiving end is not using TCL at that moment but is in the middle of a program the message will appear on his screen. This is one good reason not to use MESSAGE too much. Because if your friend *is* using a program and has lots of important information on the screen, your message could overwrite some of it, and you may find your friend less friendly in future. Notice that the MESSAGE command tells the receiver who sent the message. This saves you the trouble of signing your messages, but it does mean you can't really disown any messages that don't go down too well.

There is another problem with MESSAGE in that the length of a message is limited. A TCL command is not allowed to be longer than 140 characters. And the space for your message will be shorter than this by the fifteen or so characters required for the verb "MESSAGE" and the recipient's user name. So the MESSAGE command is not really suitable for anything longer than a short note.

If you attempt to send a message to a person who is not logged on to the computer you will get a reply like this:

```
>MESSAGE JACK WHERE'S THAT TEN QUID YOU OWE ME?
[337] User is not logged on
```

and there is nothing for it but to communicate your message to them in person.

As MESSAGE is quite a long word and you might need to type it often, Pick provides the verb MSG which is shorter than, but exactly synonymous with MESSAGE. Thus "MSG JACK TIME FOR TEA?" would have worked equally well in the example above.

4.2.5   TIME & DATE

Typing "TIME" makes the computer display the current time and date according to its internal clock/calendar. The DATE verb does exactly the same thing. There is no difference between these two. If you type them one after the other you will see something like this:

```
>TIME
16:21:32 29 Oct 1990
>DATE
16:21:37 29 Oct 1990
```

Having seen examples of simple TCL verbs we now move on to verbs which do things with particular files.

4.2.6   CREATE-FILE, CLEAR-FILE, DELETE-FILE & DELETE

Pick provides a number of verbs for creating and destroying files, and for deleting data from them.

CREATE-FILE. CREATE-FILE is the verb you use to make a new file. Creating a file is a moderately tricky operation because you need to decide not only what you want to call it, but also what you want its modulo and separation (see §3.2.1) to be.[6] The general rules for choosing the mod and sep are as follows:

(i) The separation should always be 1.[7]

(ii) The modulo should be set to the number of frames you want to reserve for the storage of the data in the new file, which is dependent on how much data you expect to put in the file.

(iii) The modulo should always be a **prime number**. A prime number is a whole number that cannot be divided exactly by any other number except 1. Table 4.1 contains a list of all the prime numbers up to 1000, so all you have to do is choose your modulo from the numbers in this table.

---

[6] The ideal mod and sep are the ones that will make your machine run fastest, but it will run fine with any reasonable values. For most purposes mod and sep of 11 and 1 are perfectly acceptable.

[7] So universal is this rule that in the new operating system, Advanced Pick, released by Pick Systems in 1989, the sep has been abolished altogether, and is automatically taken to be 1 for all files, without your having to put a 1 in the file-defining item at all.

Table 4.1.   Prime numbers up to 1000, for use as file modulos.

1	2	3	5	7	11	13	17	19	23
29	31	37	41	43	47	53	59	61	67
71	73	79	83	89	97	101	103	107	109
113	127	131	137	139	149	151	157	163	167
173	179	181	191	193	197	199	211	223	227
229	233	239	241	251	257	263	269	271	277
281	283	293	307	311	313	317	331	337	347
349	353	359	367	373	379	383	389	397	401
409	419	421	431	433	439	443	449	457	461
463	467	479	487	491	499	503	509	521	523
541	547	557	563	569	571	577	587	593	599
601	607	613	617	619	631	641	643	647	653
659	661	673	677	683	691	701	709	719	727
733	739	743	751	757	761	769	773	787	797
809	811	821	823	827	829	839	853	857	859
863	877	881	883	887	907	911	919	929	937
941	947	953	967	971	977	983	991	997	1009

Thus the steps to choosing the correct mod and sep for a new file are:

1. Work out approximately how much data the file will hold when it is full by estimating the average length in bytes (characters) of each item and multiplying it by your estimate of the number of items there will be in the file.

2. Divide this total by the number of bytes of data to a frame on your computer (which is probably 500, but could be 1000 or 2000) to get the number of frames the data in the file will occupy when it has all been typed in.

3. The modulo of the new file should be the next number bigger than this in Table 4.1, and the separation should be 1.

Let us illustrate this procedure with an example. In the last chapter we drew diagrams of several typical items in a fictional file "STAFF". Each of these items was about fifty characters long if we remember to count all the spaces and punctuation marks as well as the letters. If there are, say, a hundred employees whose details are to be stored in this file, then the file is going to occupy around $100 \times 50 = 5000$ bytes when all the data have been fed in. If the frames on your computer contain 500 bytes of data, then these 5000 bytes are equivalent to 10 frames. (These numbers don't have to be accurate—rough estimates are fine.) Consulting Table 4.1, we find that the first prime number after 10 is 11. So the modulo should be 11 and the separation 1.

Usually when you create a file you want to create both a dictionary and a data portion for it. Thus in creating the file you need to specify what it is to be called and the modulo and separation, separately, of both its portions. The mod for a dictionary should be 1 (and the sep should be 1 too, as usual). Suppose then that you want to create a new file called "SUPPLIERS" which is to have mod and sep of 1 and 1 on the dictionary portion and 7 and 1 on the data portion. Then you type

```
>CREATE-FILE SUPPLIERS 1 1 7 1

[417] File 'SUPPLIERS' Created. Base=23514, Modulo=1, Separ=1.
[417] File 'SUPPLIERS' Created. Base=23515, Modulo=7, Separ=1.
```

Here **CREATE-FILE** is followed by the desired name of the new file, followed by the mod and sep of the dictionary portion, followed by those of the data portion. The computer has created both portions of the file. It creates both completely empty; there are no data in the data portion and no words in the dictionary. The two messages it has printed out here are for the two portions of the file; it has not created two files.

If for some reason you want to create a new file with only a dictionary or only a data portion you can use the slightly different forms

```
>CREATE-FILE DICT SUPPLIERS 1 1
```

and

```
>CREATE-FILE DATA SUPPLIERS 7 1
```

to accomplish these tasks. This however will most likely be a rare occurrence.

CLEAR-FILE. Once you have created a file you will presumably start to fill it up with your data using a method such as that described in Chapter 6, or using some Pick BASIC program that you have written or bought. A large part of many computer users' working lives is spent feeding in the data that make up a database. But very occasionally it also happens that you want to clear all the data out again. Destroy it. Forget it. **CLEAR-FILE** is the verb which achieves this. It must be used with *extreme caution* because once all the data are cleared from a file there is no getting them back. The computer business abounds with appalling stories of people who have inadvertently destroyed the fruits of weeks or months of work by the misuse of commands like **CLEAR-FILE**. (The prudent owner of a Pick computer will keep 'backup' copies of all his or her valued data on disks or tapes away from the computer to prevent this sort of tragedy. Chapter 7 explains Pick's excellent provisions for making such copies.)

Imagine then that you have given up your old line of business and, setting off along the road with your computer on your back, you have sought and found a new and exciting economic niche to exploit. To supply your new trade you need a new and different set of wholesalers, and the old ones are no longer of any use whatsoever. So you want to purge your SUPPLIERS file

of every last trace of the old regime and start afresh, typing in the details of
your new suppliers. To do this you type

>CLEAR-FILE DATA SUPPLIERS

which means "clear everything out of the data portion of the file SUPPLIERS".
It will erase all the data and leave a file with an empty data portion as if it
had just been created. The word "DATA" is mandatory. If you miss it out the
computer will complain. There is no way to clear out both the dictionary and
the data portions of a file simultaneously. This however is the only safeguard
there is against doing the wrong thing. The data are erased the moment you
hit the RETURN key and there is no getting them back unless you have a copy
stashed away somewhere else. We find this rather disturbing. It is easy to
make a program that asks you "Are you sure you really want to erase all this
stuff?" before it actually does it. In fact there is exactly such a program
given as an example in §9.2.3 and it might be as well to use this, or one very
like it; clearing files is a delicate business.

Similarly, if you want to purge all the entries from a file's dictionary
before constructing a new one, you should type

CLEAR-FILE DICT SUPPLIERS

But this is a far less common operation.

DELETE-FILE.   An even more drastic verb is DELETE-FILE which not
only erases all the data in a file, but completely destroys the file itself to boot.
In a way it is the opposite of CREATE-FILE. If you were to type

>DELETE-FILE SUPPLIERS

then, as soon as you had pressed RETURN, the file SUPPLIERS would be no
more. You can also type "DELETE-FILE DICT SUPPLIERS" or "DELETE-FILE
DATA SUPPLIERS" to delete just the dictionary or data portions of the file
respectively.

DELETE.   In addition to being able to delete a whole file you can also
delete just one item from it. This is done with the DELETE verb. You type
"DELETE" followed by the name of the file from which you wish to delete an
item, followed in turn by the name of the item. For example, if we have an
item "GIMCRACK" in our SUPPLIERS file, we can remove it leaving the rest of
the file intact by typing

>DELETE SUPPLIERS GIMCRACK

Or we can delete several items at once, by giving a list of their names. Thus

>DELETE SUPPLIERS GIMCRACK JONES-D-Q MACMILLAN-H-X MURPHYS

has the effect of erasing the four named items only from the SUPPLIERS file.

4.2.7   COPY

Sometimes you want to copy data, *verbatim*, from one file to another, or between items in the same file. Pick provides the verb "COPY" for this job. Suppose you have an item "BLOGGS-J" in the file "STAFF" and you want to copy its entire contents into the item "OTHER-A-N", also in the file "STAFF", so that in future STAFF will contain two copies of the data in BLOGGS-J. Then you type the following:

```
>COPY STAFF BLOGGS-J
TO:OTHER-A-N

    1 BLOGGS-J

    1 items copied
>
```

Here "COPY" is followed by the name of the file containing the data you want to copy, followed by the name of the item in that file. Provided the item actually exists in the file you name, the machine will respond with "TO:" meaning "Okay. I found it. Where do you want it put?" and you in your turn give the name of the item you want it put in. Note that it is the name of an *item* that you give it. The data are copied to another item *in the same file*. The message "1 BLOGGS-J" is a list of all the items of which copies were successfully made as a result of this command. In this case it is a list with only one entry, but we will shortly see how we can use one command to copy several items at once.

If on the other hand the item "BLOGGS-J" in the file "STAFF" does not exist, the machine will say

```
'BLOGGS-J' NOT ON FILE
0 items copied
```

and the matter will be taken no further. Normally the machine has to create a new item "OTHER-A-N" in the file "STAFF" because there is no item with that name there already. If there *is* one there already then Pick will *not* copy the new data into it. It will do nothing. For all it knows you might want the data in that item, and it would be rather unfortunate if you copied in the new data and went back later to find that you've lost a vital address or something—there's not room for two sets of data in one item. There are times when you *do* want the old data erased and the new put in its place, and copy will do this for you. The trick is to put an O (the letter O not the number 0) in brackets at the end of the COPY command. Such a letter in brackets is called an **option**. We will come across several examples of these in TCL commands. O stands for "overwrite", because you are writing the new data 'on top of' the old. Thus, if Mrs. Other already has an entry in our STAFF file

and we want Joe Bloggs' data to replace what's in it, the last example won't
work and we need an "(O)":[8]

```
>COPY STAFF BLOGGS-J
TO:OTHER-A-N

    0 items copied
>COPY STAFF BLOGGS-J (O)
TO:OTHER-A-N

    1 BLOGGS-J

    1 items copied
>
```

In the first case no items were copied because the computer found that
there was an item called `OTHER-A-N` in `STAFF` already, but in the second case
we told it to ignore this and just copy the data anyway. So it did. Hence the
message "1 `items copied`". (Pick's English grammar is a bit dodgy here.
It's easy to make a `COPY` program that gets this right, but Pick's designers
evidently thought this would be a pointless frill.) Notice that when an item is
copied the original version still remains. The data haven't been moved from
one place to the other; a copy has been made and now there are two.

   In addition to copying items within a single file, the verb "`COPY`" can also
be used to copy items from one file into another. You specify the item you
want to copy in exactly the same way as before, but when the machine asks
`TO`: you put a left bracket "`(`" followed by the name of the file in which you
want the copy made. Thus to move Bloggs' entry in `STAFF` to another file
called "`EMPLOYEES`" you should type:

```
>COPY STAFF BLOGGS-J
TO:(EMPLOYEES

1 BLOGGS-J

1 items copied
>
```

and the data will be copied to the item "`BLOGGS-J`" in `EMPLOYEES`. There is no
way to copy the data from `STAFF` to any other item in `EMPLOYEES`; when you
are copying between files the item IDs in the two files are always the same.
If you wanted Bloggs' data to go into the item "`JOE-B`" in the `EMPLOYEES`
file you would first have to copy it into the `EMPLOYEES` file as above and then
make another copy in the item "`JOE-B`":

```
>COPY EMPLOYEES BLOGGS-J
TO:JOE-B

1 BLOGGS-J

1 items copied
>
```

---

[8] In fact it is not necessary to put in the closing bracket after an option—if you are
feeling lazy you can type "`COPY STAFF BLOGGS-J (O`" and the machine will know what you
mean.

Table 4.2.   Options for use with the verb "COPY"

Option	Effect
D	Delete the original item, once the copy has been made
I	Do not display a list of the items copied
N	Don't copy any item unless another one with the same name already exists in the destination file
O	Overwrite any old items with the same names as new ones
S	Suppress any error messages produced during the copying

The copy in the item "BLOGGS-J" in the file "EMPLOYEES" is still there when you have done this. If you don't want it any more, you can now rub it out using the DELETE verb described in §4.2.7—type

```
>DELETE EMPLOYEES BLOGGS-J
```

and it is gone.

In fact you can achieve both the last two steps (the copying of the data to JOE-B and the removal of BLOGGS-J) in one easy move by using another of COPY's options: this time a D in brackets at the end of the COPY command.

```
>COPY EMPLOYEES BLOGGS-J (D)
TO:JOE-B

    1 BLOGGS-J

    1 items copied
>
```

The "(D)" tells the computer to delete the data in BLOGGS-J after it has copied it to the item "JOE-B", so that there is only one copy of it in the file at the end.

If we want both to overwrite old data with our copies *and* delete the first copy as the second is made (that is, if we want both the O and D options with the same COPY command) then the two letters should be placed at the end of the command between one pair of parentheses:

```
>COPY STAFF BLOGGS-J (O,D)
```

The D and the O can be in either order and should be separated by a comma.

COPY admits several other options—the most interesting of these are given in Table 4.2. The complete list is in the Pick Manual.

It often happens that you want to copy a whole bunch of items one after the other and it would be very tiresome if you had to type "COPY FILE-NAME ITEMID" for each one. So COPY allows you to give a whole list of items to be copied. For example, if we want to copy the items "BLOGGS-J", "BINNEY-J-J" and "NEWMAN-M-E-J" in the file "STAFF", into the items "JB", "JJB" and "MEJN", also in STAFF, then we can do it like this:

```
>COPY STAFF BLOGGS-J BINNEY-J-J NEWMAN-M-E-J
TO:JB JJB MEJN

    1 BLOGGS-J
    2 BINNEY-J-J
    3 NEWMAN-M-E-J

    3 items copied
>
```

The only thing to be careful about is to get the names of the items in which you want the copies placed in the same order as the names of the items that are to be copied. If you wanted the three items to be copied to a different file then you would type

```
>COPY STAFF BLOGGS-J BINNEY-J-J NEWMAN-M-E-J
TO:(EMPLOYEES

    1 BLOGGS-J
    2 BINNEY-J-J
    3 NEWMAN-M-E-J

    3 items copied
>
```

and the items "BLOGGS-J", "BINNEY-J-J" and "NEWMAN-M-E-J" in the file "STAFF", are copied into the file "EMPLOYEES".

It may happen that you want to copy *every* item from one file into another. In that case you put an asterisk "*" in place of the item name in the COPY command. Suppose, for example, you want the EMPLOYEES file to be an exact copy of the file "STAFF". Then you should type

```
>COPY STAFF *
TO:(EMPLOYEES

    1 BINNEY-J-J
    2 BLOGGS-J
    3 NEWMAN-M-E-J
    4 OTHER-A-N
    . . . .
```

and the list of items copied will be all the items in the file. When the copying is done the computer will tell you how many items there are. You can use options like "(O)" and "(D)" with lists of items and asterisks as well.

4.2.8   SET-FILE

There is one other special verb we should mention, which can save you a lot of time when you are using TCL. This is the verb "SET-FILE". SET-FILE creates a Q-pointer in your MD pointing to any file you specify. Let us illustrate its use with an example. Imagine you wish to delete the item "GIMCRACK" from the file "STAFF". The file-defining item for STAFF is in the PERSONNEL MD. If this MD is your MD then there is no problem—you just type "DELETE STAFF GIMCRACK" and the item gets deleted (see §4.2.7). However, if you do not share the MD "**PERSONNEL**", but use another MD, then in order to delete this item you need a Q-pointer (see §3.2.2) to **STAFF** first. You may already have such a Q-pointer in your MD; if so, well and good. But if not, rather than create one the long way by editing it into your MD using the system editor as described in Chapter 6, you can create one by typing

```
>SET-FILE PERSONNEL STAFF
'QFILE' FILED.
```

This puts a Q-pointer called "QFILE" in your MD pointing to the file "STAFF" under the account "PERSONNEL". Then all you have to do to delete the unwanted item is type

```
>DELETE QFILE GIMCRACK
```

And out it goes.

The Q-pointer created by **SET-FILE** is always called "QFILE". If you already have a Q-pointer called QFILE in your MD because you have used the verb "SET-FILE" previously, then it will be deleted to make way for the new one when you use **SET-FILE** again.

4.3 ACCESS verbs

At the moment you probably have lots of programs that run on your computer to look at the contents of your database and print out reports and invoices and such. But there are also several very useful verbs in TCL that can be used to search through a file for certain information. These verbs are called **ACCESS** verbs. If you need to look through large files for items with particular characteristics, like people with surnames between B and N, or people who live in Surrey or something like that, then you may find that the flexible ACCESS commands are actually handier tools than the programs you are using at the moment. These commands are one of Pick's most impressive and original features.

There are only a small number of ACCESS verbs that find frequent use, but they are quite complicated, so we will examine them in some detail.

4.3.1 SORT

The most important of the ACCESS verbs is the verb "SORT". Furthermore, once you have mastered its use the others will all seem very simple, since all ACCESS verbs work in much the same way.

Listing the contents of a file. SORT is the verb that you use to tell the computer to print out some information from a file. Suppose, to take a concrete example, you are interested once more in the file "STAFF". If you type "SORT STAFF" the computer will print out the IDs of all the items in the file on the screen.[9] The reason the verb is "SORT" and not "PRINT", say, is because it prints them out in alphabetical order, which means it has to sort them out before it prints them. So if STAFF has just four items in it, we might see this:

```
>SORT STAFF

STAFF.........

BINNEY-J-J
BLOGGS-J
NEWMAN-M-E-J
OTHER-A-N
>
```

The word "STAFF" at the top of the list is just the computer telling you that this is a list of the items in STAFF.

This list is not much use as it stands; you want to see some of your staff's personal details. The way to do that is to say what other information you want immediately after the filename. For example, suppose each item in STAFF has an attribute called "FORENAME" (see §3.5 on dictionaries), then you can find out everybody's forename by saying

```
>SORT STAFF FORENAME

STAFF......... FORENAME.......

BINNEY-J-J     James
BLOGGS-J       Joe
NEWMAN-M-E-J   Mark
OTHER-A-N      Annabel
>
```

Note that we type "FORENAME" not "FORENAMES" here. The dictionary defines the word "FORENAME", singular, to mean the contents of the appropriate attribute, and "FORENAMES", plural, is a completely different word as far as Pick is concerned. This means that the resulting SORT command isn't really a good English sentence, but it's close enough for most people to understand what it means.

We can ask to see any number of attributes from each item. For example, if we want to know the FORENAME, SURNAME and TELEPHONE number of each member of staff, then we should type

---

[9] Well, this is usually what happens. If you want to, you can instruct the computer to print out some of the other data from the file as well as the IDs when you type "SORT STAFF" by the way you set up the dictionary for the STAFF file. This facility is explained under the heading "Default reports" at the end of this section.

```
>SORT STAFF FORENAME SURNAME TELEPHONE

STAFF......... FORENAME....... SURNAME........ TELEPHONE..

BINNEY-J-J     James          Binney              314159
BLOGGS-J       Joe            Bloggs              141421
NEWMAN-M-E-J   Mark           Newman              271828
OTHER-A-N      Annabel        Other                57721
>
```

The columns of data are printed in the order in which we ask for them in the
SORT command.

If you ask for so much data on each person that the computer cannot fit
it all on one line then it will use a separate line for each attribute, like this:

```
>SORT STAFF FORENAME SURNAME TELEPHONE

STAFF......BINNEY-J-J
FORENAME...James
SURNAME....Binney
TELEPHONE..    314159

STAFF......BLOGGS-J
FORENAME...Joe
SURNAME....Bloggs
TELEPHONE..    141421

STAFF......NEWMAN-M-E-J
FORENAME...Mark
SURNAME....Newman
TELEPHONE..    271828

STAFF......OTHER-A-N
FORENAME...Annabel
SURNAME....Other
TELEPHONE..     57721
>
```

If you ask for so much data that the entire listing does not fit on the screen
then the computer will print out only the first screen-full to begin with, and
then stop. When you have scrutinized this at your leisure, you press RETURN
and the computer will print another page. And so on until all the data you
requested have been displayed. If you get tired of looking at the pages of such
a list and do not want to work your way through the whole lot, you can bring
it to an end at any moment by typing Ctrl-X. These conventions are the
same as those used by the LISTFILES and LISTVERBS commands described in
§4.2.3.

One small complication to SORT arises when you ask for an attribute
which contains several values. You may recall that it is possible for one
attribute in an item to contain not merely one piece of data, like a number
or a sentence, but several, each one individually known as a 'value' (see §3.4).
Suppose the FORENAME attribute in each item of the file "STAFF" contained not
merely the first name of the relevant person, but all his names as a series of

separate values. Then if you asked to see everyone's FORENAMEs, SORT would
print out each value on a separate line, like this:

```
>SORT STAFF FORENAME SURNAME TELEPHONE

STAFF......... FORENAME....... SURNAME........ TELEPHONE..

BINNEY-J-J       James          Binney              314159
                 Jeffrey
BLOGGS-J         Joe            Bloggs              141421
NEWMAN-M-E-J     Mark           Newman              271828
                 Edward
                 John
OTHER-A-N        Annabel        Other                57721
                 Natalie
>
```

Sorting out the list.   All the lists we have seen so far have been sorted
into alphabetical order of ID. However, it might be more convenient if they
were sorted by, say, first name instead. This is easily done. You type

```
>SORT STAFF BY FORENAME FORENAME SURNAME TELEPHONE

STAFF......... FORENAME....... SURNAME........ TELEPHONE..

OTHER-A-N        Annabel        Other                57721
BINNEY-J-J       James          Binney              314159
BLOGGS-J         Joe            Bloggs              141421
NEWMAN-M-E-J     Mark           Newman              271828
>
```

and out comes the list in order of first names. You put "BY" and the name
of the attribute by which you want them sorted, and the computer does the
rest. It may seem a bit silly that you now have the word "FORENAME" occurring
twice in the one command, but it is important that it should because the two
occurrences are fulfilling completely different rôles. The first says that we want
the list arranged in order of forenames, and the second says that we want to
see the forenames printed out as part of our list. It is perfectly possible (if
a little pointless) to make a list which is arranged in order of forenames, but
doesn't actually show the forenames. You'd do it like this:

```
>SORT STAFF BY FORENAME SURNAME TELEPHONE

STAFF......... SURNAME........ TELEPHONE..

OTHER-A-N        Other                57721
BINNEY-J-J       Binney              314159
BLOGGS-J         Bloggs              141421
NEWMAN-M-E-J     Newman              271828
>
```

Pick knows about numerical order as well and if you ask it to print out
a list ordered by telephone number, say, you will get a list looking like this:

```
>SORT STAFF BY TELEPHONE FORENAME SURNAME TELEPHONE

STAFF......... FORENAME....... SURNAME........ TELEPHONE..

OTHER-A-N      Annabel         Other                57721
BLOGGS-J       Joe             Bloggs              141421
NEWMAN-M-E-J   Mark            Newman              271828
BINNEY-J-J     James           Binney              314159
>
```

Listing data selectively.   SORT can do much more for you than just printing data on the screen. It can also search through the file looking for particular
entries. You are allowed to specify which items you want to see by giving the
value of any attribute in the item. For example, you can ask it to print out
all the items in **STAFF** with the **SURNAME** "Bloggs" by saying

```
>SORT STAFF WITH SURNAME "Bloggs" FORENAME SURNAME TELEPHONE

STAFF......... FORENAME....... SURNAME........ TELEPHONE..

BLOGGS-J       Joe             Bloggs              141421
>
```

and only the one item is listed. This command affords us one example of a
situation in which it *is* vitally important to distinguish between capital and
lower-case letters. The name given between the quotation marks must be in
exactly the form in which it appears in the file, or the computer will not find
Bloggs' data. If we say **"BLOGGS"** in capitals and the entry in the database
says "Bloggs", then there will be no items in our list instead of one. And
conversely, if the entry in the database reads "BLOGGS" or maybe "bloggs",
the command above will not work and the list will again be empty. This is an
important point. Its consequences are far reaching. It means that you must
be absolutely meticulous when entering data into your files. You must decide
how you are going to type names, addresses and so on, where the capitals are
going to be, and you must ensure that everyone who enters data into your
files abides by those decisions.

You can also ask for items by ID. The command

```
>SORT STAFF = "BLOGGS-J" FORENAME SURNAME TELEPHONE

STAFF......... FORENAME....... SURNAME........ TELEPHONE..

BLOGGS-J       Joe             Bloggs              141421
>
```

with no "WITH" anything before the equals sign lists the item with the ID
"BLOGGS-J".

When searching it is not necessary to specify exactly which name or
number you are looking for. You can also ask for names beginning or ending
with a certain letter or letters, or even names containing a certain string of
letters within them. For example, we can print a list of all the personnel with
surnames beginning with B thus:

```
>SORT STAFF WITH SURNAME "B]" FORENAME SURNAME TELEPHONE

STAFF......... FORENAME....... SURNAME........ TELEPHONE..

BINNEY-J-J     James           Binney           314159
BLOGGS-J       Joe             Bloggs           141421
>
```

The "]" after the B means "As long as there's a B there I don't care what comes after it". So it finds Binney and it finds Bloggs. It would find Bowler and Baker and Bronk and any other B names there were in the file. Even the letter B on its own, with nothing following it at all, would be included in this search, were there anyone outlandish enough to have a surname consisting of a B and nothing else. Here are a few other possible WITH clauses we could put in a SORT command:

```
WITH SURNAME "Bi]"          Surnames starting Bi
WITH SURNAME "[ey"          Surnames ending with ey
WITH FORENAME "M]"          Forenames starting M
WITH SURNAME "[nn]"         Surnames with nn anywhere in them
```

In the last example we use both a "[" and a "]" to mean, 'As long as there's an "nn" there I don't care what comes before it *or* after it'. A SORT command containing this WITH clause would pick out names beginning with "nn", names ending with "nn" and names with "nn" anywhere in the middle.

We could also ask for all the items with IDs beginning with B like this:

```
>SORT STAFF = "B]" FORENAME SURNAME TELEPHONE

STAFF......... FORENAME....... SURNAME........ TELEPHONE..

BINNEY-J-J     James           Binney           314159
BLOGGS-J       Joe             Bloggs           141421
>
```

But SORT is even cleverer than this. You can ask it to list items from a file by indicating a whole range of values that some attribute may take. You might want a list of all the personnel with surnames in the second half of the alphabet from N to Z. To get this you should say

```
>SORT STAFF WITH SURNAME AFTER "N" FORENAME SURNAME

STAFF......... FORENAME....... SURNAME........

NEWMAN-M-E-J   Mark            Newman
OTHER-A-N      Annabel         Other
>
```

Notice that "Newman" is regarded as being after "N" in the alphabet. This may seem fairly odd to you but it is supposed to be similar to the way "n" is the first word in the dictionary under N, and "new" and all the other N words come after it. This command is interpreted to mean "with surname after N in the dictionary sense". We can also get the items with names in the first half of the alphabet by the obvious ploy of typing "SORT STAFF WITH SURNAME

Table 4.3. Words and symbols for use in WITH clauses

Word	Meaning
=	Equal to
EQ	Equal to
None	Equal to
>	Greater than
GT	Greater than
AFTER	After
<	Less than
LT	less than
BEFORE	before
>=	Greater than or equal
GE	Greater than or equal
<=	Less than or equal
LE	Less than or equal
#	Not equal to
NE	Not equal to
NO	No

BEFORE "N" SURNAME FORENAME". Again "BEFORE" is taken to mean before in the dictionary sense so that Mzzzz is before N but Naaaa is not.[10]

BEFORE and AFTER are not the only words you can use in a WITH clause. The complete list is given in Table 4.3. You will see that there are quite a few which do exactly the same thing. For example "AFTER", ">" and "GT" are all synonymous.[11] This is merely for convenience. It makes them easier to remember. For example, while it may be natural enough to say "WITH SURNAME AFTER "N"" or "WITH DATE AFTER "29 OCT 1990"", it would sound pretty silly to ask for all personnel "WITH SALARY AFTER "20000"". Much better to say "WITH SALARY > "20000"". And the good news is that you *can* do this, and the machine will know what you mean. Here then are a few more examples of lawful WITH clauses:

WITH FORENAME "James"	People whose first name is "James"
WITH FORENAME = "James"	People whose first name is "James"
WITH FORENAME EQ "James"	People whose first name is "James"
WITH SURNAME NOT "Ne]"	Surnames not starting with "Ne"
WITH SURNAME # "Ne]"	Surnames not starting with "Ne"
WITH DATE BEFORE "29 OCT 1990"	Date before 29th October 1990

[10] A fuller explanation of the way the computer thinks of alphabetical order is given in §8.4.4.

[11] The arrow-like symbol ">" is the mathematical symbol for "greater than" and GT is an abbreviation for the same.

```
WITH DATE < "29 OCT 1990"          Date before 29th October 1990
WITH DATE <= "29 OCT 1990"         Date on or before 29 th October 1990
WITH NO TELEPHONE                  No phone number in the file
```

The last example here shows how we can use the word NO to select all the items in a file in which one particular attribute has not been filled in at all; in this case the telephone number. This could mean either that they have no telephone, or that their number has not been entered for some reason. Thus if you are in the middle of entering the numbers of all the personnel in the file and you come back from your coffee break to resume the task, you might find it very helpful to have a list of the IDs of all the people whose numbers you have not yet entered. To get this you should type

```
>SORT STAFF WITH NO TELEPHONE
```

You can do more thorough searches still by using two or more WITH clauses in one command. For example you might want to know the addresses of all the people in STAFF with surnames between N and T in the alphabet. To get this you need to type

```
>SORT STAFF WITH SURNAME AFTER "N" AND WITH SURNAME BEFORE "T"
```

The really difficult thing to remember about this sort of command is that the words WITH SURNAME have to occur twice. The natural thing to type is "WITH SURNAME AFTER "N" AND BEFORE "T"" but this will not work. This idiocy takes a lot of getting used to and is worth noting against those inevitable occasions on which the machine responds to an apparently valid ACCESS command with some cryptic error message. Holdups like this are frequently caused by typing errors or spelling mistakes and putting them right is just a matter of carefully checking the command till you find the problem. But stare as you will at the line you have typed you may be unable to see the error if everything is spelled right and it reads almost like proper English. So bear in mind that ACCESS is *not* English and that there are occasions on which the correct thing to type is clumsy, while the natural one is wrong.

Two obvious extensions of the WITH clause are:

(i) Several WITH clauses: there is no limit to the number you are allowed. You can have WITH this AND WITH that to your heart's content. It is perfectly lawful (if somewhat pointless) to have a command that says

```
>SORT STAFF WITH SALARY < "20000" AND WITH SURNAME "Bloggs" AND WI
TH FORENAME "Joe" AND WITH TELEPHONE "141421" SURNAME
```

(ii) Use of the word "OR" in the same way as the word "AND". You can ask for a list of all the people whose surnames are either "Binney" or "Newman" by typing the command

```
>SORT STAFF WITH SURNAME "Binney" OR WITH SURNAME "Newman" FORENAM
E SURNAME
```

Note the two WITHs again. They are important.

There is one other subtlety that is worth mentioning in connection with
"WITH". Namely how it deals with attributes split into more than on value.
Suppose, as we did at the beginning of this section, that the FORENAME attribute of each item in the file "STAFF" contains not merely the first name of
the relevant person, but all his names as a series of separate values. Then the
command

```
>SORT STAFF WITH FORENAME "Joe" FORENAME SURNAME
```

would make the computer search through all the values in the FORENAME attribute of each item in the file for the name "Joe". And if *any* of a person's
forenames were "Joe", it would print out his ID and surname, and each of his
forenames on a separate line (see above). If then the J in M. E. J. Newman
stood for Joe (which it doesn't) the command above might produce:

```
STAFF......... FORENAME....... SURNAME........

BLOGGS-J       Joe            Bloggs
NEWMAN-M-E-J   Mark           Newman
               Edward
               Joe
```

Options.   The last modifications to SORT commands that we will consider
are the options. As explained in §4.2.8 an option is a letter that goes in
brackets at the end of a command which slightly alters the way the command
works. In connection with the COPY verb we saw how the O and D options can
be used to make COPY overwrite or delete data at the same time as making
a copy. The SORT verb also allows a number of different options of varying
utility. The full list is given in the Pick Manual. We decribe only the three
most important. The first is the P option which stands for 'printer'. If we
type in a SORT command followed by "(P)" then the list produced will appear
on the printer instead of on the screen of your terminal.[12] Clearly it would
often be useful to have a permanent record of your data like this. The next
most frequently used option is the I option. In the examples we have seen so
far the IDs of the items listed have always appeared. We didn't ask for them
to be printed in the way we asked for SURNAMEs for example, but the computer
printed them anyway. An "(I)" (for ID) at the end of a SORT command will
stop it from doing this.

```
>SORT STAFF FORENAME SURNAME TELEPHONE (I)

FORENAME....... SURNAME........ TELEPHONE..

James          Binney          314159
Joe            Bloggs          141421
Mark           Newman          271828
Annabel        Other            57721
>
```

---

[12] As with COPY's options, the closing bracket after the letter is actually optional—"SORT
STAFF (P" will work fine.

The last option we mention is the N option. An "(N)" after a SORT command will stop the computer waiting at the end of each page. If you specify this option, reports longer than one screen-full will be printed out in a continuous stream, with no pauses for you to press RETURN between each page and the next (see above).

If you want to invoke two or more options simultaneously, then you should put all the ones you want in one pair of brackets at the end of the SORT command, with commas separating them. They can be in any order. For example, if you want the printing of IDs suppressed *and* you want the list printed on the printer, then you should put both the letters I and P in the brackets at the end of the command, thus:

```
>SORT STAFF FORENAME SURNAME TELEPHONE (P,I)
```

All the different features and refinements of the SORT commands that we have described can be combined with one another in virtually any way you please. ACCESS verbs are very flexible. And just to prove it here is a really convoluted example with all the features used in one command:

```
>SORT STAFF WITH SURNAME "Ne]" AND WITH SALARY > "20000" AND WITH
NO TELEPHONE BY FORENAME FORENAME SURNAME (I,P)
```

which instructs the computer to print out the first names and surnames of all the personnel on £15,000 or more who have no known telephone number and whose surnames begin with 'Ne', in alphabetical order of first names, without giving the item IDs. The different elements of the command can be combined in almost any order. The options in the brackets have to go at the end, but the WITH clauses can go in any order and the BY clauses can go before them or after them, and the list of attributes you want printed, like FORENAME and SURNAME, can go before or after these, or even in between the WITH bits and the BY bit. You can choose any arrangement that suits you—there is no need to remember a special order.

Default reports.   At the beginning of this section we demonstrated the simplest example of a SORT command, "SORT STAFF", which simply lists the IDs of all the items in the file "STAFF" in alphabetical order. In fact, you can set up your files so that a laconic command of this type will list not only the IDs of the items in a file, but also any set of attributes you want, even though you don't explicitly ask to see those attributes. It would for example be possible to set up the STAFF file so that on typing "SORT STAFF" the computer responded with staff members' names, as well as their IDs:

```
>SORT STAFF

STAFF......... FORENAME....... SURNAME........

BINNEY-J-J     James           Binney
BLOGGS-J       Joe             Bloggs
NEWMAN-M-E-J   Mark            Newman
OTHER-A-N      Annabel         Other
>
```

A list like this with attributes that appear automatically is called a **default report**. To get a default report when you SORT a file all you have to do is define a word called "1" in the dictionary of the file which describes the data you want printed in the first column of the default report after the ID. Similarly, you define words "2", "3" and so on, which describe the data you want to see in the second and third columns after the ID. Thus, to produce the default report seen above, we would have to define a word "1" in DICT STAFF thus:

| File: DICT STAFF | Item: 1 |

```
Attribute
  Number    Contents of Attribute
       1    A
       2    2
       3    FORENAME
            ...
```

and another similar one called "2" for the surname. These dictionary items can make use of any of the standard dictionary features of Pick—conversions, correlatives, etc. So if we had been feeling very keen, we could have defined a single numbered word "1" in DICT STAFF making use of the concatenation correlative (see §3.5.3) thus:

| File: DICT STAFF | Item: 1 |

```
Attribute
  Number    Contents of Attribute
       1    A
       2
       3    NAME
       4
       5
       6
       7
       8    C;2 1
       9    L
      10    20
```

This would produce the default report

```
>SORT STAFF

STAFF......... NAME................

BINNEY-J-J     James Binney
BLOGGS-J       Joe Bloggs
NEWMAN-M-E-J   Mark Newman
OTHER-A-N      Annabel Other
>
```

The one thing to be careful of when setting up default reports, is not to make a break in the numbering of the numbered words. If there is a break in the numbering of the words—for example, if the IDs of the numbered items go 1, 2, 4, 5, etc.—then the ones after the gap, after the first two in this example, will not get printed in the default report.

Default reports apply to all SORT commands which contain no information on which attributes you want listed; they apply to commands containing BY and WITH clauses, as well as to ones of the simpler type shown above. It is only if you specify explicitly which data you want to see, with words like "SURNAME" or "FORENAME" that the default report gets overridden.

Default reports also affect the action of the verb "LIST" (see the next section).

4.3.2   LIST & COUNT

Once you understand how to use the SORT verb, there are two other ACCESS verbs that can be explained in just a few lines. The first is LIST. The LIST verb does exactly the same thing as the SORT verb, except that it will not sort the items in the list into alphabetical order for you. Consequently BY clauses have no effect in LIST commands. In all other respects the two verbs are used in exactly the same way. Thus we might type

```
>LIST STAFF WITH SALARY < "20000" FORENAME SURNAME (P)
```

to get a list of the names of personnel on less than £15,000 p.a. The names are printed in the order in which they are stored on the disk, which to the ordinary user would most likely appear completely random. Since this is probably not a stunningly convenient way to have your lists arranged, there is not really much use for the LIST verb. It is superseded by SORT. (The only time you might want to use it is when listing very large amounts of data. If you were making a list five thousand items long using a SORT command you might find that the computer took a minute or two to sort them into the right order. If this is inconveniently slow and you don't really need the data in alphabetical order then you could use a LIST command which would print them all out in a muddle, but would do it quickly.)

The second and more useful new verb is COUNT. If we type one of the SORT commands shown in this section with the word "SORT" replaced with "COUNT", but otherwise identical, then the computer will search the database as it would for the equivalent SORT command but it will not print out the items it finds. It will just count them and when it is finished it will print the total number that it has counted. Since it is not printing out any data, the words like FORENAME, SURNAME and TELEPHONE that we use to tell SORT which attributes we want printed are no longer necessary. And as with LIST the BY clause is redundant also and so should not be typed in. COUNT commands thus tend to be simpler than the equivalent SORT commands. As an example of the use of the verb "COUNT", imagine you need to know how many people called Bloggs there are in the STAFF file. You would type

```
>COUNT STAFF WITH SURNAME "Bloggs"

1 items counted
>
```

4.3.3   SSELECT

The last ACCESS verb that we will consider is the verb "SSELECT", which is very similar again to the SORT verb. In fact it does exactly what the SORT verb does, but instead of printing out the list of items that you asked it to search for, it stores their IDs away in the computer's memory. A list of IDs stored in memory like this is called a **select list**. When you have made a select list by typing an SSELECT command we say that the select list is **active**. There are cunning ways in which you can use a select list to save yourself a lot of work. For example, if you want to delete from your STAFF file everyone with name after N in the alphabet, you can make a select list of those people with the command

```
>SSELECT STAFF WITH SURNAME AFTER "N"
```

The computer stashes the list away in its memory, and you can then delete the SSELECTed items with the command "DELETE STAFF". (An explanation of this mysterious procedure follows shortly.)

The SORT commands we have demonstrated in this section can be made into SSELECT commands merely by replacing the word SORT by the word SSELECT. Since SSELECT, like COUNT, lists no data on either the screen or the printer, words such as SURNAME, TELEPHONE, etc., which in a SORT command tell Pick which attributes you would like listed, no longer have a use and should be left out.

The word "SSELECT" actually stands for "sort and select" because the computer sorts the items into alphabetical order before storing the list away.[13]Normally this means alphabetical order of ID, but if we put a BY clause in the command like "BY SURNAME" then they will be sorted in order of surname instead. Here are a few examples of lawful SSELECT commands:

```
SSELECT STAFF
SSELECT STAFF WITH SURNAME "[nn]"
SSELECT STAFF WITH FORENAME "Joe" AND WITH SURNAME "Bloggs"
SSELECT STAFF BY FORENAME
SSELECT STAFF WITH SURNAME AFTER "N" BY SURNAME
```

In Chapter 8 we will see how a select list can be used by a BASIC program through a READNEXT statement. Meanwhile here are two examples of its use with TCL verbs.

---

[13] There does exist a verb "SELECT", which is exactly the same as SSELECT except that it will not sort your records for you. It is something of a redundant verb however—it is superseded by SSELECT in the same way as LIST is superseded by SORT (see §4.3.2).

DELETE. We have seen this one already. Normally the verb "DELETE" should be followed by the name of the file and a list of the IDs of the items in that file which you wish to delete. If we have a select list active, all items in a file with IDs in that list can be deleted by typing just "DELETE" followed by the name of the file. Thus to delete all the Binneys and Newmans from **STAFF** you would type

```
>SSELECT STAFF WITH SURNAME "Binney" OR WITH SURNAME "Newman"

2 items selected
<DELETE STAFF

2 items deleted
>
```

Notice how the usual prompt ">" is changed to "<" after the **SSELECT** command has been obeyed. This is Pick's way of reminding you that a select list is active. If there is no select list active when you give the **DELETE** command, with no item IDs specified, the computer will assume you meant to specify the name of an item yourself, and will prompt you for it with the message

```
Item id:
```

to which you may reply either with the name of an item which you would like deleted, or with nothing at all (simply hit the RETURN key) in which case no items will be deleted.

The file searched to create the select list (that is the one whose name is given in the **SSELECT** command) does not have to be the same file as that from which the items are deleted. Suppose you have two files called "STAFF" and "EMPLOYEES" which contain the same data, except that not everyone in **STAFF** appears in **EMPLOYEES**. And suppose you decide to delete from **STAFF** all those who already have copies of their records in **EMPLOYEES** on the grounds that it is silly to keep two copies of the same data in different files. Then you would type

```
>SSELECT EMPLOYEES

13 items selected
<DELETE STAFF

13 items deleted
>
```

The **SSELECT** command creates a select list of all the item IDs in **EMPLOYEES** and the **DELETE** command deletes the corresponding items from **STAFF**.

COPY. You can copy a select list of items from one file to another in a very similar way. When you type just "COPY" and the name of the file containing the items, the IDs in the select list will be copied. So, for example, to copy all the records in **STAFF** which have telephone numbers starting with "01" into the file **LONDONERS** we would type

```
>SSELECT STAFF WITH TELEPHONE "Ø1]"

5 items selected
<COPY STAFF
TO:(LONDONERS

5 items copied
>
```

5 Using printers

Your Pick computer will have at least one printer connected to it to allow you to print things out on paper. Bigger computers may have several printers. A printer is plugged into a port on the computer in the same way as an ordinary terminal[1] (see §1.2), and the computer can make it print things by shipping data out of this port. Data to be printed are divided into **reports**. A report is any collection of things that you want printed out in one block on the printer. It might be a 'real' report, from your finance director for example, or it might be a list of the balances of all your accounts for the tax year just ended, or it might be a load of data from your personnel files, or whatever.

When you (or one of your programs) asks for a thing to be printed, the computer does not send your data off to a printer immediately. In between your telling the computer to print a thing and its coming out on paper, a lot of to-ing and fro-ing goes on. All reports sent to the printer are first processed by a program called the **spooler**. The spooler is a special program which runs all the time, though you don't normally notice it since it runs 'inside' the computer, and not on any particular terminal.[2]

What the spooler does is this. It receives from users all reports destined to be printed and it stores them temporarily on the disk. This collection of reports we shall call the **printer list**, and we shall refer to the entries in it as the **printer list elements**.[3] The spooler forms the elements of the printer list into **queues** in the order in which it intends to print them. If you have several printers attached to your computer there will be a separate queue for each printer. Some printers may even have several queues. For the purposes

---

[1] Actually, in contrast to terminals, there is more than one type of port into which you can plug a printer—see Appendix 1.

[2] The computer *does*, for its own purposes, give the spooler a line number, but it is not the line number of any terminal on the computer. Usually it is one greater than the highest line number of any of the computer's ports.

[3] The official Pick terminology in this area is extremely confused. You may see elements of the printer list referred to as "spool files", "hold files" or "print files", though strictly they are not files at all. We shall avoid all of these terms, and confine ourselves to "printer list", "printer list element" and "report".

of identification each queue has a unique number, which we will call a **queue number**. One by one, in the order in which they appear in the queues, the spooler feeds the printer elements out to the appropriate printers and deletes them from the list. New elements are added to the printer list as users send in ('spool') fresh reports, and each is added to the end of one of the queues for printing when its turn comes. As we shall see, Pick provides a way for you to specify to which queue you would like your reports added, so that you can have them directed to the printer of your choice.

5.1   Using the spooler

The original object of a spooler was two-fold:

(i) To resolve conflicts between different users who try to print out reports simultaneously, by temporarily storing them in the printer list, and then printing them out one after another.

(ii) To allow programs to run faster. Even the fastest of printers can take ten or fifteen minutes to print a really long report and it would be very frustrating if one were obliged to sit so long at the terminal, twiddling one's thumbs while the printer did its stuff. But even a long report can be added to the printer list in a twinkling, and then you can get on with your work, while the spooler feeds it out to a printer at its leisure.

However, spooler programs have come a long way since they first appeared, and the Pick spooler can do much more for you than just this. There exist a handful of TCL verbs for telling the spooler what you want done with your reports. For example, you can specify to which printer you want your reports sent, inspect a report before it is printed, or cancel the printing of any report, even after it has started to spew from the printer. In this chapter we describe the most important of these verbs. For the ordinary user, the verbs "SP-ASSIGN", "LISTPEQS" and "SP-KILL" will be of most interest. Most of the other sections will be of interest primarily to system managers, and the more enthusiastic Pick users.

5.1.1   SP-ASSIGN

The fundamental verb for sending instructions to the spooler is SP-ASSIGN. All SP-ASSIGN commands affect only those reports sent to the spooler from the terminal on which the command was typed, so there is no chance you will upset other people by experimenting with them. The verb "SP-ASSIGN" is normally followed by a string of letters that indicate what you want the spooler to do. These letters are known as **options**, because they are all

Table 5.1. Options for use with the verb "SP-ASSIGN"

Option	Function
None	Cancel the effect of all previous SP-ASSIGN commands.
H	Hold all subsequent reports for later examination.
S	Do not print any subsequent reports.
3	Print 3 copies (or any other number you specify) of all reports.
F1	Put all subsequent reports in queue number 1.
R4	Limit the effect of this SP-ASSIGN to report number 4.
I	Start printing when the first lines of the report reach the spooler.
C	Slow down printing program to the rate at which printer prints.
O	Leave the printer list element open after the report is finished.
T	Send subsequent reports to the tape unit not the printer.

optional.[4] The complete list of options is given in Table 5.1. We now explain the use of each one in detail.

The plain SP-ASSIGN command. The simplest SP-ASSIGN command is just the verb SP-ASSIGN all on its own:

>SP-ASSIGN

This has the effect of cancelling any previous SP-ASSIGN commands and putting the spooler back in its normal state, in which it prints one copy of every report and then deletes it from the printer list. If a printer ever starts playing games with you, one good thing to try is an "SP-ASSIGN" all on its own—this may well sort things out. (But see also §5.2.1 on SP-STATUS.)

The H (hold) option. Probably the most useful of the options is the H option. H stands for 'hold'. If we specify this option, that is, if we type

>SP-ASSIGN H

at TCL, the spooler will mark all elements subsequently added to the printer list for 'holding'. This means that the element will not be deleted in the usual fashion after it has been printed. The verb "SP-EDIT" enables you to inspect elements of the printer list that have been put on hold (see §5.1.4).

Like all other SP-ASSIGN commands, the command "SP-ASSIGN H" affects only the reports produced by the person using the terminal on which the command was typed. And, like most of the other options for the verb "SP-ASSIGN", the H option affects only reports produced *after* you type the

---

[4] In §4.2.8 we introduced the word options to describe the single letters that go in brackets on the end of some TCL commands, to modify the effect of those commands. The options for the verb "SP-ASSIGN" do *not* go in brackets, so, in a sense, we are using the word "options" in two different ways, which is regrettable. However, this is official jargon and we feel obliged to stick to it.

SP-ASSIGN command. Previously created reports, even if they are still in a queue waiting to be printed, are not affected.

The S (suppress output) option.   Specifying the option S thus:

>SP-ASSIGN S

will stop the printer from printing any reports subsequently sent to the spooler. This might be useful, for instance, if you were just trying out a program that printed lots of stuff and you didn't want it to print all this stuff yet. A more common use for the S option is in conjunction with the H one. You can give both the S and H options together like this:[5]

>SP-ASSIGN S H

This will tell the spooler to hold onto your reports so that you can inspect them later (see §5.1.4 on the verb "SP-EDIT"), but not to print them just now.

The order in which you put the options after an SP-ASSIGN command is immaterial. So the command above could also have been given as

>SP-ASSIGN H S

and it would have had exactly the same effect.

The number of copies.   If you put a number after SP-ASSIGN the spooler will print out that many copies of all your reports. So for example the command

>SP-ASSIGN 6

when typed at TCL, would make the spooler print six copies of all your subsequent reports.

The F (queue number) option.   If you follow the SP-ASSIGN verb with an "F" and a number, the spooler will send all your subsequent reports to the queue with that number.[6] They will then appear on the printer that is responsible for printing reports added to that queue. For example the command

>SP-ASSIGN F3

will make the spooler add all subsequent reports to queue number 3. Notice that there is no space between the F and the 3. This is important. If you type "SP-ASSIGN F 3" with a space, the spooler will add your reports to queue number *zero*, and print out three copies of all of them, which is not at all what you meant!

Provided you know the appropriate queue numbers, you can, by deft manipulation of SP-ASSIGN commands, arrange for your data be printed on any of the computer's printers.

---

[5] The space between the S and the H is optional. You could type "SP-ASSIGN SH" and it would have precisely the same effect. However, there are occasions when a space is mandatory between one option and another, and rather than remember rules about where to use one and where not to, it is probably sensible always to put one in.

[6] The letter F stands for 'form', an obsolete synonym for queue which became unfashionable because it is so unclear.

The R (report number) option. There may be times when you don't want an `SP-ASSIGN` command to affect all the reports you print, only one particular one. Under certain circumstances you can achieve this using the R option.

If you are using a Pick BASIC program to produce a report, then the report will have a 'report number' (see §8.2.2), and you can limit the effect of an `SP-ASSIGN` command to just that report by including an R option in the command, followed by this number. For example, suppose you are running some program that produces many reports. Suppose also that you have to run it several times to get several different printouts from it, but that one of its reports (say number 4) is the same every time you run the program. If you don't want to keep printing out this same report over and over again, then you can suppress the printing of just that one report by issuing the following TCL command before running the program:

```
>SP-ASSIGN R4 S
```

Any other reports produced by the program will printed as usual.

As another example you might decide that you wanted all the reports produced by one particular program to be printed on your dot-matrix printer (which is fast, and cheap to run) except one, number 6, which you want printed on your laser printer (which produces much higher quality print). If the dot-matrix printer prints the reports in queue number 1 and the laser printer those in queue number 2, then you could achieve the desired effect by issuing the following two commands:

```
>SP-ASSIGN F1
>SP-ASSIGN R6 F2
```

The first `SP-ASSIGN` command tells the spooler that *all* subsequent reports are to be printed on the dot-matrix printer (queue number 1), and the second slightly countermands the first by telling the spooler that it is actually to print report number 6 on the laser printer (queue number 2).

The disadvantage of the R option is that, in order to use it, you have to know the numbers of your reports, and these can only be found by inspecting the code of the program that produces them. If you didn't write the program yourself, and you don't know the person who did, this may be difficult.

The I (immediate) and C (choke) options. Giving the I option thus:

```
>SP-ASSIGN I
```

will make the spooler start printing your data as soon as they reach it. Normally the spooler doesn't even begin printing a report until it has the whole report in its hands. But with the I option in effect printing starts immediately the first data are produced. In conjunction with this option you may also want to use the C option. If you give the command

```
>SP-ASSIGN I C
```

at TCL before sending a report to the spooler, then Pick will slow down the running of the program or command producing the report so that it doesn't get too far ahead of the printer in the data it sends for printing. Computers produce data very quickly, much faster than printers can print them. So without the C option you may find that you get way ahead of the printer, and that there is a large backlog of data waiting to be printed when the program or command finishes. This is not normally a problem—the data are stored in the printer list until the printer is ready for them. However, if you are printing a very large report and space is at a premium on your disk, then you may not have room for a big printer list element like this. In that case the C option is the one for you. Its precise effect is to suspend execution of the program or command when the backlog of unprinted data exceeds 20 frames, and only to start it going again when the printer has printed enough to rectify the situation. Thus with the C option in effect, you can be sure that the spooler will not need more than 10K of space on your disk to print any given report.

The O (open) option.   Giving the O option tells the spooler to keep your printer list elements 'open' even when it would normally 'close' them. Elements are usually closed when the program or command that produced them finishes.[7] Once an element is closed, no more data can be written in it, and the spooler is free to start printing it. If you use the O option to specify that elements in the printer list be kept open, the printing of those elements will be delayed, and you will be able to add further stuff to them later. For example, suppose you are using a Pick BASIC program which produces two reports, with report numbers 1 and 2, say, then two elements are added to the printer list, one for each report. Normally, when the program ends, these elements are closed, and the spooler is free to print them. However, if you type

>SP-ASSIGN O

at TCL before running the program, then the printer list elements will be kept open for you after the program ends, and they will not be printed. What's more, if you now run another program, which produces two more reports, with report numbers 2 and 3, say, then the new report number 2 will be appended to the same printer list element as the old one, and a new element will be created for report number 3. The elements are again left open, and unprinted, when the program finishes. The command

>SP-ASSIGN

all on its own, will cancel the O option, allowing the spooler to close the elements and add them to the relevant queues for printing.

---

[7] You can instruct the spooler to close a printer list element from within a BASIC program, using the "PRINTER CLOSE" statement—see §8.2.2.

Thus, by skillful use of the command "SP-ASSIGN O" you should be able to contrive that the reports from several different programs all go into one element in the printer list and get printed at once. This might be useful, for example, if there are many people using the computer and you want to avoid those annoying situations in which you find ten pages of somebody else's boring junk between two of your wonderful reports. Notice however, that there is nothing you can do to get several reports all produced by the same program into one printer list element. The spooler automatically puts these into different elements whether you like it or not. Luckily this is not usually a problem because the elements created by one program will almost always all be closed at exactly the same instant, usually when the program ends, so they will follow one another in the printer queue and there is little chance of somebody else's report squeezing in between two of them.

The T (tape) option.   There is one other rather specialized option which we will just mention. This is the T option. Giving the command

>SP-ASSIGN T

at TCL will make the spooler send all subsequent reports to the tape drive (see §7.3.1) instead of the printer. (If you use floppy disks not tapes then they will be sent to the floppy disk drive. If you have both floppies and tapes, then you can choose to which the data will be sent by using the verbs "SET-SCT" and "SET-FLOPPY"—see §7.4.1.) The data can be examined at a later date by giving the command "SP-TAPEOUT", which copies one report off the tape and sends it to the spooler. Unless you have told it to do otherwise with an SP-ASSIGN command, the spooler will then print the report.

5.1.2   LISTABS

If you use the verb "SP-ASSIGN" a lot, you may not always be able to keep track of which options are currently in force. In this case you may find the verb "LISTABS" a handy one. If you type "LISTABS" at TCL, the machine will list, for each of your machine's terminals, all the SP-ASSIGN options currently in force. (Remember that there can be different options in force on each terminal, because an SP-ASSIGN command only affects reports produced by the person working on the terminal on which it was typed.) Here is an example of what you might see on typing LISTABS:

>LISTABS

LINE #	STATUS	COP IES	FORM #
Ø	P	1	1
1	P	1	1
2	PH	2	1
3	P	1	2
4	P	1	1
5	P	1	1

Table 5.2. STATUSES reported by the verb "LISTPEQS"

Letter	Meaning
P	This report will be queued for printing when it is complete.
C	The report is completed and the printer list element closed.
H	This report has been put on hold.
S	The report has been put in a printer queue to await printing.
O	This report is being printed right now.
L	The report is locked so you cannot SP-EDIT it.

The first column in the output contains the line number (see §4.2.4) of each terminal.[8] (Use the verb "WHO" (see §4.1.1) to find out the line number of your own terminal, if you don't know it.) The second contains the SP-ASSIGN options for the corresponding terminals. The letters in this column mean exactly the same as the options in the SP-ASSIGN commands, except that you get a P when the data sent to the spooler are to be printed, instead of an S when they aren't (see §5.1.1 on the S option). The third column gives the number of copies of each report that are to be printed (see §5.1.1 on the number of copies). The fourth gives the number of the spool queue to which data from each terminal will be added.

Thus the standard settings for your computer might, for example, be P, 1 and 1 as on line 1 above. This would mean that one copy of each report is to be printed on the printer which deals with queue number 1. If your terminal were attached to line number 2, then the above display would tell you that you were set to produce two copies of each of your reports and not to delete the printer list elements containing them when they have been printed out. If your terminal were attached to line number 3, then in our example you would be set to print all your stuff on the printer that deals with queue number 2, rather than the one that deals with queue number 1, which everyone else is using.

5.1.3 LISTPEQS

Another thing you may well need to discover is what data you have already sent off to the spooler, and what the spooler is doing with them. LISTPEQS is the verb to tell you this.[9] It displays the details of all the elements in the printer list. Here is a typical example of its use:

---

[8] In case you've not met it before, the symbol "#", is the American abbreviation for "number".

[9] LISTPEQS stands for "list printer elements and queues".

```
>LISTPEQS

   PRINTER LIST ELEMENTS                  29 OCT 1990  16:54:12

   # STAT LK LN STATUSES        CP OF FRMS   DATE      TIME    ACCT
   1 48A5    2 P S O C L         2  0    2 29/10/90 16:52:03 JACK
   2 C080    2 P S C L           1  0    1 29/10/90 16:52:05 JACK
   3 41C1    2 P L               1  0 OPEN 29/10/90 16:52:09 JACK
   4 8080    3 H C               1  2    3 29/10/90 16:53:32 JILL
   5 8080    3 H C               1  2    4 29/10/90 16:53:42 JILL

   5 QUEUE ELEMENTS LISTED.             10 FRAMES IN USE.
```

The columns are as follows:

1: Job number (#). The first column, headed "#" is the **job number**. Each report is given its own job number when it is sent to the spooler, to distinguish it from the other reports the spooler is working on at the moment. Pick BASIC programs also give each report a number—the report number (see §8.2.2)—but this is not usually the same as the job number.

2 & 3: Status tally and forward link (STAT and LK). The second column, marked "STAT", contains the 'status tally' and the third, marked "LK", the 'forward link'. These numbers appear to be of no interest to humans, so you might as well ignore them.

4: Line number (LN). The fourth column is the line number of the terminal responsible for creating each report.

5: Status indicators (STATUSES). The fifth column contains a set of letters that indicate what the spooler is doing about each report. The most common status letters are shown in Table 5.2. If you do fancy things with the printer list using the verb "SP-EDIT" detailed in §5.1.4, then you may see other status letters in these listings, X or R for example. The full list of possible status indicators is given in the Pick Manual.

6: Copies (CP). The sixth column records how many copies of each report the spooler is set to produce (see §5.1.1 on the number of copies).

7: Queue number (OF). The seventh column is the queue number (or 'form number') of the queue to which the spooler is to add reports as they are completed. (The letter S in the STATUSES column indicates that this has already been done. The letter P indicates that the spooler intends to do it when the report is complete.)

8: Frames (FRMS). The eighth column shows the number of frames occupied on the disk by each element in the printer list. If a report is not yet complete, the entry in this column for that report will read "OPEN".

9 & 10: Date and time. The next two columns are headed "DATE" and "TIME" and they give the date and time at which the first data were added to each element.

Table 5.3.   Options for use with the verb "LISTPEQS"

Letter	Meaning
A	Display only your printer list elements, and not other people's.
C	Give a summary only, without precise details of the printer list.
P	Send the LISTPEQS display to be printed on the printer.

11: User name (ACCT).   The last column (rather sloppily headed "ACCT" for 'account') gives the user name of the user responsible for the report.

At the end of the report there is a line giving the total number of elements appearing in the list and the total number of frames that they occupy on the disk.

There are a number of options—single letters following the verb "LIST-PEQS" in the same style as the SP-ASSIGN commands described in §5.1.1—which modify the effect of the LISTPEQS verb. The full list will be found in the Pick Reference Manual. Its most useful members are summarized in Table 5.3.

Thus, for instance, if in the example above JILL, whose terminal is connected to line 3, had typed the command

>LISTPEQS A

instead of just "LISTPEQS" on its own, then a list like this would have appeared on her screen:

```
    PRINTER LIST ELEMENTS                29 OCT 1990  16:54:12

    # STAT LK LN STATUSES       CP OF FRMS   DATE       TIME    ACCT
    4 8080     3 H C             1  2    3 29/10/90 16:53:32 JILL
    5 8080     3 H C             1  2    4 29/10/90 16:53:42 JILL

    2 QUEUE ELEMENTS LISTED.             7 FRAMES IN USE.
```

with only the details of her own reports. And the command

>LISTPEQS A P

would have caused the same report to be printed on the printer.

5.1.4   SP-EDIT

In the last section we explained how you can get the spooler to put your printer list elements on hold. In this one we explain how you can then examine their contents using the verb "SP-EDIT", and so find out what your programs are sending to the printer without actually having the stuff printed out on paper.[10] To use SP-EDIT type

---

[10] We imagine this facility will principally be of interest to programmers and system managers. For the ordinary Pick user it may well be a good idea to skip this section, and

>SP-EDIT

at TCL. The computer will then go through all the elements in the printer list which are on hold and ask you in turn about each one which you created. It will start by announcing the element's job number (see §5.1.3) thus:

ENTRY #1

Immediately below this it will say

DISPLAY (Y/N/S/D/X/(CR))?

to which you are expected to reply with one of the letters listed, or just by hitting the RETURN key (for which "(CR)" is an abbreviation).

Typing Y will make the computer display the first page of your report on the terminal. Typing N will take you on to the next question (the "STRING" prompt, see below). Type S to skip to the "SPOOL" prompt, D to skip to the "DELETE" one (see the following paragraphs), X to finish SP-EDITing and return to TCL, or RETURN (or ENTER) to move onto the next element in the printer list, leaving this one as it is.

If you reply "Y" or "N" in response to the "DISPLAY" prompt, then the next thing the machine will say to you is:

STRING:-

It is asking you to give a string of characters which it should look for in the report. If you reply with nothing (i.e., just hit RETURN) then the computer will go straight on to the "SPOOL" prompt (see below). However, if you give a string of characters at this point the computer will search through the report for those characters and stop where it finds them (or at the end of the report if it doesn't). This could be useful for example if you were printing a big report, and the printer jammed on page 42. You can use the SP-EDIT verb to print out just the second half of the report (see the "SPOOL" prompt, below) provided you can tell the computer where it is to start. You can do this by telling it to look for a string of characters that you know occurs on the 41st page (which should be easy enough, since you have the 41st page printed out on paper already). If, for example, each of your pages has the page number written at the top of it, you could type

STRING:-PAGE 41

in response to the "STRING" prompt and the computer would find "PAGE 41" and wait there.

The next thing machine says to you after this is

SPOOL (Y/N=CR/T/TN/F)?

possibly the whole of the rest of this chapter, on a first reading, and only come back to it later if it becomes apparent that a knowledge of the more sophisticated spooler facilities will be of value.

to which, once again, you are expect to respond with one of the replies listed in brackets. (This is also the question you get asked if you reply S to the "DISPLAY" prompt, see above.) This "SPOOL" prompt is the most important and useful feature of the SP-EDITing facilities. It allows you to inspect the contents of your printer list elements on the screen, or to have them printed out on the printer, or just to leave them as they are.

First, if you enter Y in response to the "SPOOL" prompt, your report will be sent back to the spooler again, starting from wherever SP-EDIT is at the moment (this will normally be the beginning of the report, but it may be further down if you entered something at the "STRING" prompt, see above). Provided the spooler is set to print out all subsequent reports, the report will be printed as soon as the printer is free. You must be careful about this however, because if the spooler is set to hold all your reports, and not print them, (because you have said "SP-ASSIGN H S" at some point), then sending a report back to the spooler will simply result in a new copy being added to the printer list, but not printed. For this reason you should issue the command "SP-ASSIGN" on its own before the command "SP-EDIT", if you intend to send your reports off for printing by replying Y to the "SPOOL" prompt. (Well, you can use the command "SP-EDIT P" instead if you want—see Table 5.4.)

Typing N (or just RETURN, which is entirely equivalent) in response to the "SPOOL" prompt, takes you straight to the "DELETE" prompt (see below). Typing T makes the computer print out the contents of the report on your terminal, stopping at the end of each screen-full for you to hit the RETURN key. If you grow tired of watching pages of garbage going past on the screen you can stop the process at any time by typing Ctrl-X. Typing TN at the "SPOOL" prompt makes the computer print out the report on the terminal without stopping at the end of each screen-full, and typing F makes it copy the report into a file, in 'RUNOFF' format.

If you have asked for a report to be sent to the spooler for printing by replying "Y" to the "SPOOL" prompt, then SP-EDIT will go straight on to the next element in the printer list. Otherwise the next thing it will say is

```
DELETE (Y/N=CR)?
```

(This is also the prompt you will be given if you reply "D" to the "DISPLAY" prompt.) If you reply Y to this prompt, the printer list element you are editing will be deleted. If you reply "N" (or just RETURN), it will be kept.

Then SP-EDIT goes onto the next element in the list:

```
ENTRY #2
DISPLAY (Y/N/S/D/X/(CR))?
```

and the process repeats until your stock of elements is exhausted.

As with LISTPEQS there are a number of options that can be used to modify the behaviour of the SP-EDIT verb. These are single characters, or groups of letters that follow the word "SP-EDIT" itself. The complete list will be found in the Pick Manual. Its most useful members are given in Table 5.4.

Table 5.4.   Options for use with the verb "SP-EDIT"

Option	Meaning
4	Edit element number 4 (or any other numbered element in the list).
2-5	Edit elements 2 to 5 inclusive, in order.
P	Send reports to the printer, even if "SP-ASSIGN S" is in effect.
MS	Send all held elements to printer without asking about each one.
D3	Delete element number 3 from the printer list.
MD	Delete all held elements without asking about each one.

The most important of the options is the D option. This allows you to delete held reports, without going through all this rigmarole of prompts for each one. The command "SP-EDIT D1" for example will delete the first element in the printer list, provided it is a held report, and it belongs to you. (See §5.2.3 for how to put ordinary printer list elements on hold, so that they can be deleted with SP-EDIT.) Two useful extensions of this command are "SP-EDIT D3-6", which will delete elements 3 to 6 inclusive, and "SP-EDIT MD" which will delete all the reports you have on hold in one go.

By now you are probably quite weary of SP-EDIT and all its wretched prompts. But perhaps the following scenario will persuade you that it may one day be of use to you.

Jill is having some problems with a stock control program, "STOCK-UPDATE", which she has just written. The program is meant to produce two reports, the first containing details of the quantities and stock codes of all the items currently in stock, and the second containing these details together with the individual and accumulated wholesale values of the items. With only ten minutes left before she must pack up for the day, Jill finally tracks down a bug in the program which could explain why all the totals on the second report are too large by a factor of ten billion. The code is fixed in an instant, but time is running out, and the program is to be demonstrated to the head of the division at nine the following morning. So, rather than running the program again and getting it to print its two lengthy reports on the printer, which will take hours, Jill sets the spooler to place her reports on hold and not print them:

```
>SP-ASSIGN S H
>RUN PROGRAMS STOCK-UPDATE
 ...
```

After doing this and running her program, Jill uses the verb "LISTPEQS" to find out the job numbers of the printer list elements the program has created and uses SP-EDIT to examine the one she is interested in:

```
>LISTPEQS

   PRINTER LIST ELEMENTS                    29 OCT 1990   16:54:12

 # STAT LK LN STATUSES         CP OF FRMS     DATE       TIME    ACCT
 1 48A5     2 P S O C L         2  Ø    2 29/1Ø/9Ø 16:52:Ø3 JACK
 2 CØ8Ø     2 P S C L           1  Ø    1 29/1Ø/9Ø 16:52:Ø5 JACK
 3 41C1     2 P L               1  Ø OPEN 29/1Ø/9Ø 16:52:Ø9 JACK
 4 8Ø8Ø     3 H C               1  2    3 29/1Ø/9Ø 16:53:32 JILL
 5 8Ø8Ø     3 H C               1  2    4 29/1Ø/9Ø 16:53:42 JILL

 5 QUEUE ELEMENTS LISTED.                1Ø FRAMES IN USE.

>SP-EDIT 5
 ENTRY #5
 DISPLAY (Y/N/S/D/X/(CR))?
```

and so on. Happily, the report turns out now to be correct, and, smiling
contentedly to herself, Jill uses SP-EDIT's MD option to delete all the reports
the spooler is holding for her, before packing up for the day and heading for
the car park.

```
>SP-EDIT MD
>LISTPEQS

   PRINTER LIST ELEMENTS                    29 OCT 1990   16:54:39

 # STAT LK LN STATUSES         CP OF FRMS     DATE       TIME    ACCT
 1 48A5     2 P S O C L         2  Ø    2 29/1Ø/9Ø 16:52:Ø3 JACK
 2 CØ8Ø     2 P S C L           1  Ø    1 29/1Ø/9Ø 16:52:Ø5 JACK
 3 41C1     2 P L               1  Ø OPEN 29/1Ø/9Ø 16:52:Ø9 JACK

 3 QUEUE ELEMENTS LISTED.                 3 FRAMES IN USE.
```

When she lists the printer elements the second time her two reports are gone.
Note that "SP-EDIT MD" only deletes *her* reports, and not other people's.
(The MD option clearly has quite a drastic effect and should be used with
caution; you can't get your reports back once they're deleted. Like it says in
the Pick manual: "Do not pass Go, do not collect $200".)

5.2   Troubleshooting on printers

There exist a number of other verbs for controlling the spooler in addition to
those mentioned above. These verbs are specifically for finding out what is
happening when things go wrong, and for setting things to rights again. These
verbs are SP-STATUS, LISTPTR, STARTPTR, STOPPTR, SP-KILL and :START-
SPOOLER. We now deal with each of these verbs in turn.

5.2.1   SP-STATUS

The verb SP-STATUS is used to find out how the spooler is set up: how many
printers it is using; which printer queues are being dealt with by which printers; whether those printers are being used at the moment and so on. To use
it you simply type "SP-STATUS". Here is a typical example:

```
>SP-STATUS

THE SPOOLER IS ACTIVE.

PRINTER #0 IS PARALLEL, ACTIVE, AND ON LINE.
THE PRINTER IS DEFINED AS PARALLEL PRINTER #0.
PRINT FILE BEING OUTPUT IS ELEMENT 1, A CLOSED FILE FOR LINE #2
   GENERATED ON ACCOUNT JACK, WHICH IS 2 FRAMES LONG.
ASSIGNED OUTPUT QUEUES: 0.
THE NUMBER OF INTER-JOB PAGES TO EJECT IS 1.
```

All printers have numbers by which they may be distinguished from other printers. Printer numbers are set by the verb "STARTPTR" (see below). Typing "SP-STATUS" tells us about each printer in order of printer numbers. The meaning of the display above is as follows:

(i) The spooler is 'active', which means that it's doing something at the moment, like printing out a report for somebody.

(ii) Printer number 0 is a parallel printer. (Printers are either serial or parallel—see Appendix 1.)

(iii) This printer is active (that is, it's printing something right now).

(iv) It is on line. Printers can be on line or off line. When a printer is on line it will print whatever the computer sends it; when it is off line it is not listening to the computer, and will print nothing. It is useful be able to put a printer off line for example when you want to feed a new box of paper into it and you don't want the machine chattering away printing out somebody's report while you are threading the paper through the mechanism. There is usually a button on the front of the printer marked "on line" for turning it on and off line. The verb "SP-STATUS" does not always get it right about when a printer is on line and when it is off line, so you should not take this bit too seriously.

(v) Printer 0 is connected to parallel port number 0. Parallel printers do not plug into ordinary ports like terminals (though serial ones do), but have their own set of parallel ports (see Appendix 1).

(vi) Printer 0 is at present printing a report for the user called "JACK", who is working on the terminal connected to line number 2. This report is job number 1 in the printer list (see §5.1.3 on the verb "LISTPEQS"), and is two frames long.

(vii) Printer 0 is handling all jobs in queue number 0. (Note that "ASSIGNED OUTPUT QUEUES: 0" does *not* mean there are *no* queues assigned to printer 0; it means that queue *number zero* has been assigned to printer 0.)

(viii) Printer 0 is set up to put one blank sheet of paper in between each report and the next. This number can be changed using the verb "STARTPTR" (see §5.2.2).

If there were any other printers attached to the system, SP-STATUS would print out all the details for those as well, but in our example there is only one.

If anything peculiar is going on with the printers on your computer, then the first thing to try is "SP-STATUS" because this will tell you if anything is amiss. For example, you might see a message like this appear:

>SP-STATUS

THE CONTROL BLOCK FOR PRINTER #0 IS IN AN AMBIGUOUS STATE.
DELETE THE PRINTER FROM THE SPOOLER SYSTEM.

You should, however, be wary of these sorts of messages; they can sometimes be produced spuriously. If you get such a message unexpectedly you should wait for a minute or two and then try typing "SP-STATUS" again. Often the message will not be present the second time, in which case things are OK, and you have nothing to worry about. If, on the other hand, the message persists when you type "SP-STATUS" again, you may well have a problem and the correct procedure is to delete the printer from the spooler system as the message says, using the verb "SP-KILL" described in §6.2.3 below, and then to reinstate it using the verb "STARTPTR".

There is one other use for the verb "SP-STATUS", which is as a spooler awakener. It happens very occasionally that the spooler 'falls asleep' and does not notice when new work comes along for it to do. The reason for this curiously anthropomorphic behaviour is unclear, but the cure is simple. If you cannot get the printer to print something for you, and you have exhausted all the things you can think of to check (like the printer being plugged in, switched on, on line, attached to the right port on the computer, etc.) then it may be that the spooler is dozing, and you should type

>SP-STATUS

at TCL to awaken it again. If the spooler *is* asleep when you do this you will usually find that the message you get back from the SP-STATUS verb is of the misleading type described in the last paragraph, and it should not be taken seriously. In fact, you may find that SP-STATUS will go on giving you this sort of message for some time as the spooler prises itself out of its sleepy haze. Not to worry. Things will clear up as soon as the backlog of print jobs waiting to be done is under control.

There is another verb—LISTPTR—which performs practically the same job as SP-STATUS as far as telling you about the state of the spooler and the printers is concerned. However, the output from LISTPTR is even more cryptic than that from SP-STATUS and the verb does not fulfill the useful secondary function of waking the spooler if it has dozed off, so we won't bother you with details of LISTPTR.

5.2.2   STARTPTR & STOPPTR

When you add a new printer to the system, you have to inform the spooler of where the new printer is plugged in, what type it is, what queues it is to be given charge of, and so on. This is done with the verb "STARTPTR". Here is a typical example of a STARTPTR command:

>STARTPTR Ø,(Ø),1,PØ

The numbers given after the verb mean the following:

1: The printer number. The first zero says that the new printer is to be referred to as printer number 0.

2: Queue numbers. The zero in brackets says that this printer is to be given the job of printing out reports added to queue number 0. A printer may be given up to three queues to watch over by putting their numbers in these brackets. For example the command "STARTPTR Ø,(Ø,3,5),1,PØ" would give this same printer the job of watching over queues 0, 3 and 5.

3: Pages to eject. The third number, 1 in this case, is the number of blank pages the printer is to stick in between one report and the next. It is useful to have at least one blank page between reports so that you don't have to tear through the middle of a sheet to separate your report from the next person's.

4: Type of printer, and port number. The "PØ" tells the spooler that this new printer is a parallel printer and that it is plugged into parallel port number 0 (see Appendix 1). If the new printer were a serial one, plugged into (serial) port number 32, say, then you would have to give the command "STARTPTR Ø,(Ø),1,S32" instead. The "S" is for serial, of course.

There is also a verb which undoes the effect of STARTPTR, and takes a printer off-duty. This verb is "STOPPTR".[11] If you type

>STOPPTR Ø

at TCL, then printer number 0 will be taken out of service, and the spooler will stop using it for printing stuff. If the printer is printing a report when you give this command, it will wait until it has finished before shutting down. If there are any other reports in the queue(s) for that printer, waiting to be printed, then they will wait for ever after a STOPPTR command, because there will no longer be a printer there to print them. STOPPTR is useful when you want to unplug a printer and move it elsewhere, or when you just want to turn it off for some other reason or when you are going to replace it with a different type of printer for which you want to issue a new STARTPTR command.

The computer does not completely forget about a printer that has been stopped. It saves the printer's details—the ones you fed in when you used "STARTPTR"—on the disk. This allows you to start the printer up again simply by typing

>STARTPTR Ø

---

[11] SYS2 system privileges are required to use this verb (see §7.8.1).

Table 5.5. Options for use with the verb "SP-KILL"

Option	Function
2	Stop printer number 2 from finishing its current job
1-4	Stop printers 1 to 4 from finishing their current jobs
B	Stop all the printers from finishing their current jobs
F3	Stop item 3 in the printer list (see LISTPEQS) from being printed and place it in a hold file
F2-6	Stop items 2 to 6 in the printer list from being printed
F05	Stop item 5 in the printer list from being printed and place it in a hold file, even if it's being printed right now
DØ	Retire (delete) printer number 0 from service
A	Limit the effect of this command to your own reports
N	Stop the message "ABORT!" being printed when the job is killed

giving only the printer number, and nothing else. The details of a printer are only actually erased if you feed in new ones using the verb "STARTPTR", or if you use the verb "SP-KILL" with the D option (see §5.2.3).

One useful modification of the STOPPTR verb is

```
>STOPPTR B
```

which stops all printers attached to the computer.

5.2.3   SP-KILL

SP-KILL is the verb to use when you want to stop a printer from printing something. It can be used to cancel a report that is in the process of being printed, or one queued for printing. Or it can be used to retire a printer from duty. The verb "SP-KILL" is followed by one or more options. The full list of options is given in Table 5.5, and its most important members are explained below.

The printer number option.   If you give just a number after the verb SP-KILL, then Pick will take that to be the number of a printer, and will stop that printer from printing whatever it is printing at that moment. Thus, for instance

```
>SP-KILL Ø
```

will stop the printing of the report that is currently being printed on printer number 0. When this happens printer 0 will print the message "ABORT!", and then get on with printing the next job in the queue, if there is one. If the aborted report has been put on hold (see §5.1.1), then it is not deleted from the printer list by the SP-KILL command, so you may inspect the text afterwards using the verb "SP-EDIT" (see §5.1.4), and even send it back to be printed once more if you want. However, if the report is not on hold, the text of the report is lost when you give the SP-KILL command. The command will have no effect if printer 0 is not doing anything at the instant you type the SP-KILL command, or if there is no printer 0.

You can also specify that a whole lot of printers are to stop printing at once, by giving a command like

>SP-KILL 3-6

which kills off the reports currently being printed on each of printers 3 to 6 inclusive. The command

>SP-KILL B

kills off the reports currently being printed on every printer attached to the computer.[12]

The F (hold report) option. The verb "SP-KILL" can also be used to stop a report being printed before it ever reaches the printer, by removing it from the print queue. In order to do this you have to know the report's job number, which you can find out using the verb "LISTPEQS" (see §5.1.3). Then to prevent the spooler sending job number 7, say, to the printer, you type

>SP-KILL F7

The report will be put on hold for you so that you don't loose it's contents. You can also remove several reports from the printer queues at once by typing, for example

>SP-KILL F4-8

This would remove the reports with job numbers 4 to 8 inclusive from whatever queues they were in and put them on hold.

If the printer has already started printing a report number 7, "SP-KILL F7" will not stop it. Under these circumstances you should use the command "SP-KILL F07" to force the spooler to stop printing the report and place it on hold.

When you have finished with your held reports you should delete them using the verb "SP-EDIT" with the D option (see §5.1.4).

The D (delete printer) option. The verb "SP-KILL" can also be used to retire a printer from duty. The command

>SP-KILL D1

---

[12] However, to kill off reports originally produced not by you, but by another user, you have to have SYS2 system privileges (see §7.8.1).

will remove printer number 1 from service with immediate effect and erase every last trace of it from the computer's memory (by contrast with STOPPTR which saves the details of the printer so that you can start it again easily). You should not kill a printer while it is printing anything out—all sorts of bizarre spooler neuroses may ensue if you do. Rather, you should stop the printer first using the verb "STOPPTR" (see §5.2.2), and only after it has finished printing, give the order to "SP-KILL" it.

As an illustration of the use of SP-KILL in stopping print jobs, consider the following events. JACK has sent two reports to the printer, but has decided that he does not want them printed after all and wishes to kill them. Typing LISTPEQS to find out what the printer is doing with his reports, he sees this:

```
>LISTPEQS

   PRINTER LIST ELEMENTS              29 OCT 1990  16:54:12

# STAT LK LN STATUSES      CP OF FRMS   DATE      TIME   ACCT
1 48A5    2 P S O C L       2  0    2 29/10/90 16:52:03 JACK
2 C080    2 P S   C L       1  0    1 29/10/90 16:52:05 JACK
3 8080    3 H         C     1  2    3 29/10/90 16:53:32 JILL
4 8080    3 H         C     1  2    4 29/10/90 16:53:42 JILL

5 QUEUE ELEMENTS LISTED.           10 FRAMES IN USE.
```

This tells him that one of his jobs (job number 2) is waiting to be printed in queue number 0 (that's what the "S" under "STATUSES" means), but that the other one (job number 1) is already being printed (because there is an "O" in the "STATUSES" column). Stopping job number 2 is easy. He types

```
>SP-KILL F2
```

at TCL, and the appropriate element is removed from the printer queue by the spooler and put on hold. To stop job number 1 JACK then types

```
>SP-KILL FO1
```

The "O" forces the spooler to stop printing the report and put it on hold too. In fact JACK could have achieved both the last two operations with the one command "SP-KILL FO1-2" if he had been feeling really adventurous.

Now JACK has two held reports, which he doesn't really want. So, clean and public-spirited citizen that he is, he deletes them from the printer list with the command

```
>SP-EDIT D1-2
```

and they are no more.

5.2.4   :STARTSPOOLER

It is worth just mentioning one other spooler verb, the verb ":STARTSPOOLER". This is the verb to use when the spooler stops working completely and cannot be woken, no matter what. This is not something that should happen to you regularly, but if ever it does ": STARTSPOOLER" is the thing to type. Notice the colon at the beginning. You have to put that in. There are various options that may follow this verb, some of them with very drastic effects. We will say no more about this verb—if you have cause to use it, you should consult your Pick manual.

Part Two

Pick for programmers and system managers

6 Editing

On a day-to-day basis it is best to enter data into the computer through programs which constantly remind the user what should be entered next and perform checks on the data entered to ensure that they are internally consistent and complete. For example, the personal details of a new employee might be entered via a program that asks in turn for the person's surname, forenames, address, telephone number, date of birth and so forth. This program would routinely check that the name entered does not coincide with the name of any existing employee (to guard against the possibility that the employee's data had already been entered by another person), and that the date of birth is a possible one (not, for example, September 31st).

However, it often happens either that one wants to check exactly what the machine holds in a file on its disk, or to alter such a file in an unpredictable way. An important case is when one is entering into the machine the lines of a Pick BASIC program (see Chapter 8). In these circumstances one wants to *edit* the file. That is, one wants to call up the file onto the screen, move the cursor to any particular place within the file and the delete or add a character by hitting the appropriate key. Unfortunately, standard Pick does not provide a facility of this sort, which is called a **screen editor**. This chapter describes various strategies for coping with this lamentable omission.

The strategies are:

1: Use the standard Pick System Editor. Pick does come with an editor, though one which is a throw-back to the bad old days of steam engines, teletype machines and vacuum tubes. The Pick **System Editor** is a **line editor**, rather than a screen editor. As the name implies, such an editor only allows you to see one line at a time. Worse than this, a line editor doesn't allow you to use the cursor to point to the text you wish to change, but insists that you describe it symbolically. For example, to correct the word "MISTAKC" with the Pick System Editor you would have to type "R/C/E/", which is short for the sentence "Replace C by E". Clearly, this is a very poor substitute for moving the cursor to the end of MISTAKC, erasing the errant C

with the backspace key and then hitting **E**. In fact it is such a poor substitute
that only a fanatic would routinely use the Pick System Editor to change files
by more than a character here and there. However, there are a few situations
in which the System Editor *is* the best tool for the job and it can be useful
to know how to use it.

2: Install a proprietary screen editor.   Like Pick, DOS, the standard
operating system on IBM-compatible computers, does not come with a screen
editor.   Nonetheless most IBM-compatible machines are used almost exclusively for word-processing with a screen editor since numerous excellent screen
editors will run on any IBM-compatible computer. Unfortunately, many fewer
software packages are sold for Pick machines than for IBM-compatible computers, and we have not encountered a serviceable screen editor for our Pick
machine. The feeble attempt at a screen editor that was delivered with our
machine was next to useless. So we wrote our own screen editor, "PickED".
Appendix 5 explains how PickED works and how it can be adapted to run
on your machine. Appendix 6 explains how to obtain a copy of PickED on a
floppy disk.

3: Edit your files on a friendly personal computer.   A screen editor
is not the easiest piece of software to write and PickED was not the first
program we wrote. So what editor *did* we use for our early software? We
certainly didn't use the Pick System Editor. We wrote PickED and a lot
of other programs with a screen editor on a micro and then transferred the
programs into our Pick machine. This scheme has several advantages:
 (i) You can use an editor with which you are familiar and comfortable.[1]
 (ii) You can program on any handy machine, including one at home.
(iii) You can easily share programs and data with like-minded friends and
      colleagues simply by sending them a floppy.

In fact, the ability to transfer data between a personal computer and your
Pick machine is so useful that proprietary software packages are available for
just this purpose. However, we now explain how you can do this job just fine
without any special software for your Pick machine.

6.1   Transferring data between a micro and your Pick machine

We assume that you have a personal computer equipped with a serial port
and a **terminal emulator**. Many terminal emulators are now available for

---

[1] However, if you use a word-processor such as WORD or WordPerfect, you must set
up the word-processing program so that it writes to disk "plain ASCII" text rather than
the mixture of text and formatting characters that word-processors normally save on disk.
Consult your word-processor's manual to see how to set it up for ASCII text.

micros. One of the best is a public-domain program from Columbia University, New York, called **Kermit**.[2] To be specific we'll describe how to work with Kermit, but essentially identical operations could be carried out with any other terminal emulator.

The serial port of your micro should be connected to one of your Pick machine's ports (see Appendix 1 for a discussion of serial port characteristics). Then start up your terminal emulator and set it so that it talks to the right serial port on the micro at the correct baud rate and parity (usually 9600 bits per second and no parity), with the "Xon/Xoff" flow-control protocol in force, and so that it is emulating the kind of terminal your Pick machine is set to converse with (see §7.10). The screen should then clear and with any luck a Pick logon banner will appear and you can log onto the Pick machine in the usual way.[3]

6.1.1   Copying data from Pick to a micro

Once you have logged on, your micro can be used indefinitely as a 'dumb terminal', that is, one which simply sends keyboard input to the Pick machine and displays the latter's responses on the screen. So, for example, you could use ACCESS to generate various useful lists of employees or whatever (see §4.3). Now suppose you want to send one of these lists to a colleague in another office over the phone, perhaps by leaving it for him in an electronic mail box, and you have software for this sort of thing on your micro. Then your next step would be to move the list from the Pick machine onto one of your micro's disks, whence your telecommunications software can send it down the phone line. Capturing material on a micro in this way is often referred to as **downloading** the material onto the micro.

If you are using Kermit you can download the output from an ACCESS enquiry like "SORT STAFF WITH SURNAME = "B]"" as follows:

1. Type

   >SORT STAFF WITH SURNAME = "B]" (N)

   but *do not* hit RETURN. Notice the **(N)** option at the end of this command; this stops the machine including in the list terminal control characters that would upset your communications software (see §4.3.1).
2. Wake up your micro by typing Kermit's escape sequence (**Ctrl-_** and then **C** if you use our version of Kermit[4]).

---

[2] A "public-domain" program is one whose general, non-commercial duplication has been authorized by its copyright holder. You can obtain a copy of Kermit, along with a selection of Pick software, by sending a formatted disk to the publisher—see Appendix 6.

[3] If you don't get a logon prompt, hit RTN a couple of times. If you still don't get a logon prompt, try typing Ctrl-_ followed by B.

[4] By Ctrl-_ we just mean hold down the key marked CTRL and hit whatever key bears the symbol "_". There's no need to hold down SHIFT as well even if you would need to to type "_".

3. When the "Kermit>" prompt appears at the bottom of your screen, enter "LOG SESSION FILENAME", where FILENAME is the name of the file on the micro in which you wish to save the data, say LIST.DAT.

4. Enter C to get back into contact with the Pick machine and hit RETURN.

5. When the Pick machine stops printing, wake your micro up again by typing Kermit's escape sequence (Ctrl-_ C or whatever) and tell Kermit to close the micro file by entering "CLOSE" at the Kermit> prompt.

6. Your data are now safely stored on the micro in the file "LIST.DAT" and you may return to the Pick machine by entering C.

One sometimes wants to download to a micro the contents of an entire item. For example, suppose you wanted to copy to your micro a Pick BASIC program that is stored in the item "TRIAL" of the file "PROGRAMS". With Kermit you would do this as follows:

1. Use Kermit to log onto the Pick machine and get to TCL.

2. Type "ED PROGRAMS TRIAL". The machine will respond like this

```
>ED PROGRAMS TRIAL
Top
.
```

3. Enter "S". The machine will respond like this:

```
.S
Suppress On
.
```

4. Type "L1000" *but do not hit* RETURN *a second time*. Instead type Kermit's escape sequence (Ctrl-_ C or whatever) and then "LOG SESSION FILENAME", where FILENAME is the name of the file in which you wish to store the item on the micro, for example, "TRIAL.PK".

5. Return to the Pick machine by entering C and then hit return. Pick will type out the requested item and Kermit will capture it in the file "TRIAL.PK" as it flows over the screen.

6. When the item has stopped moving up the screen, close the capture file by typing Kermit's escape sequence followed by "CLOSE".

7. Type C to return to the Pick machine and finish up by typing "EX". Now you are back at TCL and your item has been copied into a file on the micro.

6.1.2   Copying data from a micro to Pick

Suppose now you have used your favourite editor to write a Pick BASIC program "TEST" on your micro and wish to transfer it to the Pick machine so you can try it out. You **upload** the file as follows. Use the micro's editor to put the following statements at the head of the micro file, immediately above the material you want transferred to the Pick computer:

```
DELETE PROGRAMS TEST
ED PROGRAMS TEST
I
```

And at the very end of the file on the micro put

```
(blank line)
FI
```

These extra lines have the following effect. When the file is fired from the micro to the Pick computer, the first line instructs the machine to delete the item "TEST",[5] the second line starts the Pick System Editor and the third line tells the editor to insert what follows into the item "TEST" of the file "PROGRAMS". Your program will then flow smoothly into the Pick machine. Immediately after your program comes the blank line you added before the FI. This blank line will stop the Pick System Editor inserting the contents of your micro file into the item "TEST" and cause it to sit up and take notice of what you say next. This will be FI, which will cause the editor to file TEST on the disk and return to TCL. So once you have fired the micro file containing your program at the Pick machine, the program will be safely inserted into PROGRAMS TEST.

With Kermit you fire the file at the Pick machine like this:

1. Use Kermit to log onto the Pick machine, and get to TCL.
2. Wake up your micro by typing Kermit's escape sequence (Ctrl-_ C or whatever).
3. When the Kermit> prompt appears, type "TRANSMIT FILENAME", where FILENAME is the name, say "TEST.PK", of the micro-file that contains your program. When you hit RETURN at the end of the name, Kermit will start sending your file to the Pick machine. From the point of view of the Pick machine all that is happening at this point is that an awfully quick (and accurate!) typist is using the System Editor to type in a new version of TEST. From your point of view the file is being painlessly transmitted.
4. When the file ceases to flow up the screen, you can return to the Pick machine by entering C.

6.1.3   Transferring databases between a micro and your Pick machine

If you move up to a Pick machine from a micro-computer of some sort, you will undoubtedly need some way to copy your existing data onto the new machine. Fundamentally, copying a database from a micro is no different from transferring a simple item such as a program. To transfer to the Pick machine a database "STAFF" you first produce a micro file like this:

---

[5] If there is no item "TEST" already in the PROGRAMS file, it is obviously unnecessary to tell the machine to delete TEST. But it is a harmless precaution.

Table 6.1.   Generating attribute, value and
sub-value marks on a micro

Mark	Key	BASIC	Pick disk
Attribute	Ctrl-^	CHR$(30)	ASCII 254
Value	Ctrl-]	CHR$(29)	ASCII 253
Sub-value	Ctrl-\	CHR$(28)	ASCII 252

```
ED STAFF BLOGGS-J
I
Bloggs
Joe
M
21/04/50
14 Home Ave↔Working↔Surrey△
(0347) 145763
(blank line)
FI
ED STAFF OTHER-A-N
I
Other
Annabel↔Natalie
......
```

When this file is fired at the Pick machine, it will create an item called
"BLOGGS-J" in the STAFF file. The first attribute will be "Bloggs", the second
"Joe", the third "M", and so on. The fourth attribute, "21/04/50", is Bloggs'
birthday in human-readable form. As was explained in §3.5.1, Pick likes to
have its dates in 'Pick internal format'. However, once we have Bloggs' birthday in the machine in the form 21/04/50 we can use a Pick BASIC program to
convert it to internal format (see §8.5). So we don't worry about converting
dates at this stage.

The fifth attribute in Bloggs' entry in STAFF should contain his address
as a multi-valued attribute. So the lines of his address should be separated
by **value marks**. On the Pick database these are ASCII character 253 (see
Appendix 2). However, one cannot generate this ASCII character directly
from the keyboard. So the System Editor has been programmed to write
ASCII 253 into the file when you simultaneously depress CTRL and]. This
key-combination actually generates ASCII 29. So on the micro it is necessary
to separate the lines of Bloggs' address with the character ASCII 29 (see Table
6.1). The double-headed arrow "↔" is how ASCII 29 appears on our IBM-
compatible micros. On many machines Ctrl-] will produce *two* characters
on the screen, for example "^]". This will also work fine although it is rather
confusing to have two characters instead of one.

In similar fashion, if we wished to break a value into a series of sub-
values, in the micro file we would separate subvalues with the ASCII character
28, which one gets by typing Ctrl-\.

The sixth attribute of Bloggs' entry should be his postcode. Unfortunately we don't know what it is so it must be left blank. If we were just to leave a blank line in the micro file, the System Editor would interpret this as terminating the stream of data to be inserted into the item "BLOGGS" and would take the next line to be an instruction rather than data. So we don't generate a blank attribute by inserting a blank line into the micro file but by inserting an **attribute mark** at the end of the previous attribute. On the Pick database this is the character ASCII 254, but since this character cannot be directly generated on the keyboard, we insert instead ASCII 30, which the Pick System Editor has been programmed to interpret as an attribute mark. The triangle "△" at the end of Bloggs' address is how ASCII 30 appears on the screens of our IBM-compatible micros.

To generate two blank attributes one would simply end the last filled attribute with a pair of characters ASCII 30.

After Bloggs' address we give his telephone number, which will become the sixth attribute of his item. Then there is a blank line which terminates data input by the System Editor. The FI that follows the blank line causes the editor to file the item "BLOGGS-J" on the disk and we can get straight on entering data for Mrs Other.

When the details of every member of staff have been added to our micro file we fire this file at the Pick machine as described in §6.1.2. These data will then be automatically formed into a Pick file ready to be interrogated by ACCESS and other Pick software.

Imagine that we have done this. We can now use the System Editor to check that Bloggs' data have arrived safely. The conversation would go like this:

```
>ED STAFF BLOGGS-J
Top
.P
001 Bloggs
002 Joe
003 M
004 21/04/50
005 14 Home Ave]Working]Surrey
006
007 (0347) 145763
BOTTOM 007
.
```

The next section explains what's going on here.

6.2   Snooping with the System Editor

Your database program is showing some unintelligible gibberish on the screen instead of Joe Bloggs' employment history. What is wrong? Have Bloggs'

personal details been incorrectly entered, or is the database program displaying correctly entered data incorrectly? The way to find out is to look at the
item "BLOGGS" in the STAFF file with the System Editor; this will show you
exactly what you have on file about Bloggs, and you can take the problem
from there. If the data are at fault by a character or two, you can use the
System Editor to put things right. On the other hand, if the data are totally
messed up, you will probably prefer to use some tool other than the System
Editor to straighten things out. For now, we show you how with the System
Editor you can peek into any file and change things here and there.

You always start by issuing a TCL command of the form "ED FILENAME
ITEMNAME":

```
>ED STAFF BLOGGS-J
Top
.
```

Here we have told the System Editor to read the item "BLOGGS-J" in the file
"STAFF" and the machine has replied that it has found the desired item and
awaits our next gambit. The dot is the System Editor's prompt; it means
"OK, so what's next?". How should we reply? It is useful to divide the
possible replies into three categories:

6.2.1   Moving around the item (the L, P, A, G & B commands)

We have already met the P command. P is a very simple command; it just
says "Page", and the next page (up to 24 attributes) of the item being edited
are printed out. L can be used in a very similar way; "L2" Lists (i.e., prints)
two attributes, "L20" lists 20 attributes:

```
.L2
001 Bloggs
002 Joe
.
```

But L stands for "Locate" as well as for "List" since we can use L to locate a
sequence of characters within the file. Suppose at the top of Bloggs' item you
type "L"14". Then the quote sign before the number "14" tells the machine
that you want it to look for the first occurrence of "14" in BLOGGS-J, *not* list
the next 14 attributes. Thus the conversation would go like this[6]

```
>ED STAFF BLOGGS-J
Top
.L"14
005 14 Home Ave]Working]Surrey
.
```

---

[6] The character "]" is how the System Editor denotes the end of one value and the
beginning of another. Similarly, sub-values are separated with the character "\".

On being instructed to look for the number "14" the machine runs through the item "BLOGGS-J" until it finds an attribute with "14" in it, prints that attribute out and sits waiting for further instructions.   Had you entered "L"Home" the result would have been exactly the same.

Suppose this isn't the occurrence of "14" you are interested in. Then you can find the next occurrence of "14" either by repeating "L"14" or by typing "A" for Again; "A" just repeats the last L command. Thus you could continue the conversation like this

```
.A
007 (0347) 145763
BOTTOM 007
.
```

The machine has found the "14" in Bloggs' telephone number.   Had there been no second occurrence of "14", the machine would have gone to the end of the item and said

```
BOTTOM 007
.
```

Suppose now you are worried that Bloggs' first name has been incorrectly entered. His forenames are stored in attribute 2, so you now type either "G2" for "Go to 2" or simply "2" which means the same thing:

```
.2
002 Joe
.
```

We shall soon see that it is not always possible to move up an item in this way—you may have to issue an F command first (see the next section).

If you want to know how long a very long item is without waiting for all its attributes to be printed out, the thing to do is to type "B". The machine will reply by printing the last attribute. For example

```
.B
007 (0347) 145763
BOTTOM 007
.
```

Summary

- To edit an item in a file, type "ED FILENAME ITEMNAME" at TCL.
- The L command can be used to either list a number of attributes, as in "L14" or to locate a string in the file, as in "L"14".
- The A command repeats the last L command.
- The P command prints a screen-full of attributes.
- A G followed by a number causes the machine to go to the attribute whose number you give. Actually the G is redundant; the number on its own has the same effect.
- The letter B causes the machine to go to the bottom of the item.

6.2.2   Changing things (the DE, R, F & I commands)

Suppose you want to eliminate altogether the third attribute of every item
in the file "STAFF" because you have decided it is sexist to even notice the
gender of employees. Suppose furthermore that in your folly you decide to use
the System Editor rather than Pick BASIC for this job. Then after calling up
the item of each employee by typing a variant of[7] "ED STAFF BLOGGS-J" you
would go to the third attribute by typing "3" and then delete that attribute
by typing "DE" thus:

```
>ED STAFF BLOGGS-J
Top
.3
003 M
.DE
004 21/04/50
.
```

On elimination of the third attribute, the fourth attribute is printed out to
indicate that this has become the current attribute. Then the machine prints
its prompt ".".

To continue our example, let us imagine that the anti-ageists have been
on at you as well as the anti-sexists and that you have decided to delete
attribute 4, which contains dates of birth, alongside the sexist attribute 3.
Then your conversation with the machine would run as follows:

```
>ED STAFF BLOGGS-J
Top
.3
003 M
.DE2
005 14 Home Ave]Working]Surrey
.
```

Here, by entering "DE2" rather than just "DE" you have deleted two attributes
instead of one and your computer can henceforth discriminate on grounds of
neither sex nor age.

This important egalitarian work done, you notice that Bloggs' home town
is given as "Working" not "Woking" as you think it should be. This is easily
fixed with the R command. Thus

```
.R/r//
005 14 Home Ave]Woking]Surrey
.
```

The command "R/r//" tells the machine to find the first occurrence of "r"
and to replace it with nothing. The machine demonstrates its compliance by
printing out the amended attribute. Now it dawns on you that Bloggs really
lives in Workington. The emendation looks like this:

---

[7] Actually there is a way to edit every item in a file automatically, one after another;
you type ED STAFF *.

```
.R/Woking/Workington/
005 14 Home Ave]Workington]Surrey
.
```

The R command needs two character sequences, or "strings" as they are known in computerese; the thing to be replaced and the thing it is to be replaced by. In the examples just given these strings are delimited by the slash character "/". But you can actually delimit your strings with any non-numeric character you like provided the character you choose does not occur in either of the strings you wish to pass to the R command. It is important to be able to choose a delimiter other than slash since there might be a slash in one of your strings. Thus to replace "23/4" with "23-4" you could type

```
.R?23/4?23-4?
```

Here the machine knows you are using "?" as a delimiter because it is the first character after R.

Now you have second thoughts about deleting all those genders and want to restore Bloggs' third attribute. So you wish to insert after the existing second attribute a new attribute consisting of the letter M. The I command, which stands for "insert" is the command for this job. But before you can actually make this change you have to make a clean copy of Bloggs' item. The reason for this is that things that come lower down the item have changed— for example attribute 5, the address. So to avoid getting into a muddle about which attribute numbers refer to which attributes, Pick insists on your starting over from the top of an updated copy of the item. To make this updated copy you issue the F command, which stands for "Flip". It looks like this:

```
005 14 Home Ave]Workington]Surrey
.F
Top
.
```

Now you can go to attribute 2 and issue an Insert command:

```
Top
.2
002 Joe
.I
002+M
002+
.
```

On receiving the I command the machine issued the prompt "002+" to indicate that what followed would be added after attribute 2. It would then have inserted everything that followed into new attributes labelled 3, 4, etc., until it met a blank line. In this case the second line input in response to the 002+ prompt was blank, so only one extra attribute was created. If you Flip the item and Page it, you will now see the following:

```
.F
Top
.P
001 Bloggs
002 Joe
003 M
004 14 Home Ave]Workington]Surrey
005
006 (0347) 145763
BOTTOM 006
     .
```

Notice that following the deletion of the age attribute, the old fifth attribute
has become the fourth and so on down the item.

Summary

- The DE command deletes attributes. "DE" or "DE1" deletes the current
  attribute, "DE2" deletes the current attribute and the following one, and
  so forth.

- The R command replaces one string in the current attribute by another.
  The strings are delimited by a punctuation character, often either "/" or
  "?". For example, one might type "R/this/that/" to replace "this" by
  "that".

- The F command makes a fresh copy of the item and sends the editor to the
  top of it. It is usually necessary to issue an F command prior to inspecting
  an attribute that precedes attributes that have been changed since the F
  command was last issued.

- The I command allows material to be inserted after the current attribute—
  after issuing the I command everything you type goes into fresh attributes
  until you enter a blank line. Only after a blank line has been entered does
  the editor again interpret what you type as instructions rather than data.

6.2.3   Exiting from the System Editor (the EX, FI & FD commands)

So far nothing has been written on the disk. So nothing is yet permanently
lost if the editing session has not been a success. In fact, you can exit the
editor leaving the item on disk just as it was by issuing the EX command. If
you have changed the item in RAM the machine will ask you to confirm that
you wish to quit, thus:

```
.EX
Item may have changed. Type Y to EXIT item 'STAFF BLOGGS-J':Y
'BLOGGS-J' exited
```

If the editing session has been a success you can save it on the disk by
issuing the command "FI", which stands for FIle:

```
.FI
'BLOGGS-J' filed
```

If you are fed up with Bloggs and wish to delete his wretched item from the STAFF file altogether, you issue the command "FD":

```
.FD
Type Y to DELETE item 'STAFF BLOGGS-J':Y
'BLOGGS-J' deleted
```

Summary

- The EX command allows you to finish editing an item without writing your changes on the disk.
- The FI command causes the machine to write the amended item on the disk and quit editing the item.
- The FD command causes the machine to erase the current item from the disk.

6.2.4   Other System Editor commands

The Pick System Editor understands several other commands, which we have not discussed here because we have not found them useful. The most important of these are probably the MErge command and the Pn command; the ME command allows you to copy an attribute from any file in the database into the item you are editing. The Pn command allows you to execute a complicated series of editor commands that you have Prestored on the disk. If Pick BASIC did not exist, these would undoubtedly be useful commands. However, it's safer to carry out all delicate or repetitive operations on files through BASIC programs since (i) you then don't have to remember how to use complicated editor commands, and (ii) you have in the BASIC program a record of exactly how you have changed the database. Having such a record can be useful if you later discover that you didn't do things right; discovering exactly what you did wrong is the first step towards putting things right. If you change the database interactively, it is easy to get into a muddle and then to be uncertain exactly what you have done.

7 System management

Every computer system should have a **system manager**, a caretaker in charge of the upkeep of the computer. On a Pick computer there are several important tasks which fall into the hands of the system manager and we have collected together the details of these tasks in this chapter. If you are the system manager of a Pick computer, then this is the chapter for you.

7.1 The SYSPROG account

Every Pick system has an account containing the programs and data that a system manager needs to accomplish his system management tasks. On most systems this account is called "SYSPROG", though it is just possible it has another name on your computer. We shall always refer to it as SYSPROG.

In §3.3 we explained how with every account there is associated a special user, whose user name is the same as the account name, and whose MD is that of the account. However, we argued against the existence of such users, maintaining that one should normally keep the names of accounts and the names of users separate; the former reflecting the nature of the files in the accounts, and the latter being the names of the people who use the machine. In SYSPROG however, we see the one important counter-example to this principle: it is standard practice for the system manager to log on by giving the user name "SYSPROG" and an appropriate password, thus making the MD "SYSPROG" his MD and gaining access to all the system management software. The reason for this is that in the interests of security it is highly desirable to limit the number of users sharing the SYSPROG MD to as small a number as possible (see §7.8). Under the scheme described this number is one, which is the smallest it can be. There is normally no reason for any user other than SYSPROG to have access to the SYSPROG MD. If two or more people need to be able to perform the system manager's job, then they should both log on as SYSPROG after giving SYSPROG's (carefully guarded) password.

124

On most Pick computers the system manager has other work to do in addition to his system management tasks. Like other users of the machine, he will do this ordinary work when logged on as a regular user in his own name, under whatever account is appropriate for the work he does. He will log on as SYSPROG only when he wants to do something specifically connected with the maintenance of the system. For example, if Joe Bloggs is the system manager on your system and he works in the finance department, then he should have a user name "BLOGGS", say, with its own password, and share the FINANCE MD with the other members of his department. He should only log on as SYSPROG to discharge his responsibilities as system manager. Conversely, the system manager should never attempt to perform system management tasks while logged on under any name other than SYSPROG. It *is* possible to allow other users, not sharing SYSPROG's MD, access to the system manager's files, by putting appropriate Q-pointers in their MDs. Occasionally this can be useful. However, your system will be much more secure if the system manager is always logged on as SYSPROG when performing tasks specifically connected with system management—in a properly secure system the programs that accomplish these tasks will not work unless run by the user SYSPROG, even though other users may have Q-pointers to the files containing them. This restriction is desirable because an unauthorized person playing with the system manager's programs could do a lot of damage. In §7.8.2 we explain how ordinary users can be prevented from gaining access to sensitive files.

7.2   Creating and deleting accounts and users

We now discuss in detail a Pick system manager's responsibilities. The first of these is the maintenance of accounts and users.

7.2.1   Creating accounts

New accounts are created by using the verb "CREATE-ACCOUNT". Unfortunately, CREATE-ACCOUNT is not a standard Pick verb—it is not a true part of the operating system. It is rather, a program, usually written either by the manufacturer, or by the supplier of the computer, to make create accounts on your particular computer. This means that the way it works, and what exactly it needs to be told when you run it, will vary from one computer to another. Below we give an example of how to make a new account on a Pick system, but you should be aware that on your computer the procedure may be slightly different from the illustrated one in step 4.

1. Log onto the computer as SYSPROG and get to TCL if you are not already there.
2. Now type

    ```
    >CREATE-ACCOUNT
    ```

3. Answer the computer's questions as shown in the following example (see
the following paragraph for an explanation of them):

```
ACCOUNT NAME?PERSONNEL          (Desired name of account)
L/RET CODE(S)?P                 (Retrieval lock)
L/UPD CODE(S)?P                 (Update lock)
PASSWORD?                       (Password, does not appear)
PRIVILEGES?SYSØ                 (System privileges)
MOD, SEP?29,1                   (Mod and sep of new MD)
```

As a result of this dialogue a new account is created with its own MD and
the account name "PERSONNEL".

Some of the computer's questions are less than self-explanatory, so we
will go over them one by one:

1: Account name. The first question asks you to enter the name that you
wish the new account to have (which is the name by which you will refer to
its MD—see §3.3). In this example we create an account called "PERSONNEL".

2: Retrieval lock. The second question, "L/RET CODE(S)?", is asking you
to give the 'retrieval lock' with which the new account's MD is to be locked.
The use of retrieval locks is explained in §7.8.2. If you do not use retrieval
locks on your system, then you should just hit RETURN in response to this
question.

3: Update lock. The next thing you are asked for is the 'update lock' to
be placed on the new MD. Update locks are also explained in §7.8.2. Again
just hit RETURN if you don't want the MD locked at all.

4: Password. As described in §3.3 and briefly mentioned above, whenever
you create a new *account* you also create a new *user* whose user name is the
same as the account name, and whose MD is the MD of that account. The next
two questions refer to this user. In a well run system this option of having
a special user "PERSONNEL" associated with the account "PERSONNEL" will
not be used (see §3.3.2), but nonetheless you should answer these questions
with care, particularly the first, concerning the password, if you don't want
intruders breaking into your computer through this 'back door'.

The fourth question, "PASSWORD?", is asking you what password you wish
to give this unsatisfactory extra user. If no one is to be allowed to log on under
this user name (i.e., as user "PERSONNEL" in our example) then the safest thing
is to make up some random jumble of letters as the password and then forget
them as soon as you've typed them in. That way there is no danger of anyone
ever guessing or finding out what the password is. For the sake of secrecy the
password does not appear on the screen when you type it in, in the same way
as your password does not appear on the screen when you log onto a Pick
computer.

5: System privileges.   The fifth question concerns the system privileges the user is to have. System privileges are explained in §7.8.1. If nobody is ever to log on as this user, then the correct procedure is to give the user the lowest privilege rating, "SYS∅", as above. Simply hitting RETURN in response to this question is equivalent to typing "SYS∅" so we could also have done that in our example.

6: Mod and sep of new MD.   The last thing you are asked to enter is the mod and sep of the MD of the new account. §4.2.7 explains how to choose the mod and sep for a file. If you are unsure about how large the new MD is going to be then stick in a mod of 29 and a sep of 1, which are suitable for most purposes. (On many computers you get these values by default if you just hit RETURN.)

On some Pick systems the verb "CREATE-ACCOUNT" serves to create new *users* as well as new accounts. If you have such a system, you will find that the computer will ask you some question like "REAL ACCOUNT OR SYNONYM (R/S) ?" before all the others, by which it means, "Do you want to create an account, or a synonym user?" If you want to create an account, the correct response to this question would be "R" for "real account". After this the dialogue should proceed much as above.

When the computer creates a new account it does four things:

(i) It creates an MD bearing the account name.

(ii) It makes a new item in the system dictionary, which tells the computer where to find that MD, as described in §3.3.

(iii) It puts a Q-pointer to the new MD in SYSPROG's MD.

(iv) It copies into the MD a whole load of useful PROCs (see Chapter 9) and other items. These allow the users of the new MD to do all the things one normally takes for granted on a Pick computer. For example, the verb "OFF" is actually a PROC which is copied into each MD when the MD is first created, so that the users of that MD can log off the computer by typing "OFF".

The items that are copied to the new MD are stored in the SYSPROG account, in a file called "NEWAC". Thus, if you have a program or PROC which you would like all users to have access to, a convenient way to ensure they do would be to add a short PROC to the file "NEWAC", which calls your program or PROC. If, on the other hand, there is some system facility that you don't want people to use, (the old-fashioned line-editor for instance, see Chapter 6), then you could delete the appropriate item ("ED" in this case) from NEWAC so as to disable it.

7.2.2   Creating users

Creating new *users* presents something of a problem on many Pick systems; Pick's designers have, strangly, omitted to provide a verb for this job. On some more recent releases of the operating system, the verb "CREATE-ACCOUNT" is used to create synonym users as well as new accounts. If the CREATE-ACCOUNT on your computer lacks this flexibility, then your best courses of action are:

(i) To use an editor to add new user-defining items to the system dictionary by hand (see §3.3.2 for details of the exact form these items should take).

(ii) Use the program "CREATE-USER" given in Appendix 4.

On computers equipped with a CREATE-ACCOUNT which *can* create synonym users, the procedure will be similar to that below (though possibly differing in minor ways).

1. Log onto the computer as SYSPROG and get to TCL if you are not already there.

2. Now type

   >CREATE-ACCOUNT

3. Answer the computer's questions as shown in the following example:

   REAL ACCOUNT OR SYNONYM?S   (Create a user rather than an account)
   ACCOUNT NAME?JILL   (Desired name of user)
   L/RET CODE(S)?Z]U]F   (Retrieval keys)
   L/UPD CODE(S)?Z]U   (Update keys)
   PASSWORD?   (Password, does not appear)
   PRIVILEGES?SYS0   (System privileges)
   REAL ACCOUNT NAME?PERSONNEL   (Account name of MD to share)

As a result of this dialogue, a new user JILL is created who uses the MD with account name "PERSONNEL".

Let us go over these questions and answers one by one:

1: Real account or synonym user.   Since the same verb "CREATE-ACCOUNT" is used for the creation both of accounts *and* synonym users, the computer first asks you which you wish to create in this particular instance. In this case we want to create a new user, rather than a new account, so we reply "S". In a properly run system you will create users far more often than you will accounts.

2: User name.   Next you are required to enter the name of the user you wish to create, "JILL" in this example.

3: Retrieval keys.   Then you have to enter the retrieval keys that the new user is to have. The use of retrieval keys is explained in §7.8.2, so for the moment we merely note that if the user is to have more than one retrieval key then the different keys must be separated by value marks (see §6.1.3 for how to enter a value mark at the keyboard) which will appear on the screen as the symbol "]", as shown above. If you do not use retrieval keys on your system, or if the new user is not to have any, then you should just hit RETURN in response to this question.

4: Update keys.   The next thing you are asked for is the new user's update keys. These too are explained in §7.8.2. The comments on retrieval keys in the previous paragraph apply equally to update keys.

5: Password. Next you have to type in the password the new user is to have. Just in case there is anyone peering uninvited over your shoulder as you type it, the password does not appear on the screen.

6: Privileges. In response to the "PRIVILEGES?" question you should enter one of SYS∅, SYS1, SYS2. If you just hit RETURN that is equivalent to entering SYS∅. System privileges are explained in §7.8.1.

7: Real account name. In §3.3.2 we explained that synonym users do not have their own MDs. So when you create a new synonym user you have to specify which of the MDs already on the disk the new user is to share. The question "REAL ACCOUNT NAME?" is asking you to give the account name of this dictionary. In our example we suppose that the new user, JILL, is to work in the personnel department, and should therefore share the MD of the account "PERSONNEL".

7.2.3 Deleting accounts

On rare occasions you will also want to delete an account. Deleting an account means deleting from the disk the MD for that account, and all files for which it contains file-defining items, (though not those for which it only contains Q-pointers). Deleting an account is a drastic measure, and not something to be undertaken lightly. Be very sure you want to delete an account before you do it. (You should be making daily 'backups' of your files on magnetic tapes or floppy disks—see §7.3. So if the worst comes to the worst, you should be able to recover deleted files from these backups.)

The deletion of an account is accomplished using the verb "DELETE-ACCOUNT". Like "CREATE-ACCOUNT" this verb is usually a program written by the manufacturer of the computer. Though it may be slightly different on your computer, the procedure for using it is always roughly along the following lines:

1. Log onto the computer as SYSPROG and get to TCL if you are not already there.
2. Now type
   >DELETE-ACCOUNT
3. The computer will ask you to name the account you wish to delete, and you reply by giving the account name.
4. The computer will print a list of the names and other details of the files whose file-defining items reside in the MD of the account you have named, and ask you if you are sure you want to erase them all.
5. If in response you type any word beginning with the letter Y, either capital or lower-case, (like "YES" or "Y" or "yogurt") then the MD, and all the files whose names are on the list will be deleted.

To take an example, here is how you would delete the account "PERSON-NEL" and all the files it contains:

```
>DELETE-ACCOUNT
ACCOUNT NAME? PERSONNEL

FILE                BASE    MOD   SEP

MD                  26942   29    1
STAFF               27181   1     1
STAFF               27182   7     1
PAY                 20853   1     1
PAY                 20854   3     1
....

DO YOU STILL WANT TO DELETE THE ACCOUNT? YES

>
```

And the account, and all the files it contained, are gone.

7.2.4   Deleting users

No special verb is needed to delete users, since a user consists only of an item
in the system dictionary and nothing else (see §3.3.2). To delete a user you
only have to delete the relevant item in SYSTEM and they are gone. You can do
this using the verb "DELETE" described in §4.2.6. For instance, suppose one of
your employees has left your company and accepted a managerial post with
your hated enemies the Gimcrack Corporation of America. This guy is not
going to need to use your computer again, and it seems wise to protect yourself
against intrusion by removing his user name, "ACE", from the machine. To
do this:

1. Log onto the computer as SYSPROG and get to TCL if you are not already
   there.

2. Now type

```
>DELETE SYSTEM ACE
```

and ACE's user name is deleted.

   This example is, perhaps, a little melodramatic—it makes sense to delete
any user name that is no longer needed. If you don't, the system dictionary
will only become clogged up and hard to maintain.

7.3   Making backups

Little though you may like to contemplate it, there is always the possibility
that your computer will one day break down and destroy some of your data.
A more likely, but equally disastrous possibility is that one of your staff will
make a slip and delete a few hundred frames of your database by mistake.
Even if your hardware and your personnel are one hundred per cent reliable,
there is always the chance that you will be struck down by an Act of God—a
fire, a burst water main, a gas explosion, a lightning strike, a sixteen wheel

juggernaut driving through reception by mistake... Most computerized companies are so heavily dependent on the information stored in their computer, that losing a large portion of it like this would be catastrophic. Of course this is not just a phenomenon of the computer age—there has always been the possibility of trashing the wrong drawer in the filing cabinet or shredding the wrong pile of papers—but computerized systems *are* different (i) because these mistakes are easier to make, and (ii) because there exists a simple way to guard against them: you can keep 'backups'.

A **backup** is a copy of all the data on your disk, made on some portable medium like magnetic tape or floppy disks. If you make regular backups of the data on your disk and keep them in some safe place, then, no matter what happens to your computer, you will always have a copy of your precious data.

Pick computers provide a simple means by which these backup copies of the data can be made, and fed back into the machine should the need arise. Making backups is now standard practice on *all* well-run computers, down to the smallest home-computer, and if you run a computer system it is your undeniable duty to make sure that backups of your data are made regularly, preferably every day. Anyone who tells you otherwise needs his head examined. Making backups on a Pick computer is so easy, and the possible consequences (however unlikely) of not making them so appalling, that there can really be no argument about it.

Well, enough of this lecturing; if you're not won over yet, then you never will be. "How," we hear you ask, "do I make these wonderful backups?" First you need to decide whether your backups are to go on 'tapes' or 'floppies'.

7.3.1 Magnetic tapes or floppy disks?

Your computer may use either **magnetic tapes** or **floppy disks** for backups. Generically, tapes and floppy disks are both examples of **magnetic media**.[1] The most common type of magnetic tape looks like an ordinary audio cassette blown up big, and it works on exactly the same principles.[2]Physically, it is about six inches long, three inches wide, and maybe half an inch thick. A floppy disk (or 'floppy') is just a disk of magnetic material (the same stuff the tapes are made of). It is contained in a thin protective plastic envelope, which may be either $3\frac{1}{2}$ or $5\frac{1}{4}$ inches square. If you are unsure whether your machine uses tapes or floppies then you may find it instructive to inspect the computer casing. The computer will be equipped with either a **tape drive** for reading and writing tapes, or a **floppy-disk drive** for reading and writing floppies. Outwardly these drives manifest themselves as slots in the computer, into which you are expected to push your tapes or floppies and, because a tape

---

[1] The word media, like data, is one of these irregular Latin imports. It's singular form, of which we will make occasional use, is 'medium'.

[2] On large or old installations tapes may be wound on big, loose reels, rather than packed into cassettes. These are sometimes called **nine-track tapes**.

is a different shape from a floppy, the sizes of these slots should give away
the nature of the drives concealed behind them. If you are still not sure after
looking at the machine then it's probably time to consult your supplier.

Some machines are fitted with both a tape drive *and* a floppy-disk drive,
so that you can choose which you want to use. In such cases tapes are almost
invariably the medium of choice for making backups because they can store far
more data than floppy disks. If you have a machine like this you will probably
find that the programs supplied for making backups (see §7.3.2 below) use
tapes rather than floppies by default.

If you are going use floppies for making your backups then before you
record any data on them you will have to **format** your floppies. Formatting
a floppy means preparing it for use by writing a load of preliminary data on
it which specify how much space there is available on the disk, and how it is
arranged. To format a floppy you should simply place it in the floppy-disk
drive and then type

```
>FORMAT-FLOPPY
```

at TCL. (On some systems it is `FORMAT-DISKETTE` or `FFORMAT`.) The drive
will whirr away to itself for a while (anything up to five minutes) and when
it stops the floppy will have been formatted.

Other than in the matter of floppy formatting, the procedures for making
backups with tapes and floppies are identical so we will not go through them
separately. In the following the word "tapes" should be interpreted as meaning
either tapes or floppies.

7.3.2   The FILE-SAVE verb

The basic verb for making a backup is "`FILE-SAVE`". You should be logged on
as `SYSPROG` before you use it. Ideally, you should also ensure that nobody else
is using the computer when you make the backup, because (i) the computer
performs other work very slowly while saving its files, and (ii) if you ever have
to copy the data back onto the disk, you will want to know exactly which data
are stored on the tape, and this will be difficult if people have been changing
them as they were being saved. However, unless you make your backups out
of working hours (and on most systems `FILE-SAVE` does provide facilities for
doing this) then this is probably not practical.

`FILE-SAVE` copies onto the tape everything on the disk, except the ABS
frames which contain the operating system (see §3.1). `FILE-SAVE` is the verb
you should use once a day to backup your data. Unfortunately, `FILE-SAVE`
is not a standard Pick verb. It is a program, usually written either by the
manufacturer, or by the supplier of the computer, to make backups on your
particular computer. This means that the way it works, and what exactly it
needs to be told when you run it, will vary from one computer to another.
Below we give an example of how to make a backup on a Pick system, but

you should be aware that on your computer the procedure may be slightly different from the illustrated one, particularly in step 4.

Here, then is what you do:

1. Place a tape or floppy in the appropriate slot in the computer.
2. Log onto the computer as SYSPROG and get to TCL if you are not already there.
3. Now type

   ```
   >FILE-SAVE
   ```

4. Answer the computer's questions as shown in the following example:

   ```
   Do you want to print the file names to the printer (Y/N) [N] :N
   Tape label :JB12DEC90
   Full, Summary or No file-stats report to printer (F/S/N) [F] :S
   Do you want to verify the tape automatically (Y/N) [Y] :Y
   Do you want to disable the ports (Y/N) [N] :Y
   Current time is - 17:27:24
   Starting time for save (CR = now) :04:00
   File-save will start at 04:00:00
   ```

Let us go over each of these question in turn.

1: `...print the file names...` If you answer "Y" to this question, the computer will print out the name of each file on the printer as it saves it on the tape. If you answer "N", then it will still print out the names, but on your terminal, not on the printer. The "[N]" at the end of this question is Pick's way of saying that if you just hit RETURN in reply, it will understand you to mean "No".

2: `Tape Label`. Any string of characters you type on this line will be stored on the tape (not written on the actual tape label of course!), and can then be read back off the tape at a later date using the verb "T-RDLBL" (see Table 7.1). In our example we have supposed that it has been agreed that the 'tape label' should be the initials of the person responsible for making the backup followed by the date on which it was made.

3: `...file-stats report...` As well as printing a list of file names, the computer can be instructed to print a 'file statistics report' when it has finished making the backup. These reports are exactly the same as those produced by the verb "LIST-FILE-STATS" (see §7.5.1). Replying "F" tells Pick to print a 'full file statistics report', replying "S" tells it to print an 'account totals report', and replying "N" tells it not to print a file statistics report at all.

4: `...verify the tape...` If you answer "Y" or just RETURN in response to this question, the machine will 'verify' the tape when it has finished making the backup. That is, it will rewind the tape and go back over it, checking that the data on it are the same as those on the disk, and signalling any differences it finds on the terminal. Though faults with magnetic tapes or floppies are very rare it does no harm to ward against them by saying "Y" in answer to this question.

5: ...disable the ports. If you answer "Y" in response to this question, the computer will put all its ports out of action while it is making the backup. This makes absolutely sure that no one will change anything on the disk while the backup is being made, but again, it is clearly impractical if you are making your backups during working hours.

6: Starting time... Pick next displays the current time, and asks you at what time you want it to start making the backup. If you simply hit RETURN in response to this question the file-save will begin immediately. If however you enter a time, in twenty-four hour clock form, then the computer will wait until that time to perform the file-save. This allows you to set the computer before you leave work in the evening to make a backup in the middle of the night. You can then safely instruct it to disable all the ports while the backup is being made, because this instruction will not take effect until the appointed time is reached and everyone in their right mind has gone to bed.

The backup will now go ahead automatically, at the time you have specified. When it is complete, Pick will automatically log you off as a security precaution, since it wouldn't do for any old Tom, Dick or Harry to come in before you in the morning and find your terminal sitting there, with you still logged on as SYSPROG.

If you make backups on floppies you will probably find that there is too much data on your disk to fit onto one floppy. The same can happen with tapes too, if you have a very large disk. In this case the computer will fill up the first floppy or tape you feed it, and when that is done it will display a message on the terminal asking you to put the next one in the drive. When you have done this, the computer will proceed with the backup. Obviously you can't ask the computer to make such a backup in the dead of night— someone has to be there to feed the clean tapes in. (This can be a real pain. It's one very good reason why you shouldn't use floppies for making backups.)

It is a good idea to have a large number of tapes or floppies to make your backups on. You do not want to be using the same tape every day and erasing the previous day's backup when you make the new one, because one of your users might destroy some data by mistake and not realize it until he or she came to look for them three days later. The prudent system manager would have the appropriate three-day-old tape to hand, to recover the lost information, but for the tight-fisted one with only one backup tape it would be too late—the information would already have been rubbed out. A sensible routine for keeping backups would be to have one tape for each day of the week so that you are only re-using tapes after the data on them are a week old. Also, every so often, every month maybe, take one of your daily tapes out and put it in another box, replacing it with a new tape for that day of the week. That way you will have a box of monthly backups stretching back to the earliest times, just in case you should ever need to go back a really long

way. It may sound to you as if this procedure is going to be very expensive
on tapes, but tapes are cheap compared with the value of your data, and an
old tape may save your skin in the end.

Tapes on which backups have been made should be kept in a safe place
away from the computer. This reduces the risk that a disaster like a flood or
a fire, that wipes out your computer, wipes out all your backup tapes as well.

7.4 Restoring lost data from backups

Some day, for whatever reason, you are going to need to recover some data
from one of your backup tapes. This process is called **restoring** the data.
According to the circumstance, you can restore all the data on the tape,
(i.e., every file on the computer), just the files contained in one account, just
one file, or even just selected items from a file. Pick provides TCL verbs to do
these jobs for you, but before you can use them you will need to know a little
more about using tapes/floppies with your computer.

7.4.1 Tape and floppy management

Pick provides a number of TCL verbs to help you control tape and floppy
drives.[3]

SET-SCT and SET-FLOPPY. First, if you have a machine that will
accept either tapes or floppies, then, before you can retrieve data from a tape
or floppy, you have to tell your machine which you are going to use. Probably
you use magnetic tapes, in which case you should type

> `>SET-SCT`

at TCL.[4] (On a some systems it is **SET-CTAPE** or **SET-HALF**, or **SET-9** for systems
with nine-track tape drives.) On the other hand, if you want to read data off
a floppy you should type

> `>SET-FLOPPY`

(or on some systems **SET-FLOP**), to inform the computer of this.

Once you have told your computer which type of magnetic medium it
should use, all subsequent operations are identical in the two cases. Floppies
are treated in every respect like tapes on a Pick computer. You have to
instruct the computer to 'rewind' a floppy, to 'fast forward' it, to go back or
forward a step, exactly as if it were a tape. (This may seem odd to people who
have used floppy disks on other computers, but it's the way the Pick system
works. On a Pick computer floppies are 'sequential' devices, not 'random

---

[3] These verbs are only available to users with SYS1 or SYS2 system privileges—see §7.8.1.

[4] You may possibly find it mnemonic to know that the letters SCT stand for "streaming
cartridge tape".

access' ones.) Thus everything we say about magnetic tapes in the rest of this section, and in the sections succeeding it, applies equally to floppies.

The verbs for handling tapes/floppies are listed in Table 7.1. The most important and frequently used of them are:

T-ATT. Before you can use the tape drive you must lay claim to it—you must **attach** it to your terminal—by typing

>T-ATT

Once you have done this the computer will give you sole use of the drive. Anyone else attempting to bag it (by typing T-ATT at their own terminal) will get the message

[95] Tape/diskette attached to line 2

(or whatever your line number is) and they will have to wait until you are finished.

T-DET. When you have finished using the tape drive you should surrender it for the use of others—**detach** it from your terminal—by typing

>T-DET

After you have done this the tape drive is available once more for the use of anyone who cares to type T-ATT at his or her terminal.

T-REW. After attaching the tape drive, you should put your tape into the slot in the computer and rewind it to the beginning by typing

>T-REW

Always do this after putting a tape in the tape drive, even if you believe the tape to be rewound already—it's a good habit to get into, and it can do no harm. If you use floppy disks for your backups you still have to type "T-REW" when you first put them in, to tell Pick to start at the beginning of the data on the disk, even though the computer doesn't have to physically wind the disk back to the beginning.

7.4.2   ACCOUNT-RESTORE

Each of your backup tapes will contain a complete record of everything on your computer's disk. However, the most common use for backup tapes is the recovery of single files or accounts which have inadvertently been deleted, so Pick provides ways of searching through a backup tape to find just the data you want and restoring them, (i.e., copying them back onto the computer's disk). These jobs are done by two verbs. The simpler of them is the verb "ACCOUNT-RESTORE". This verb restores an entire account from a tape. That is, it copies the contents of all the files whose file-defining items reside in a particular MD off a tape onto the disk.

Suppose then that you come back from your coffee break one morning to discover that all your financial records have been mysteriously destroyed,

Table 7.1.   TCL verbs for controlling tape and floppy-disk drives.

Verb	Function
T-ATT	Attach (claim sole use of) the tape drive
T-BCK	Move one file backwards on the tape
T-CHK	Go through one file on the tape checking for parity errors
T-CHK (A)	Go through the whole tape checking for parity errors
T-DET	Detach (surrender your claim to) the tape drive
T-EOD	Wind the tape forward to the end of the data stored on it
T-FWD	Move one file forward on the tape
T-RDLBL	Read the tape's 'label' and print it on the terminal
T-READ	Display on the screen the contents of the next file on the tape
T-REW	Rewind the tape to the beginning
T-SPACE	Move a given number of files forward on the tape
T-UNLOAD	Rewind the tape and free it from the drive (not all systems)
T-WEOF	Write an end-of-file marker
T-WTLBL	Write a new 'label' on the tape

and you wish to restore from a backup the contents of all the files under the account "FINANCE". The procedure is as follows:

1. Log onto the computer as SYSPROG and get to TCL if you are not already there.

2. If your computer can make backups on more than one type of magnetic medium you should tell it which type you want to recover your data from, by typing

    >SET-SCT

    or whatever the appropriate verb is (see §7.4.1 above).

3. Next attach the tape drive to your terminal (see §7.4.1) by typing

    >T-ATT

4. Place the appropriate backup tape or floppy disk in the slot in the computer. If your backup is spread over several tapes or floppies, you can find out which one contains the account you want from the 'full file statistics report' (see §7.5.1 on the verb "LIST-FILE-STATS").

5. Rewind the tape or floppy by typing

    >T-REW

    Remember that you have to do this even if you are using a floppy disk.

6. Now you type

    >ACCOUNT-RESTORE FINANCE
    ACCOUNT NAME ON TAPE?FINANCE

The computer will search the tape until it finds the appropriate data, and then copy them back onto the disk.

Account names are stored on the tapes along with the data in those accounts, and the computer asks you to give the name under which the account is stored on the tape (the bit about "ACCOUNT NAME ON TAPE?") since it is possible that the name of the account has been changed since the tape was made, or that you wish the data to be placed in a new account that is not the one from which they were originally copied. The name you give after the verb "ACCOUNT-RESTORE" is the name of the account in which the restored data are to be placed.

The computer will not restore an account from a tape if that account already exists on the computer's disk. So if most of the data had been deleted from the files under the FINANCE account, but the account was still on the disk, albeit in a sorely depleted form, the procedure above would not work. Before the account could be restored, its remaining fragments would first have to be deleted using the verb "DELETE-ACCOUNT" (see §7.2.3).

7.4.3   SEL-RESTORE

There will also be times when you want to restore only a single file or item from a tape, not a whole account. This can be achieved using the verb "SEL-RESTORE". (SEL-RESTORE is short for "selective restore".) Imagine for example that the file "STAFF" under the account "PERSONNEL" has been deleted by mistake and that you wish to restore just this one file from the previous day's backup tape, without setting all the files in the account "PERSONNEL" back a whole day. To do this there must be a Q-pointer to the file "STAFF" in SYSPROG's MD; in the example below we create one using the verb "SET-FILE" (see §4.2.9). You restore the file as follows:

1. Log onto the computer as SYSPROG and get to TCL if you are not already there.
2. If your computer can make backups on more than one type of magnetic medium you should tell it which type you want to recover your data from, by typing

   >SET-SCT

   or whatever the appropriate verb is (see §7.4.1 above).
3. Next attach the tape drive to your terminal (see §7.4.1) by typing

   >T-ATT

4. Place the appropriate backup tape or floppy disk in the slot in the computer. If your backup is spread over several tapes or floppies, you can find out which one contains the account you want from the 'full file statistics report' (see §7.5.1 on the verb "LIST-FILE-STATS").
5. Rewind the tape or floppy by typing

```
>T-REW
```

Remember that you have to do this even if you are using a floppy disk.

6. Now you type

```
>SET-FILE PERSONNEL STAFF
>SEL-RESTORE QFILE
ACCOUNT NAME ON TAPE?PERSONNEL
FILE NAME ON TAPE?STAFF
```

SET-FILE sets the Q-pointer "QFILE" to point to the file "STAFF" in the account "PERSONNEL". Then the SEL-RESTORE command restores the file from the tape.

As the tape runs through the machine, all the names of the files stored on it will be displayed as the computer finds them. When it comes to the one you have asked for, it will copy the file onto the disk.

SEL-RESTORE can also be used to restore individual *items* from a backup tape. Suppose, for instance, that the items "BINNEY-J-J", "NEWMAN-M-E-J" and "BLOGGS-J" in the file "STAFF" have been erased in error, and you wish to retrieve them from yesterday's backup tape. To do this there must be a Q-pointer to the file "STAFF" in SYSPROG's MD; in the example below we create one using the verb "SET-FILE" (see §4.2.9). The procedure is as follows:

1. Log onto the computer as SYSPROG and get to TCL if you are not already there.

2. If your computer can make backups on more than one type of magnetic medium you should tell it which type you want to recover your data from, by typing

   ```
   >SET-SCT
   ```

   or whatever the appropriate verb is (see §7.4.1 above).

3. Next attach the tape drive to your terminal (see §7.4.1) by typing

   ```
   >T-ATT
   ```

4. Place the appropriate backup tape or floppy disk in the slot in the computer. If your backup is spread over several tapes or floppies, you can find out which one contains the account you want from the 'full file statistics report' (see §7.5.1 on the verb "LIST-FILE-STATS").

5. Rewind the tape or floppy by typing

   ```
   >T-REW
   ```

   Remember that you have to do this even if you are using a floppy disk.

6. Now you type

   ```
   >SET-FILE PERSONNEL STAFF
   >SEL-RESTORE QFILE BINNEY-J-J NEWMAN-M-E-J BLOGGS-J
   ACCOUNT NAME ON TAPE?PERSONNEL
   FILE NAME ON TAPE?STAFF
   ```

The computer will search the tape and recover just those items from the backup of the file "STAFF" and put them back in the file "STAFF" in the account "PERSONNEL" on the disk.

7.4.4   Restoring all your files

In the event of the ultimate disaster in which all the records on your computer's disk are erased by some awful software goof, or the computer is annihi-
lated by an Act of God, you will want to get everything back from yesterday's
backup tape—you will want to do a **full file restore**. Pick provides a way of
doing this too. What you do as follows:

1. First make sure no one is using the computer. After the last person
   has stopped work and logged off, you must wait for about a minute to
   ensure that the computer has finished doing whatever it is doing with the
   disk drive. You must not go onto (2) until it has or you risk destroying
   programs and data.[5]

2. Next, if the computer has a 'reset button' (usually on the back of the
   computer casing, often actually marked 'reset'), press it. If it hasn't,
   just turn the computer off, wait a minute or two to let the disk come
   completely to rest and then turn it on again.

3. The computer will lumber into action, and go through its warming-up
   routine, which varies from machine to machine. After some time it will
   start printing messages on the terminal connected to port number 0 (see
   §4.2.4). Eventually it will come up with a prompt asking you for a single
   letter reply. Though the exact form of this prompt will vary from one
   machine to the next it typically says something like

```
FILE RESTORE (F), WARMSTART (W) OR EXECUTE (X) ?
```

4. The normal response to this would be X for execute, which just makes
   the machine start up with the minimum of fuss. However, in this case
   you should go to the computer and place your backup tape in the tape
   slot on the machine. Then return to the terminal and type F.

The computer will start to copy the entire contents of your tape or floppy
onto its disk. When it has finished it will start up all the other terminals and
you should find yourself back in the position you were in before the disaster
occurred.

7.5   Taking care of your disk

The speed and efficiency with which your computer operates is heavily dependent on the way your data are arranged on your disk. A good system manager
will make sure his or her computer is always running at top performance by
keeping an eye out for the problems that can develop if the disk gets into a
mess, and fixing them before they get too bad. The problems in question are:

---

[5] On some computers a verb "FLUSH" is provided which tells the computer to finish up
anything it is doing on the disk straight away. If your computer has this verb then you can
dispense with the precautionary delay—just logon as SYSPROG and type "FLUSH" at TCL.

(i)   running out of space on the disk;

(ii) over-full or under-full files;

(iii) 'fragmentation'.

Let us examine these problems, their diagnosis and their cure.

Running out of disk space.   This is an easy problem to understand: if you go on putting more and more data onto your disk, then sooner or later you are bound to run out of space to store them in. And this situation is to be avoided at all costs, since if you do let the disk fill up right to the brim, your computer will seize up completely and refuse to do anything at all. It is a Law of Life that no matter how large your disk or how small your company, you will *always* fill up the disk in the end. And disks always seem to fill up faster than you were expecting, so no one can reasonably ignore this problem.

Over-full or under-full files.   When you create a new file (see §4.2.7) you have to specify how much space is to be reserved for it on the disk, by giving it a mod and a sep. If the data you then feed into the file are so numerous and bulky that they will not fit into this space, the file will overflow (see §3.2.1). While a small number of overflow frames are acceptable in any file, having too many will slow the retrieval of data from that file.

Conversely, if the amount of space reserved for a file is much larger than the amount needed to store the data in that file, then you are wasting disk space, space you will be glad of when your disk becomes full. This sort of problem can sometimes arise simply as a mistake in the creation of the file, whereby some stupid numbers find their way into the mod and sep attributes of a file-defining item, instead of the sensible ones you thought of.

Even if you do get the mod and sep right when you first create a file, with data always being added to and deleted from files, they can easily overflow their allotted space, or shink to a tiny fraction of their former size.

Fragmentation.   When you delete items from a file, or a whole file from the disk, you leave an empty space or 'hole' on the disk where those data were. Though the computer makes a note of where that space is, and will fill it up again later with new data when it gets the chance, there will inevitably be many gaps waiting to be filled after you have been using the computer continuously for months, adding and deleting all the time. The longer you have left it untended the more patchy, or **fragmented**, your disk will be. This is not a good thing because (i) it slows down the retrieval of data from the disk by making the disk heads (see §1.1.1) race around to find what you want, and (ii) it wastes space.

7.5.1   Examining your disk

Pick provides two useful verbs, "POVF" and "LIST-FILE-STATS", to allow a system manager to assess the state of his or her disk, so that action can be taken if any problems appear. The first, POVF,[6] tells you how much free space you have left on your disk, and how fragmented it is. To use it:

1. Log onto the computer and get to TCL if you are not already there.

2. Type

```
>POVF
```

3. The computer will respond something like this:

```
13187-13189 :      3    13192-13194 :      3    13200-13203 :      4
13209-13218 :     10    13242-13247 :      6    39425-39431 :      7
39791-39887 :     97    39893-39895 :      3    39899-73197 : 33299

Total number of contiguous frames    : 33432

>
```

The most important line in this report is the one at the bottom. It tells you how many frames on your disk are still free. It is this figure that tells you when your disk is becoming full (see §7.5.2). The other figures tell you where on the disk these free frames are located. They form a list in three columns (or two on some systems). Each entry in the list gives the addresses of the first and last frames of a free area on the disk, and the length in frames of that area. These figures warn you when your disk is becoming fragmented (see §7.5.2).

LIST-FILE-STATS tells you how many frames on the disk are reserved for files under each account, and how much of the space in those frames is actually being used for storing data. In addition it can also tell you how many frames are reserved for, and are being used for the storage of each individual file.[7]

To use LIST-FILE-STATS proceed as follows:

1. Log onto the computer as SYSPROG and get to TCL if you are not already there.

2. Now type

```
>LIST-FILE-STATS
```

3. The computer will then ask you the following two questions:

---

[6] POVF is short for "print overflow frames".

[7] In fact, the information printed in the file statistics reports is generated by the FILE-SAVE verb when you make a backup, and stored in a file called "STAT-FILE" under the SYSPROG account. The verb "LIST-FILE-STATS" simply retrieves this information and displays it on the screen. This means that the information produced by LIST-FILE-STATS can never be more up to date than your most recent backup. However, if you are making daily backups this should not present a problem. Note also that on most systems the FILE-SAVE verb itself can make a file-statistics listing, and rather than using LIST-FILE-STATS you may prefer just to get it to do this and then use the listings so produced to assess the state of your disk. In this case you can skip the following paragraphs on the use of LIST-FILE-STATS and go straight to the meaning of the file statistics reports and how you can use them to diagnose disk problems.

```
Report to printer (Y/N) [N] :Y
Account totals only (Y/N) [Y] :Y
```

If you reply "N" or RETURN to the first question, the data you ask for will be printed on the screen. If you reply "Y" they will be sent to the printer. If you reply "Y" or RETURN to the second question, only the total amount of space occupied by the files under each account will be listed, whereas if you reply "N" the details of each individual file will be given.

4. The computer will start to print the requested data. In the example given above it would print them on the printer, and they would look something like this:

```
Page    1                File Statistics report              10 Dec 1990

Account Name......    GP SIZE    TOT SIZE    ITEMS  FRAMES        PAD GFE

ACC                     2,361       2,361       64      15      27,639
COLDSTART              16,764      16,764      535      12       7,236
CONFIG                 30,896      30,896      268      60      89,104
FINANCE             1,858,914   2,202,914     6442   1,426     649,086
INVESTMENTS            70,209      70,209      668     155     239,791
LIBRARY               394,428     394,428     2781     951   1,507,572
MARKETING           3,080,017   3,540,017    54726   2,901   2,261,983
PERSONNEL           1,827,699   2,057,699     3152   1,053      48,301
SALES                 658,778     686,778      808     354      21,222
STOCKS              2,141,362   2,143,362    15831   9,264  16,384,638
SYSPROG               293,709     887,709     4316     598     308,291
SYSTEM                  9,521       9,521      100      31      52,479
SYSTEM-ERRORS           1,392       1,392       24       5       8,608
                   ========== ========== ======= ======= ========== ===
                   10,386,050  12,044,050    89715  16,825  21,605,950

123 Items listed
>
```

Let's go over this report and explain what all the columns mean.

The account totals report.   This report lists the name of each account on the computer in alphabetical order. Next to each name there are five columns of figures. The columns are:

GP SIZE. This column gives the number of bytes of data in the files within each account, excluding 'Pick BASIC object code' (see the introduction to Chapter 8). This is not the same thing as the amount of space taken up on the disk by the files because the groups on a Pick disk are very rarely completely full, and the "GP SIZE" figure does not include all the little bits at the end of groups that are not being used. This figure is just the actual number of bytes of data in the groups in the files.

TOT SIZE. This column gives the number of bytes of data in the files within each account, including Pick BASIC object code. The difference between this column and the first is usually extremely slight, but the TOT SIZE column more accurately reflects the space required to store the data associated with an account.

ITEMS. This column gives the total number of items in the files under each account.

FRAMES. This column gives the total number of frames, including overflow frames, occupied by the files under each account.

PAD. This column gives the total amount of space wasted in the unused bits at the ends of frames for each account (see (1) above). This is sometimes referred to as 'pad space'.

There is a sixth column in the list headed "GFE". Usually, however, there won't be anything in this column. Numbers in this column record the number of 'group format errors' found in the files under each account. Group format errors are very nasty things. You don't want any of these. If you get any numbers appearing in the GFE column you've got trouble. In §7.11 we explain the strategies available for dealing with group format errors.

At the bottom of the account totals report there is a line which gives the accumulated values of all the columns—total amount of data stored on the disk, total number of items, total number of frames, and so on. The very last line of the report says something like "123 Items listed". This line is never correct, so don't worry about it.

The full file statistics report.   If you reply "N" to the question "Account totals only", the computer will produce the full file statistics report, which includes all the data produced by the account totals report, plus details of every file in every account on the disk. The files are divided up by account, and within each account are listed in alphabetical order, with dictionary portions preceding data portions. The data portions of files are denoted by printing the name of the file twice, with a star "*" in between. For instance, the statistics relating to the dictionary portion of the file "TRASH" would be listed under "TRASH", and those relating to the data portion would be found on the next line under "TRASH*TRASH".[8]

For each individual file there are columns giving the same data as those on the account totals report (amount of data excluding object code, total amount of data, items, frames, pad space, group format errors), and also there are nine extra columns. Seven of these contain information about the size and usage of the files:

BASE. This column gives the base frame address of each file (see §3.2.1).

MOD. This column gives the mod of each file.

_____

[8] In fact the word before the star is the dictionary name, and the word after the star is the name of the data portion. Though for all the files described in this book the names of dictionary and data portions are the same, it is possible to create a file with different names for the two. If somebody has been particularly cunning in setting up your computer, you may therefore find items in your file statistics report with different names before and after the star.

S. This column gives the sep of each file.

AV/ITM. This column gives the average number of bytes of disk space taken up by each item in a file.

ITM/GP. This column gives the average number of items per group in each file.

FRM/GP. This column gives the average number of frames per group in each file. If a file has no overflowing groups, this number will just be the same as the sep, which will normally be 1. However, if a file has overflowing groups, this number will be greater than 1. If it is greater than 2 the file is badly overflowing and should be resized (see §7.5.2).

%UT. This column gives the percentage of the space allotted to each file according to its mod and sep that is actually in use storing data. This column provides a simple, quick way of checking for under-full or over-full files (see §7.5.2).

Following the list of files for each account, the full file statistics report gives the totals for that account of the principal columns—the same totals that are printed on the account totals report. And at the end of the entire report the accumulated totals for the whole disk are given, just as in the shorter report.

There are two more columns on the full file statistics report which we have not mentioned. These contain information about the last backup made on your machine, and are printed on the far left of the report, before the file names. They are:

R#. This column gives the **reel number** for each file. If you make backups on floppy disks, you will probably find you need many disks to store one backup on. The same can happen with tapes too, if you have a very large disk (see §7.3.2). The reel number for a file tells you which tape or floppy ('reel') contains the backup copy of that file; the tapes are numbered starting from one, in the order you fed them into the machine when the backup was made. If your backups fit onto just one tape then this column will always say "1". The reel number can be useful if you want to restore just one file from a backup—it can save you having to search through every reel looking for the data you want.

ID. This column gives the **file number**. The files are numbered in the order in which they were stored on the last backup. This gives you some idea of where the file is on the backup tape if you need to restore it.

7.5.2   The diagnosis and cure of disk problems

Armed with the verbs "POVF" and "LIST-FILE-STATS" you are in a position to anticipate and deal with most of the problems that can arise with your disk.

Running out of disk space.   You know when you are running out of space on your disk by watching the last line of the report produced by POVF, which gives the number of unused frames left on your disk. When this number falls to zero, your disk is full up. A temporary cure for this problem is to delete any unwanted data from the disk—the LIST-FILE-STATS report will tell you which accounts are eating up the largest chunks of space—but the only permanent cure is to buy a bigger disk. And it is definitely better to buy one well before the disk fills right up, because a Pick computer with a nearly full disk will work very slowly, and one with a completely full disk will not work at all. As a good rule of thumb you should start thinking about getting a bigger disk when less than a quarter of your disk is still free.

Over-full or under-full files.   You can guard against cumbersome over-full files and space-wasting under-full ones by keeping your eye on the "%UT" column in the full file statistics report. If this percentage is small for a particular file—less than 20, say—then you are probably wasting space on that file. On the other hand if it is very large—greater than 80, say—then it is often a good indicator that the file is overflowing badly in some groups. If you suspect that a file is over-full then you should also check the "FRM/GR" column. The figure in this column should normally be around 1. If it is a little bigger then don't worry, that's quite healthy. If, however, it is more than 2 the file is over-full.

The cure for both over-full and under-full files is to **resize** them. That is, to change their mod and sep to new values more suitable to the amount of data they contain than the ones they have at the moment. Pick provides a simple, and indeed rather elegant mechanism whereby you tell it how you want a file resized, and it does the resizing when next you perform a full file restore (see §7.4.4). The procedure is as follows:

1. Decide what you wish the new mod and sep of your file to be. The sep should always be 1 and the mod should be an appropriate prime number. The rules for choosing mods and seps are outlined in §4.2.7.

2. Edit your new mod and sep into the file-defining item of the file that you want resized.[9] The two numbers should go in the 13th attribute of the item, in brackets, separated by a comma. The modulo should be first.

3. Now the next time the file is restored from a tape or floppy, its mod and sep will be changed to the new values. If you don't often perform a file save and full file restore (see §7.4.4), then you may like to do one specially to resize your files. But, as we shall explain in the section below on fragmentation, there are good reasons why you should regularly perform file restores, even when you don't actually need to restore any files. Thus it is usually quite adequate to simply edit your new mod and sep into the appropriate file-defining item, and then forget about them, because the file will automatically be restored from a backup tape and therefore resized sometime soon, in the course of your ordinary routine.

[9] This can be done using an editor such as the System Editor or by using the program "RESIZE" given in Appendix 4.

Let us illustrate the resizing procedure with an example. Suppose that you wish to resize the file "STAFF", whose file-defining item is held in the MD "PERSONNEL". Its current modulo is 7, and you want to change it to 19, because the company has grown so much that the file is overflowing with the personal records of all the people you have employed. You should change the 13th attribute of the file's defining item so that you see something like this:

File: MD	Item: STAFF

Attribute Number	Contents of Attribute	
1	D	
2	27182	
3	7	
4	1	
5		
6		
7		
8		
9	L	
10	15	
11		
12		
13	(19,1)	(New mod and sep)

Then, after your next file restore, the restored file "STAFF" will have a mod of 19 and a sep of 1.

Fragmentation.   The verb "POVF" (see §7.5.1 above) can also warn you when your disk is becoming fragmented. The tell-tale sign is when POVF produces a *long* list of free areas on the disk (more than twenty, say). However, on a well run system, this situation will never arise. The reason is that fragmented disks are a recurrent problem and the best way to guard against them is to reorganize your disk regularly to get rid of the 'holes'. This is actually a very simple operation. All you have to do to patch up the holes in a fragmented disk is perform a full file restore (see §7.4.4). When it copies all your files back onto the disk from a backup tape in the course of a full file restore, Pick arranges them on the disk as economically as possible with no gaps in between, irrespective of how they were arranged when the tape was made. So, simply by recording all your data onto a backup tape or floppy using the verb "FILE-SAVE" (see §7.3.2) and then reading them off again as described in §7.4.4, you can speed up your machine, and save yourself some disk space. The best policy is to get into a regular routine of doing this, say once a month, so that the system is always running at top performance.

Clearing or deleting files.   While we are discussing these secondary uses of the full file restore—resizing and rearranging files—we should also just mention one other facility: you can use a full file restore to clear or delete files. If you change a file's file type (stored in the first attribute of its file-defining item) to "DX" (or "DCX" for a BASIC program file, see Chapter 8) then the data in the file will not be stored on any subsequent backup tapes and the file will be deleted from the disk completely the next time you perform a full file restore. If you change a file's file type to "DY" (or "DCY" for a BASIC program file) then the data in the file will not be stored on any subsequent backup tapes and the file will be *cleared* (but not deleted) the next time you perform a full file restore.

As an example, you could make the file "ACC", in which the computer records the times at which users log on and off (see §7.9), a file of type "DY". Then it will be cleared out every month on the occasion of your routine full file restore.

7.6   Dumping data on a tape

Apart from storing backups, there is one other common use for magnetic tapes (or floppies) on a Pick computer: they can be used for transferring data from one Pick machine to another. One way of doing this would just be to play the backup tape from one machine into another. This would allow you to copy whole files or individual items between the machines. For many people this is perfectly adequate and they have no need of anything more sophisticated. However, there are occasions when you might need something more flexible than the automatic FILE-SAVE program. For these occasions Pick provides the verb "S-DUMP".

S-DUMP is an ACCESS verb. The form of an S-DUMP command is exactly the same as that of an SSELECT command (see §4.3.3). Its effect is to select and sort a set of items from a file, and then write *all* the attributes in each of those items on a magnetic tape. This is called **dumping** the items onto the tape. All the modifications which work for the verb "SSELECT", like BY clauses, WITH clauses and so on, work in exactly the same way for S-DUMP. Thus, to take an example, suppose that you wish to write all your stock records on a magnetic tape, so that you can send them to your newly opened branch in New York. This is what you should do:

1. Log onto the computer, and get to TCL if you are not already there.
2. If your computer can use more than one type of magnetic medium you should tell it which type you want to dump your data on by typing

   >SET-SCT

   or whatever the appropriate verb is (see §7.4.1).
3. Next attach the tape drive to your terminal (see §7.4.1) by typing

   >T-ATT

4. Insert a tape or floppy disk into the appropriate slot in the computer, and rewind it by typing

   >T-REW

Remember that you have to do this even if you are using a floppy disk.

5. Now type

```
>S-DUMP STOCK
```

The computer will write all the items in STOCK onto the tape.

The complementary verb to S-DUMP is the verb "T-LOAD", which copies items written on a tape by an S-DUMP command off the tape into a file. Thus, if you were on the staff in the newly opened New York branch and received the tape of stock data created in the example above, you could feed those data into your own STOCK file using a T-LOAD command. Here is what you would do:

1. Log onto the computer, and get to TCL if you are not already there.

2. If your computer can use more than one type of magnetic medium you should tell it which type you want to dump your data on by typing

```
>SET-SCT
```

or whatever the appropriate verb is (see §7.4.1).

3. Next attach the tape drive to your terminal (see §7.4.1) by typing

```
>T-ATT
```

4. Insert the tape or floppy disk into the appropriate slot in the computer, and rewind it by typing

```
>T-REW
```

Remember that you have to do this even if you are using a floppy disk.

5. Now type

```
>T-LOAD STOCK
```

and the computer will copy all the items on the tape into the file "STOCK".

There also exists the verb "T-DUMP", which is exactly the same as S-DUMP except that it will not sort your records for you. This makes T-DUMP fairly redundant—it is superseded by S-DUMP in the same way as LIST is superseded by SORT (see §4.3.2).

7.7 Setting the computer's clock

Although the computer's clock is probably an accurate one, you will occasionally need to change the time on it—when switching between summer time and winter time for example. This is achieved using the verb "SET-TIME". To set the time, type "SET-TIME" followed by the time in hours, minutes and seconds like this:

```
>SET-TIME 15:21:50
15:21:50 30 JUN 1990
```

As you can see the computer responds with the new, corrected time which saves you from typing "TIME" (see §4.2.2) to check that it has worked. If split-second timing is not important in your business or you are not that sure of the time anyway you can miss the seconds off:

```
>SET-TIME 15:21
15:21:00 30 JUN 1990
```

which is precisely the same as saying "SET-TIME 15:21:00".

There is also a SET-DATE verb to let you set the date. To use it type "SET-DATE" followed by the date:

```
>SET-DATE 30 JUN 1990
15:22:13 30 JUN 1990
```

The date may be given in almost any way you choose—Pick is very tolerant. You can say "30 JUN 1990" as in the example above, or you can say "30 Jun 90" or "30/6/90" or "30-06-1990", or almost anything else you can think of provided it's unambiguous, and the computer will understand.[10]

7.8   Security

In these days of hackers and the Data Protection Act, every system manager must give some thought to the security of the data on his or her computer. Of course, everyone needs a password to gain entry to a Pick computer system, but passwords are rarely the well kept secrets they should be, and besides, they can often easily be guessed by experienced intruders. Luckily, Pick provides a variety of security measures to ensure that the sphere of influence of any one user can be restricted to only those data he or she needs to examine. So a hacker gaining unlawful entry by using that person's user name and password will find his capacity for vandalism, fraud or espionage limited. Moreover, since things like pay and personal records are usually very sensitive, it makes sense to restrict access to files containing these sorts of data to only those users who absolutely must look at them. This section deals with the steps you can take to protect your data.

Pick's security provisions fall into a number of categories:

(i) System privilege codes—privilege codes are used to restrict a user's access to facilities like MDs and the magnetic tape drive.

(ii) Update and retrieval codes (locks and keys)—update and retrieval codes are used to prevent users reading or writing files that are none of their business.

(iii) Permission to use TCL—users can be denied permission to use TCL, which restricts them to running whatever programs you provide for their use.

---

[10] American computers are usually set up to print the month before the day, rather than after. If your computer is like this then you should feed in the date in that order too: "06-30-90", for example.

(iv) The BREAK keys—the BREAK key on any terminal can be put out of action by issuing an appropriate command. This prevents users from breaking out of programs, or from using the debugger.

Let us take a closer look at each of these categories in turn.

7.8.1 System privilege codes

The most basic security device on a Pick computer is the "system privilege code". As explained in §3.3, every user of a Pick computer has an item in the system dictionary in which Pick stores the things it needs to know about him, such as his password, and the account name of his MD. Attribute 8 of this item specifies the user's **system privileges**. This attribute may read "SYS∅", "SYS1" or "SYS2". When you feed in the details of a new user (using the verb "CREATE-ACCOUNT" (see §7.2), or perhaps the CREATE-USER program of Appendix 4) you must specify, amongst other things, which of these privilege levels the user is to have. The effects of such specifications are as follows:

SYS2. The user who has SYS2 privileges can do anything not forbidden by some other security measure (see §§7.8.2–7.8.4).

SYS1. The user who has SYS1 privileges is barred from using the system debugger. When such a user hits the BREAK key or types Ctrl-C, he will be taken to the debugger as usual, but will find that, once there, the only debugger commands he is allowed to use are OFF, which will log him off, END which will take him to TCL, G which will take him back to whatever he was doing before he hit BREAK (running a Pick BASIC program, for example) or P which just prints out a few numbers on the screen. The computer will not respond to any of the other debugger commands, which can have disastrous effects if they are misused.

Also Pick will not allow a user with SYS1 privileges to use the verbs "FILE-SAVE", "SEL-RESTORE", "ACCOUNT-RESTORE" (see §§7.3 and 7.4), or "STOPPTR" (see §5.2.2) or one of a small number of other specialist system-management verbs.

SYS0. A user who has been given SYS∅ privileges is the most constrained of users. In addition to the restrictions placed on a SYS1 user, Pick will not allow him to create or delete files, or to change the contents of his MD in any way, or to use magnetic tapes or floppies.

The correct awarding of system privileges is an important part of keeping the data on a Pick system secure. Note that SYSPROG must have SYS2 privileges, so that he or she can make backups.

7.8.2 Update and retrieval codes (locks and keys)

The main work of keeping your computer safe is done by **update and retrieval codes**. Update codes prevent users from updating (i.e., changing the contents of) files unless they have specific permission to do so. Retrieval codes prevent users from retrieving (i.e., looking at) data without permission.

Every file has two **locks** on it, an **update lock** and a **retrieval lock**. These locks are strings of characters, like "A" or "AAA" or "cat", which are stored in attributes 5 and 6 of the file's file-defining item in the MD (see §3.2.1). Attribute 5 contains the retrieval lock and attribute 6 the update lock. On most systems update and retrieval locks are only permitted on genuine (D- or DC-type) file-defining items, not on Q-pointers. A file-defining item for the file "STAFF" with both update and retrieval locks in place might look like this:

```
┌─────────────┬──────────────┐
│ File: MD    │ Item: STAFF  │
└─────────────┴──────────────┘
Attribute
   Number      Contents of Attribute
        1      D
        2      27182
        3      7
        4      1
        5      M                        (Retrieval lock)
        6      J                        (Update lock)
        7
        8
        9      L
       1∅      15
```

Every *user* has *one or more* **update keys** and one or more **retrieval keys**. Each of these keys is also a string of characters. The retrieval keys are stored as separate values in attribute 5 of the user's user-defining item in the system dictionary; the update keys are stored as separate values in attribute 6. A user-defining item for the user JACK, with update and retrieval keys in place, might look like this:

```
┌─────────────┬──────────────┐
│ File: SYSTEM│ Item: JACK   │
└─────────────┴──────────────┘
Attribute
   Number      Contents of Attribute
        1      Q
        2      PERSONNEL
        3
        4
        5      A]F]J]M                  (Retrieval keys)
        6      A]F                      (Update keys)
        7      C3347E∅2
        8      SYS∅
        9      U
```

Let us take the examples of the file "STAFF" and the user JACK to illustrate the effect of these locks and keys. Suppose JACK decides to look something up in the file "STAFF", say, by using the verb "SORT" to search though the file. This operation involves only *looking* at the contents of the file, not changing them. So this is a matter of retrieval codes. When JACK issues his command, asking for data from the file "STAFF", Pick checks the retrieval locks on the file, and the retrieval keys in JACK's user-defining item. If JACK has a key which comprises exactly the same sequence of letters as the lock on the STAFF file,[11] then the computer searches the file as requested. However, if none of JACK's retrieval keys 'fit' the retrieval lock on STAFF, he will be told that he is not allowed to look at that file. As it happens, JACK *does* have an appropriate key in this case and he would be allowed to examine the contents of the file—the retrieval lock on the file is just the letter "M", and JACK has just such a single letter "M" in his bunch of retrieval keys.

If JACK were to issue a command which involved, or might conceivably involve, *changing* the data in a file, then he would need an update key to match the update lock on the file before the computer would obey that command. Thus he might, for instance, try to edit an item in the file "STAFF" using the System Editor, (an action which does not necessarily change the contents of the file, but which might do so). Before letting him do this Pick would check whether he has an update key which exactly matches the update lock on the file. In this case he does not. The update lock on the file is just the single letter "J", and JACK has update keys "A" and "F", but not "J". So the computer will tell him that he is not allowed to edit this file. It will say:

FILE 'STAFF' IS ACCESS PROTECTED.

and that will be that.

It is also possible to put update and retrieval locks on MDs—you put the locks in the MD's defining item in the system dictionary. The retrieval lock goes in the fifth attribute and the update lock in the sixth, in exactly the same way as in file-defining items. Then any user wishing to look at or change the contents of that MD will need the appropriate retrieval or update lock before the computer will let him do it. However, putting a *retrieval* lock on an MD has another important consequence. In order to examine or change the contents of *any* file, Pick needs to know the base frame address, mod and sep of the file (see §3.2.1)—information which is stored in the file's file-defining item in the MD of the account to which the file belongs. If an MD has a retrieval lock on it, then a user who does not possess the key to this lock will be unable to examine or change any of the files whose file-defining items reside in that MD, because the computer will not be able to get at this vital information. It would therefore be wise to show some caution in putting retrieval locks on MDs.

On the other hand, it is very important that you put *update* locks on your MDs if you want to make your system secure. If you don't, mischievous and well-informed people will still be able to gain access to every file on the disk by changing the locks on the files. This is because the locks are stored in MDs. If there are no update locks on MDs to stop users changing their contents, a user may create a Q-pointer to an MD using, for example, the verb "SET-FILE", and then he or she may use the System Editor to edit a

---

[11] In fact the key is allowed to be longer than the lock. It need only *start* with the same sequence of letters that forms the lock for the user to be granted access to the file.

file-defining item in that MD and remove the locks from it. Thus, to make
your computer completely secure you will have to adopt one of the following
two strategies:

(i) Put only update locks on the MDs, to stop the mischievous from changing
the other locks stored therein, and put separate update and retrieval locks
on each individual file to prevent people from the examining or changing
their contents.

(ii) Put both update *and* retrieval locks on each MD, so that only people
with the appropriate keys can write or read any of the files within an
account, and then if you wish, put separate locks in each file-defining
item to specify which subset of those people will be able to examine or
change the contents of individual files.

The first of these is perhaps the simpler, and therefore the easier to
maintain, but the second involves a smaller number of locks, and so might be
less work to set up. You can take your choice. Whichever scheme you adopt
bear in mind that every user *must* be given the key to any retrieval lock placed
on his or her MD. Otherwise he or she will be unable to examine any file on
the computer. And any user who is to be allowed to create or delete files
or Q-pointers should in addition have the key to any update lock placed on
the MD, since these operations entail the creation, deletion or modification of
items stored there.

Though the system of locks and keys is clearly a neat and flexible one,
we should bring to your attention a few rather subtle points which you ought
to consider before you start putting locks on all your own files.

Update locking the system dictionary.   The keys for each user are
stored in the relevant user-defining items in the system dictionary. If you
allow users to change the contents of this dictionary freely, then they can give
themselves any keys they like, just by changing the fifth and sixth attributes
of their own item, thereby gaining access to any file on the system, no matter what locks it has. Thus, if you intend to put locks on the data files on
your disk, it is vitally important that you prevent people from changing the
contents of the system dictionary by putting a secure update lock on it. On
every Pick system there is an item called "SYSTEM" in the system dictionary
which 'points' to the system dictionary itself. This is like a file-defining item
for the system dictionary. It is in attribute 6 of this item, the item "SYSTEM"
in the file "SYSTEM", that the system dictionary's update lock should go:

File: SYSTEM	Item: SYSTEM

Attribute Number	Contents of Attribute
1	D
2	18424
3	1
4	31

```
 5                              (No retrieval lock)
 6    R                         (Update lock goes here)
 7
 8
 9    L
10    15
```

In a well run system no one should be given a key to fit this lock. Only SYSPROG should be allowed to change the system dictionary, and he or she doesn't need a key (see below). In general, the system manager should be the only person with access to every file on the disk; every other user should have only the keys to those files he or she will need to look at.

The disadvantage of putting an update lock on the system dictionary is that it stops users from changing their own passwords, since users' passwords are also stored in the user-defining items in the system dictionary, which they are now forbidden to change by virtue of the lock. In this situation, if a user wants his or her password changed, he or she will have to go to the system manager, who can change it using the verb "PASSWORD". The procedure is as follows:

1. Log onto the computer as SYSPROG and get to TCL if you are not already there.

2. Now type

    >PASSWORD

3. Answer the computer's questions as shown in the following example:

    ACCOUNT NAME:JILL
    PASSWORD:

The first question is asking you for the name of the user whose password you wish to change. (The use of the word "account" here is a bit sloppy—it covers both accounts and users.) The second is asking for the new password. The new password does not appear on the screen when you enter it, which reduces the temptation on people to peek over your shoulder while you type.

PASSWORD is an excellent example of a verb to which it would be unwise to allow any user other than SYSPROG access.

Retrieval locking the system dictionary.   Don't! Under no circumstances give the system dictionary a retrieval lock. Attribute 5 of the item "SYSTEM" in the file "SYSTEM" should *always* be left blank. If any retrieval lock is put on the system dictionary, *no one* will be able to log onto the computer at all after that, not even SYSPROG.

Users bearing the same name as an account.   As described in §3.3 and mentioned already several times in this chapter, whenever you create a new *account* you also create a new *user* whose user name is the same as the account name, and whose MD is the MD of that account. We do not recommend that you make use of this facility because it can lead to all sorts of confusions. The one legitimate user of this type—SYSPROG, see §7.1—doesn't need any keys (see below). However, you may be unlucky enough to have inherited a Pick system with users of this type already on it, and so you will need to know how to give these users keys.

As we described above, attributes 5 and 6 of an account-defining item in the system dictionary hold the retrieval and update locks respectively for that account's MD. Where then are you to put the keys that the user defined by the same item is to have? The answer is that they go in the same place, in attributes 5 and 6 of the account-defining item. The retrieval keys should be separate values in attribute 5 and the update keys separate values in attribute 6. Pick interprets only the first value in such a multi-valued attribute as a lock, but interprets all of them, including the first, as keys. To take an example, suppose you have an account called "PERSONNEL" on your computer, with an account-defining item like this:

File: SYSTEM	Item: PERSONNEL

Attribute Number	Contents of Attribute	
1	D	
2	31415	
3	1	
4	37	
5	A]F]J]M	(Retrieval lock and keys)
6	A]F	(Update lock and keys)
7	C3347E02	
8	SYS2	
9		

Then the MD "PERSONNEL" has a retrieval lock "A" and an update lock "A", and the user "PERSONNEL" has the retrieval keys "A", "F", "J" and "M" and the update keys "A" and "F".

SYSPROG's keys.   The one user for whom locks and keys are irrelevant is SYSPROG. The user who logs on as SYSPROG is automatically granted access to any file he or she asks about, irrespective of whether the correct key has been placed in SYSPROG's account-defining item. So there is really no point in giving SYSPROG any keys at all, since there is no lock that can keep him or her out. This is just one more reason why SYSPROG's password should be a very carefully guarded secret.

Locking yourself into the computer.   It is possible for someone to lock himself *into* a Pick computer by logging on as a user whose keys don't allow him access to the important files that contain TCL verbs like OFF (which are kept in the account "SYSPROG"). This is a real pain when it happens, because then he can't log off. The two things that he can do under these circumstances are:

(i) Press the BREAK key (or Ctrl-C) to get into the debugger and then type "OFF".

(ii) Have the system manager use the verb "LOGOFF" to log him off from
another terminal (see below).

7.8.3   Permission to use TCL

A user's sphere of influence within the computer can be much restricted by
preventing him from using TCL. This might be appropriate, for instance, to
a user whose only responsibility is the entering of data into a database via
some program, and who need never use any other program on the computer.
His data entry program can then be started up automatically whenever he
logs on (see §9.1 on logon PROCs) and he will never have any cause to type
anything at TCL at all.

One way to stop a user from breaking out of a program and gaining
access to TCL is to disable his BREAK key, as described §7.8.4 below. This
however, as we will explain, is not always desirable, so Pick provides another
less drastic way of achieving the same effect. The problem is that normally a
user can type Ctrl-C, or hit the BREAK key on his terminal, and this takes
him into either the system debugger or the BASIC debugger (depending on
whether or not he is using a BASIC program at that moment), at which point
he can type "END" and so get into TCL. The way to prevent him from doing
this is to place a letter R in attribute 9 of his user-defining item in the system
dictionary.[12] Such a user *is* allowed into the debugger when he hits the BREAK
key, but when he types "END", instead of depositing him in TCL, Pick goes
back and runs his logon PROC again, as if he had just logged on. This will
then start his program up again, and he will find himself back where he was
before he hit BREAK. Thus, there is no way this user can ever get to TCL, and
he can do only those things his program lets him do.[13]

A user who *is* to be allowed access to TCL should have either the letter
L or nothing at all in the place in his or her user-defining item that would be
occupied by this letter R.

7.8.4   Disabling the BREAK key

The most extreme limitation you can place on a user's scope within the computer is to put his BREAK key out of action. This prevents him from gaining
access to the debugger at all, and therefore also to TCL. There are two ways
to do this:

---

[12] If you already have a letter U in this attribute, specifying that the computer is to
record all the times the user logs on (see §7.9), then you should put "RU" in the attribute
to get both effects at once.

[13] However, if the program has a STOP statement in it (see §8.6.3) then on encountering
this statement the user *will* be taken to TCL. So for complete security you will have to be
sure there are no STOPs in his program. To do this, replace each STOP with the statement
"CHAIN "OFF"" (see §8.6.3).

1: DISBRK.   You can use the verb "DISBRK" either at TCL, or within a
PROC. For example, the lines

```
HDISBRK
P
```

within a person's logon PROC will disable his BREAK key (see Chapter 9 on
PROCs). The advantage of this method is that it is specific to the user, not
the programs he uses—another user running the same programs will be able
to break out of them and get to TCL provided his BREAK has not also been
put out of action.

The effect of DISBRK may be cancelled by the verb "ENBRK".

2: BREAK OFF.   You can also disable the BREAK key within a Pick BASIC
program with the BASIC statement "BREAK OFF" (see §8.8). The statement
"BREAK ON" enables the BREAK key again. This has the advantage of being
under the control of the program itself—the program can turn the BREAK key
on and off as it sees fit, which might be a useful facility.

There are a couple of serious disadvantages to disabling the BREAK key
on a terminal, which make it inadvisable except when you are absolutely sure
of your programs. First, once the BREAK key is out of action there is no way
to get out of a program that goes wrong. So you should never disable the
BREAK key when you are still debugging a program. (Though you could use
the verb "DISBRK" to disable the BREAK key only on other users' terminals,
and not on your own.)

Second, once the BREAK key is out of action, a user who has been confined
to a particular program cannot log his terminal off. Sooner or later you are
bound to want to log the terminal off, and in this case you will have to do it
from another terminal using the verb "LOGOFF". The procedure is as follows:

1. Log on to the computer as SYSPROG and get to TCL if you are not already
   there.

2. You need to know the line number of the terminal you want to log off.
   If you don't know it already you find out what it is by using the verb
   "LISTU" (see §§4.1.1 and 4.2.4), thus:

```
>LISTU

CH# PCBF NAME......... TIME.. DATE.......
 ØØ Ø2CØ KING          15:48  29 OCT 199Ø
 Ø8 Ø32Ø BINNEY        Ø9:45  29 OCT 199Ø
 11 Ø34Ø JACK          14:14  29 OCT 199Ø
 18 Ø4ØØ NEWMAN        13:Ø3  29 OCT 199Ø
 22 Ø41Ø JILL          12:27  29 OCT 199Ø
```

3. Suppose it is JACK that you want to log off the computer. From the first
   column of the list, we see that his line number is 11. You now type

Table 7.2.   Words defined in the dictionary for the file ACC

Word	Meaning
DATES	List of the dates on which this user has logged on at this terminal
TIMES	List of the times at which this user has logged on at this terminal
CONN	Length of time for which the user was logged on on each occasion
UNITS	'Charge units' used on each occasion (a guide to CPU time used)
PAGES	Number of pages the user caused to be printed on each occasion

```
>LOGOFF
CHANNEL:11

[534] LOGOFF SUCCESSFUL.
>
```

and JACK gets logged off.

7.9   The ACC file

Pick maintains a permanent record of when each user logs on, and on what terminal, in a file called "ACC". The file-defining item for this file is, unusually, held not in any MD, but in the system dictionary (i.e., in the item "ACC" in the file "SYSTEM"). The ACC file also contains information about which users are logged on at the present time. It is from the ACC file that Pick fetches these data when you ask for them using the verb "LISTU". ACC has a dictionary as well as a data portion, so you can use ACCESS verbs to get statistics from it on the use of the computer. A list of the most useful words defined in DICT ACC is given in Table 7.2. The form of the IDs of items in ACC is the user name of a user, followed by a hash "#", followed by the number of the line which he or she logs on to. So for example, when the user KING logs onto the computer using the terminal attached to line number 6, Pick will record the time and date of his logging on in the item "KING#6" in the file "ACC". And when he logs off again it will record that too.

Thus, suppose that you wish to know all the dates and times at which KING has logged on since you installed your computer. Then you should type

```
>SORT ACC = "KING]" DATES TIMES

ACC...... DATE. TIME...
KING#2    30/6   14:32
KING#2    29/10  10:55
2 ITEMS LISTED.
```

Clearly, KING has not made very heavy use of the computer. On the other hand if another user, JILL, say, had used the computer a lot, then you might want to limit the scope of your search through her entries in the ACC file. For example, you could list all the occasions since June 30th, 1990 on which JILL made use of the printer, with the command

```
>SORT ACC = "JILL]" WITH PAGES AND WITH DATES AFTER "30 JUN 1990"
PAGES

ACC...... PAGES
JILL#4       3
            30
             7
JILL#5       1
            14
....
```

and out will come the list. This tells us that JILL has logged on on the terminal connected to line number 4 three times, and that she printed 3 pages on the first occasion, 30 on the next, and so forth.

DICT ACC also contains a set of items defining a default report (see the end of §4.3.1) for the ACC file. This allows you to obtain a list of logon times for every user and every terminal with the single command "SORT ACC".

As far as extracting information from the ACC file on the users currently logged on is concerned, the best thing to do is just to use the verb "LISTU" described in §4.1.1, which does everything for you with a minimum of fuss.

Switching off the recording of logon times. If there are a lot of users on your computer and they all log on with moderate frequency, then you may find that the ACC file grows extremely quickly and occupies an unreasonable amount of space on your disk. There are two solutions to this problem. Either you can get your computer to clear out the file automatically every time you do a full file restore by making ACC a file of type DY (see §7.5.2), or you can stop Pick from recording data in the file altogether.

Pick provides a way of switching off the recording of data in the ACC file. The way it works is this. If you want a user's times and dates of logging on to be recorded in the ACC file, then you should put a letter U in attribute 9 of their user-defining item in the system dictionary.[14]

If you don't want a user's times and dates of logging on to be recorded in the file "ACC" then you should not put a letter U in attribute 9 of their user-defining item. If there is one there already, remove it.

These attributes in user-defining items do not affect the recording of information about which users are currently logged onto the computer. There is no way to stop Pick recording these data in the ACC file, so the verb "LISTU" will always work as it is supposed to. However, this is not a problem in the same way as the recording of logon times and dates, because the entry in the

---

[14] If there is already a letter L or a letter R there to control their access to TCL, then the letter U should go after it, like this: "LU", "RU".

ACC file which records that someone is currently logged on is deleted again
when that user logs off, and so such entries do not accumulate in the same
annoying, space-wasting way as the other kind of entry.

7.10   Terminals

You have probably noticed what an enormous number of companies there
are in the business of manufacturing and selling computers. Many produce
machines almost identical to their competitors' models, and yet with just
enough subtle differences to completely confound the poor user every time he
comes across a new one. Well, in exactly the same fashion, there is a whole
host of companies (many of them the same companies who make the computers) producing terminals, and all these terminals also have subtle differences,
which can cause no end of headaches when you have a new one that you want
to plug into your Pick machine. (The manufacturers would probably claim
that this was 'product differentiation', but in reality it's probably no more
than stubbornness, and a lack of internationally accepted standards for these
things.)

The particular difficulty with terminals lies in the way in which they
communicate with the computer. When you hit a key on one of the terminals
attached to your computer, the terminal sends a number, or possibly several
numbers, down the cable to the computer, to let it know what you did. And
similarly, when the computer needs to print a letter on your screen (or do
something more complicated like moving the cursor, or clearing everything
off the screen) it sends one or more numbers down the wires to the terminal.
And the terminal is supposed to know what to do about it. The numbers
that are exchanged are usually referred to as **codes**. The problem is that
while the codes for ordinary characters, such as letters, numbers and most of
the punctuation marks are standard,[15] those for other things, like the ones
that the terminal sends when you hit the arrow or 'cursor' keys, or the ones
the computer uses to move the cursor around the screen, are not. They vary
from terminal to terminal. To cope with this lack of standardization amongst
terminals, Pick provides a verb, "TERM", which you can use to tell it what
make of terminal is connected to any particular port, so that it knows what
codes to expect from that terminal, and what codes it should send in order
to get particular jobs done. Pick knows about a large selection of common
terminals, so there is an excellent chance that you will have to do no more
than issue the right TERM command, to get any new terminal talking happily
to your Pick computer. If you give the wrong TERM command for the type of

[15] The standard is known as the American Standard Code for Information Interchange,
or ASCII for short (pronounced 'askey'). Appendix 2 contains a table of the ASCII codes.

terminal you have connected, or if you give no TERM command at all, you will probably find that the letters and numbers the computer prints on the screen will come out OK, but that you get garbage when the computer tries to clear the screen or move the cursor. We now explain how to use the TERM verb, so that you will know what to do when this situation arises.

7.10.1   TERM

The verb "TERM" is used to tell Pick what make of terminal is connected to any particular port. It can also be used to change various properties of that port, and to specify several quantities connected with the printing of reports on the printer.

Setting the terminal type.   Each type of terminal which Pick knows about is denoted by a single letter, and in its simplest form a TERM command consists of just the verb "TERM", followed by the letter appropriate to the particular type of terminal you want to use. After such a command Pick will treat the terminal on which the command was typed as the specified type of terminal.[16] For example, to tell Pick that the terminal you are using is a VT52 type terminal, you should type:

> `>TERM Y`

A list of the most common terminal types, and their designated letters is given in Table 7.3. Not all of the terminal types on this table may be available on your computer—these things vary from one manufacturer to another.

If you are using a microcomputer, such as a Macintosh or an IBM PC as a terminal, then you will need a terminal emulator program to run on it as well (see §1.2). Most terminal emulators make your micro behave like one of several well-known brands of terminal, for example DEC VT102 or VT52. All you have to do to get your micro chattering happily with your Pick machine is to tell the terminal emulator to emulate one of the terminal types listed in Table 7.3 and then to issue the appropriate TERM command to your Pick machine.

There are many makes of terminal which are not listed in Table 7.3. If your terminal is not a type that Pick knows about, the terminal type "X" can be used. Giving the command "TERM X" will cause Pick to ignore all subsequent instructions about moving the cursor etc. on that terminal, and this will at least stop it from printing garbage on the screen when your programs try to do this. On the other hand, most programs make heavy use of these terminal facilities, and such programs will not work well if the facilities have been disabled in this way. So specifying a terminal type "X" is not a good permanent solution to the problem of a terminal of unknown type. The

---

[16] Strictly speaking Pick only knows about *ports*. If you unplug a terminal from a port, and plug in a different sort of terminal in its place, Pick will treat the new one exactly the way it treated the old, until you tell it to do otherwise with a new TERM command.

Table 7.3. Terminal types and their associated single letter codes.

Terminal	Letter
Adds 580	A
Ampex 210	B
Citoh VT52	C
Datamedia	D
IBM Monochrome display	I
Lear-Siegler ADM-3A	L
Ampex 80	M
Pertec 701	P
Adds Regent	R
TEC 2402/Televideo 925	T
Adds Viewpoint	V
Wyse 50	W
Other	X
DEC VT52	Y
DEC VT102	y

proper thing to do is first to try out all the other terminal types, to see if your
terminal actually conforms to some standard which is the same as one of the
terminals listed, or, if that fails, to pester your supplier to provide you with
a 'terminal driver' for your terminal. This is a program which adds another
terminal type to the list of permitted ones, and thus enables Pick to handle
your terminal intelligently.

More complicated TERM commands. TERM can also be used to tell
Pick various more specific things about the terminal you are using. These
complicated forms of TERM command are not used very often and it is probably
not worth your learning about them unless you are actually having difficulties
with your terminals.

In its most general form the TERM command consists of the verb "TERM"
followed by eight numbers and a letter denoting the terminal type. A TERM
command affects only the terminal on which it is typed. A typical TERM
command, for example, might be

> TERM 79,23,0,2,2,8,132,64,Y

The numbers are, in order:

1: Line length on screen. The first number is *one less than* the number of
characters you can fit on one line of the screen on your terminal. On
most terminals you can fit 80 characters on each line, in which case this
number should be 79, as above.

Table 7.4.   Effects of the fifth number n in a
TERM command on screens and printers.

n	Screen	Printer
0	Not cleared	No new page
	No delay	
1	Not cleared	New page
	No delay	
2 or	Cleared	New page
more	Delay of n characters	

2: Number of lines on the screen. The second number should be one less than the number of lines on the screen. On most terminals you can fit 24 lines on the screen, so this number should be 23, as above.

3: Number of blank lines on the screen. The third number specifies how many lines you wish Pick to leave blank at the bottom of the screen. In our example above this was zero. But if we had made the second and third numbers 20 and 3, say, then there would have been 21 lines on the screen that Pick used, and 3 blank ones at the bottom. (Still 24 in total.) Since blank lines merely waste space, the third number is normally zero.

4: Delay at the end of each line. The fourth number specifies how long the computer is to wait after it finishes printing each line on the screen, before it starts the next one. It waits exactly as long as it would take to send this number of characters down the line to the terminal. Some terminals require such a delay and some don't. 2 is a safe figure to sling in here.

5: End of page. The fifth number specifies whether the computer is to clear the screen at the end of a page of text, and if so, how long it is to wait between clearing the screen and starting the next page. It also determines whether or not the printer starts each new page of a report at the top of a new sheet of paper. Table 7.4 shows the various possibilities for this parameter, and their effects on screens and printers. A typical value for this number is 2, which means that if a report is sent to the printer, the computer will start a new sheet of paper for each page of the report. If, on the other hand, the report is sent to the terminal, Pick will clear the screen at the start of each new page. Also, Pick will put in a delay after each new page to let the terminal settle down before starting the new page.

6: Backspace character. The sixth number is the 'backspace' code. This is the code that Pick sends to the terminal to make it rub out the character just before the cursor on the screen, and move the cursor back one place. This code varies from terminal to terminal, so this parameter in the TERM command allows you to specify it for your particular type of terminal. It is usually 8, as in the example above, but 21 and 127 are both sometimes used.

7: Printer line length. The seventh number in the TERM command is the number of characters to a line on the printer. (*Not* one less than it, as it was with the line length for the terminal.) On most printers this is either 132, as above, or 80.

8: Printer page length. The eighth number is the number of lines to a page on the printer paper. (*Not* one less than it, as it was with the number of lines on the terminal screen.) A typical figure is 64, as above.

The last thing to come after the verb "TERM" is the single letter indicating what type of terminal you are using (see above, and Table 7.3). In fact you can miss out as many of the numbers immediately preceding this letter as you like, and still put the letter in, and Pick will know what you mean. For example, if you aren't really interested in what the line printer is doing in the example above, you could miss out the last two numbers, and give the TERM command as follows:

>TERM 79,23,0,2,2,8,Y

and Pick would know that this meant terminal type "Y". The two numbers missed out would just be left at whatever value they were set to before the TERM command. Furthermore, you can leave out any of the numbers in the middle of the list as well, provided you put in the commas to mark the places where they would have been. If you do this then Pick again leaves those quantities set to the values they had before the TERM command was given. Thus for example

>TERM 79,23,,,,8,Y

will set the width and depth of the screen, the backspace code, and the terminal type, but leave everything else as it was. And

>TERM 79,23

will just set the width and depth of the screen.

7.11   Group format errors

Just about the worst thing that can happen to you with a Pick computer is that you get one of the dreaded **group format errors**. You will know if you get a group format error, because one of the terminals will, without warning, come up with the message

GROUP FORMAT ERROR 31415

(though the number may be different). This happens very rarely, but when it does you have a serious problem. Your best course of action is the following:

1. Stop people from working on *any* terminal on the computer as quickly as possible, and don't let them start again until the problem is fixed. People who are already logged on should *not* log off. They should just stop working and leave the terminal alone.

2. Call the supplier, and take advice. Repairing group format errors is a tricky business, and you can loose a lot of data from your files if you get it wrong, so it's best to leave the decisions to the professionals.

If you are not in a position to do this then the simplest way to get out of trouble is to perform a full file restore from the previous day's backup tape as described in §7.4.4. This will set everybody's work on the computer back a day, to the way it was when you made the tape, but at least you will have a working computer.

8 Pick BASIC

Any computerized business system rests on twin pillars; a well organized filestore containing data useful to the business, and a suite of programs[1] designed to mine and maintain the filestore. Neither filestore nor program suite is useful by itself, and each must be tailored to the requirements of the other. In Chapter 3 we explained the structure of Pick files. In this chapter we show you how to use the programming language designed to manipulate Pick files. Once you have learnt how to program in this language there will be no operation on the filestore, whether in the inputting of data, the calculation of quantities dependent on data or the production of any type of report from the data, which you will not be able to accomplish with ease and assurance. Furthermore, you will be able to package the fruits of your labours so that they may be used by unskilled operators. By contrast, though there exist various 'fourth generation application generators' and other purported short-cuts to the generation of 'applications', someone ignorant of Pick BASIC is doomed to a life of frustration and toleration of less than perfect solutions to practical problems.

Creating a program file. Each Pick BASIC program is stored as a single item in a special program file. You can have as many of these program files as you like. But a program will run only if it is an item in a file of file type "DC" (see §3.2.1). On most systems a special TCL command is provided for creating such files; for example, to create a program file called "PROGRAMS" you type[2]

```
>CREATE-PFILE PROGRAMS 1 1 5 1
```

---

[1] In the business world computer programs are often referred to as "applications". We shall eschew this designation as we are unclear what these programs are supposed to be applications of—the hardware? the programming language? the filestore?

[2] If CREATE-PFILE does not work on your system, you will have to create the file with CREATE-FILE and then use an editor to change the first attribute of its file-defining item in your MD from D to DC.

The name PROGRAMS used here is quite arbitrary, but the P in PFILE is essential. This stands for 'pointer'—the dictionary of this file is used rather differently from the dictionary of an ordinary data file created with the verb CREATE-FILE (see below). In our example the modulo and separation (see §3.2.1) of the data portion are 5 and 1 respectively. Larger values of the modulo might be appropriate if you plan to store many programs in the file (see §4.2.6).

Compiling and running a BASIC program. Once you have created your program file you have to decide how you are going to enter your programs into items in this file. In Chapter 6 we discussed strategies for entering data into files. Any of the techniques we discussed there is suitable; all you have to do is to assemble your program as an item of your program file, each line of the program being in a separate attribute.

You can get a program printed out using the verb "RUNOFF". Suppose the item "TEST" in the file "PROGRAMS" contains your program. Then the following command issued at TCL will print your program on a printer:

```
>RUNOFF PROGRAMS TEST (P)
```

Before a program such as TEST can be run it must be "compiled", that is, inspected by a program, the **compiler**, that looks for logical errors. If the compiler finds your program to be error-free, it then translates the relatively small number of human-readable statements in your program into a greater number of simpler instructions of the type that your computer's CPU can understand (see Chapter 1). These instructions are called the program's **object code**. Finally, it stores the object code on the disk, and puts a **pointer** in the dictionary of your PROGRAMS file, which tells it where to find the code.

Successful compilation of the item "TEST" in PROGRAMS might look like this

```
>COMPILE PROGRAMS TEST
**************************
Program 'TEST' compiled. 1 frame used.
>
```

Once your program has successfully compiled you may try it out by typing

```
>RUN PROGRAMS TEST
```

which means 'run the program stored in the item "TEST" of the file "PROGRAMS"'. If you expect to run the program (or at least a modified version of it) often in the future, you will find it convenient to CATALOG it. To CATALOG TEST you issue the TCL command

```
>CATALOG PROGRAMS TEST
```

Once a program has been CATALOGed it can be run simply by typing its name at the TCL prompt:

```
>TEST
```

The machine achieves this effect by adding a special item called "TEST" to your MD. If you CATALOG every program you write, your MD is liable to become cluttered and the machine slow. So you should either CATALOG only often-used programs, or periodically remove outdated entries from your MD using the DELETE verb. Thus

```
>DELETE MD TEST
```

would delete the item "TEST" from your MD.

It usually happens that the first few times you submit your masterpiece for scrutiny by the compiler it complains that your logic is defective. These complaints rarely come singly, even when there is really only one thing wrong. Rather than launching into a long explanation of why one mistake causes the compiler to imagine others which don't really exist, we just give you the following tip, which we hope will save you from wasting hours looking for errors where there are none: concentrate on the very first error message put out by the compiler since this is likely to be a well grounded complaint to which you should attend. When you have corrected the error that gave rise to this first complaint, recompile the program without bothering to understand the later problems. With any luck your program will now compile without protest. If it does not, attend to the first complaint and then repeat the process. For example, suppose compiling TEST produces the following response:

```
>BASIC PROGRAMS TEST
********************************************************
[B110] Line 53 of TEST terminator missing
053                     CASE Key=F5
                         ^
[B107] Line 49 of TEST "ELSE" clause missing
049                     IF SP>0 THEN
                                 ^
[B102] Line 49 of TEST Bad statement
049                     IF SP>0 THEN
                          ^
[B102] Line 40 of TEST Bad statement
040                     BEGIN CASE
                         ^
[B102] Line 36 of TEST Bad statement
036             BEGIN CASE
                 ^
[B102] Line 1 of TEST Bad statement
001         BEGIN CASE
             ^
[B110] Line 1 of TEST terminator missing
[B100] Line 1 of TEST  Compilation aborted. No object code produced
>
```

In these circumstances the right thing to do is to look for an error at or near the 53rd line of your program.

8.1   Basic grammar

8.1.1   Assignment and arithmetic statements

If you have programmed in ordinary BASIC, perhaps on a PC or a home computer, you will already be familiar with much of the syntax of Pick BASIC. For example, consider the following Pick BASIC program:

```
A=5
A=A+5
B=13
C=A+B
D=A*B
E=B/A
CRT A,B,C,D,E
STOP
```

When we run this program we get the following output on our screen:

```
1Ø 13 23 13Ø 1.3
```

Each attribute of the program is a single instruction: the first attribute says "assign the number 5 to the variable A", the second attribute says "increase A by 5" and so on till the penultimate attribute says "write the values of A, B, C, D and E on the screen" (CRT stands for 'cathode ray tube', which is the technical name for a television tube). The programmer's term for one of these instructions is a **statement**. The statements in a program make up its **code** rather as the threads in a shirt make up the cloth from which the shirt is made.

It is often convenient to place several statements in a single attribute. Statements in the same attribute must be separated by semi-colons. So we can rewrite our example thus:

```
A=5; A=A+5; B=13; C=A+B; D=A*B; E=B/A
CRT A,B,C,D,E; STOP
```

Notice that in these examples CRT and STOP are written in capital letters. Pick BASIC always distinguishes between capitals and lower-case letters. *All* Pick BASIC's **reserved words** such as CRT and STOP *must* be written in capitals.

8.1.2   Comments

It is very important to add to your programs a running commentary on what is going on at each stage so that when, perhaps years hence, someone wants to adapt your program to changed circumstances, they have a hope of figuring out how your program works. Obviously we don't want to bother the machine with these remarks directed at humans. So we fence them off with exclamation marks; any attribute that starts with a ! is ignored by the compiler.[3] Thus we might annotate TEST like this:

---

[3] Comments can equally be fenced off with REM or *.

```
! Program TEST written by James Newman 17/6/90
! Object: to illustrate simple BASIC assignments
!
    A=5;!                       Assign 5 to A
    A=A+5;!                     Increase A by 5
    ......
```

Notice here the use of the combination ";!" to put a comment on the same
attribute as a BASIC statement.

Your programs can also be made more readable by judicious padding
with spaces; in most contexts the Pick BASIC compiler ignores superfluous
spaces.

8.1.3   Variable types and manipulation

One of the joys of Pick BASIC is that there is only one type of variable. For
example, the following code is lawful (if in appallingly bad taste):

```
    A=10
    B=A
    A="2"
    B=B-A
    A="This is a string"
    CRT A; CRT B
    STOP
```

When we run this program we get

```
    This is a string
    8
```

In this example we first assign the number 10 to A. Then we assign A to B
so that B becomes 10. Next we assign the string that consists of just the
character 2 (that is the character 2 rather than the number 2) to A. In most
computer languages A could be assigned a value that was *either* a number, *or*
a string, but not one after the other in this way. But in Pick BASIC we are not
only allowed to assign first a numeric and then a string value to A, but after
assigning to A the string value "2" we can subtract A from a variable assigned
the value 10 to get the number 8 just as if we had assigned the *number* 2 to
A. However, you cannot subtract any string; if your code says

```
    B=10
    A="This is a string"
    B=B-A
```

Pick will compile it without complaint, but you will get an error message
when you run the program since the machine has no idea how it can subtract
"This is a string" from 10.

Thus while all variables, A, B, etc., are equivalent, not all values are
equivalent; no matter what value we have assigned to A, we can manipulate
A as a string. But we can use A in an arithmetic expression only if A's value
is a number. Table 8.1 lists all the arithmetic operations you can apply to
numbers and to variables that have been assigned numeric values. The only

Table 8.1. Valid operations on numbers and numeric variables

Symbol	Function
+	Addition
−	Subtraction
*	Multiplication
/	Division
^	Raising to a power, e.g. $9=3^2$

operator which might not be familiar is the caret "^". One uses this to raise numbers to powers. Thus 2^3 is 8 and 3^2 is 9.

Two operations are allowed on strings: gluing them together ("concatenation") and taking them apart. You glue strings together with colons. Thus

```
A="This"
B=" is a"
C=" string"
D=A:B:C
CRT D
```

would cause the machine to write "This is a string".

Square brackets enable you to take any string apart; if in the example just given we assign E=D[1,4], then E will take the value "This" since the parenthesis [1,4] means "four characters of the string, starting with the first character". Similarly F=D[6,2] will assign "is" to F. If you want to extract everything in a string that comes after some character, you simply make the second number in [...] large. Thus G=D[6,80] will assign "is a string" to G.

8.1.4 Naming variables and dimensioned arrays

Variables don't have to have boring names like A and B, and your programs will be more readable if your variables have more interesting names. For example

```
Basic.cost=12
Profit=2
User.cost=Profit+Basic.cost
CRT User.cost
```

In this chapter we shall mostly capitalize our variables; that is, the names of variables will start with a capital but otherwise be of lower-case letters. This convention minimizes confusion between variables and either Pick BASIC's reserved words such as CRT, which are always in capitals, or ordinary English words, which are usually printed in lower-case letters.

One often wants all the variables in a set to have similar names. For example, we might write

```
Cost.3=Cost.1+Cost.2
```

and in many cases a numbering scheme of this sort would work fine. But sometimes you want to be able to refer to the ith variable in a set, where i is itself a variable to which is assigned in turn the values 1, 2, 3... In these circumstances the obvious thing to type is `Cost.i`, but the computer will think you are referring to a single variable, `Cost.i`, rather than to a collection of variables `Cost.1`, `Cost.2`... For these occasions Pick BASIC allows you to define **dimensioned arrays** like this[4]

```
DIM Price(1Ø),Cost(1Ø)
Profit=Ø.2
FOR i=1 TO 1Ø
    Price(i)=Cost(i)*(1+Profit)
    CRT Price(i)
NEXT i
STOP
```

The `DIM` statement says there shall be two groups of ten variables each called `Price` and `Cost`. Then the machine assigns 120% of the corresponding `Cost` to each `Price` variable in turn.

While we are on the topic of arrays, we should point out that Pick BASIC has another, very different kind of array, called a 'dynamic array', to be discussed in §8.3.1. As we will see, a dynamic array should not be declared in a `DIM` statement.

8.2   Communicating with screen, printer and keyboard

The reserved word "PRINT" can be used to write something either on your computer's screen or on a printer. However, Pick BASIC provides a special instruction, `CRT` for writing to the screen, and you should reserve `PRINT` for output you want sent to a printer. Printers and screens have to be managed somewhat differently and it is important to guard against treating a screen as a printer, or a printer as a screen. In particular your printer is likely to seize up altogether if you start addressing it as if it were a screen.

8.2.1   Writing to the screen

The nice thing about a screen is that you can write on any part of it at will. To facilitate this, Pick BASIC provides codes which will clear all or part of the screen, direct your output to any point on the screen and even cause it to be written in flashing characters. These screen-formatting codes are all listed in Table 8.2. Each code takes the form of an 'at' sign "@" followed by round brackets containing one or two numbers. Logically a unit such as @(-3) has

---

[4] See §8.4.3 for details of the `FOR-NEXT` construction.

Table 8.2.   Screen formatting @-codes

Character	Function
@(-1)	Clear screen
@(-2)	Position cursor at top left corner of screen
@(-3)	Clear screen from current cursor position to bottom
@(-4)	Clear screen from current cursor position to end of line
@(-5)	Start writing in blinking characters
@(-6)	Stop writing in blinking characters
@(-7)	Initiate a "protected field"– one which cannot be over-written
@(-8)	Terminate a protected field
@(-9)	Move cursor back one character
@(-1∅)	Move cursor up one line
@(x)	Move cursor to x^{th} column
@(x,y)	Move cursor to x^{th} column and y^{th} row

the status of a string; it can be glued to other strings and then written out in the ordinary way:

```
A=@(-3):"This is a string"
CRT A
CRT @(-4):"This is another string"
```

is a lawful piece of code.

The operation of the @-codes is very straightforward. The most important are: @(-1) clears the whole screen; @(-3) clears the screen from the current position of the cursor onwards; @(-4) clears everything on the current line to the right of the cursor. If an @-code's number is positive, the machine will interpret it as the number of a column and will move the cursor to that column. Then there are the @-codes that have two numbers inside the brackets. These are for positioning the cursor at a point on the screen.

Most screens consist of an array of 80 columns horizontally and 24 rows vertically. Pick numbers the columns 0–79, and the rows 0–23. Thus the character at the top left corner of the screen is at position (0,0), while that at the bottom right is at position (79,23). Notice that the horizontal (column) number comes first and the vertical (row) number comes second.[5] We can write a character H at the top left of the screen by saying

```
CRT @(∅,∅):"H"
```

After writing the H the cursor will move down to the first column of the second row just as if you had pressed RETURN after hitting the H key. If you

---

[5] This follows the convention used by mathematicians doing coordinate geometry, who write coordinates in the order (x, y). It is, however, contrary to the convention used in most basic **TAB** statements.

want to suppress this carriage return you must add a colon to the end of your CRT statement thus:

```
CRT @(0,0):"H":
```

If you want to put an H at the bottom right corner of the screen it is essential to finish your CRT statement with a colon since without the colon the cursor will try to drop down to the beginning of the next line, and as there is no such line will move everything on the screen, including your H, up a line. Thus we get an H at the bottom right corner of the screen with

```
CRT @(79,23):"H":
```

We don't have to put numbers in the brackets after the "@"—we can use variables. For example, the following will draw a line of stars diagonally across your screen:[6]

```
FOR i=1 TO 20
    j=4*i-1
    CRT @(j,i):"*":
NEXT i
```

8.2.2 Printing

Clearly, a program that produces bills, invoices or whatever needs to be able to print properly formatted documents on a printer. The Pick technical term for such a paper output is a 'report' (see the introduction to Chapter 5). It will frequently be necessary to assemble several reports simultaneously. For example, one report might consist of a series of accounts for dispatch to customers, another might summarize these for the credit manager into a list of customers being billed this cycle and a third report might be prepared for the marketing manager summarizing what items each customer has received this cycle. We don't want to produce these reports one after another. Rather, as we run through our list of customers we want to jot down his indebtedness onto the credit manager's report, add a summary of what the customer has received to the marketing manager's report and append the bill to the sequence of customer accounts.

We initiate all this frenetic printing activity simply by saying

```
PRINTER ON
```

Now no output produced with a PRINT statement will be directed to the screen; all such output will be sent to the spooler (see Chapter 5) for subsequent orderly dispatch to a printer.

Our next step will probably be to print some headings for the reports. Something like this would be appropriate:

---

[6] See §8.4.3 for details of the FOR-NEXT construction.

Table 8.3.   Screen and printer control characters

Character	Function
CHAR(7)	Causes terminal or printer to beep
CHAR(1∅)	Causes the cursor or print head to move down one line
CHAR(12)	Sends the print head to the top of a new sheet of paper
CHAR(13)	Sends the cursor or print head to the start of a new line
CHAR(27)	Causes the next few characters to be interpreted as control codes, for example, according to Epson's conventions

```
Month="AUGUST 199∅"
PRINT ON 1 CHAR(12):'     CUSTOMER ACCOUNTS FOR ':Month
PRINT ON 1
PRINT ON 2 CHAR(12):'     CUSTOMERS BILLED AT END OF ':Month
PRINT ON 2
PRINT ON 3 CHAR(12):'     GOODS DELIVERED DURING ':Month
PRINT ON 3
```

Here we have started three reports. Every report must have a **report number**—the report numbers used in this example are 1, 2 and 3. Any three distinct (not necessarily sequential) numbers in the range 0–255 could have been used. Subsequently we shall add to the "customer accounts" report by using a "PRINT ON 1" statement, and the "goods delivered" report by saying "PRINT ON 3".

You may wonder at the rôle of the expression "CHAR(12)" in the example we have just given. CHAR looks like a dimensioned array (see §8.1.4) but is actually an "intrinsic function" (see §8.5). "PRINT CHAR(12)" causes the computer to print the twelfth character from the table of ASCII characters listed in Appendix 2. We shall call this character "ASCII 12". A few ASCII characters are interpreted by essentially all printers as control characters; that is, they are not actually printed but serve to tell the printer to move the print head or paper somehow. Table 8.3 lists these printer-control characters. When a printer receives ASCII 12, it moves to the top of a new page. Thus starting each report with CHAR(12) ensures that each report starts at the top of a fresh sheet of paper.

Now that all our reports have been initialized we can grind through our list of customers adding the necessary stuff to each report. A section of the program might look like this:

```
PRINT ON 1 Item "L#4∅",Price,Discount,Discounted
PRINT ON 1 "VAT" "L#4∅"," "," ",Vat
PRINT ON 1 "Total" "L#4∅"," "," ",Charge
!
PRINT ON 2 Customer "L#4∅",Charge
!
PRINT ON 3 Customer "L#4∅",Item
```

The first statement adds to the customer's account the stock item's name, its price, his discount and the discounted price. This statement uses two devices to ensure that successive PRINT statements produce a nicely tabulated report:

(i) The "format mask" L#4∅ to be explained below pads the item's name (stored in the variable Item) with spaces to produce a string 40 characters long whose leftmost characters contain the name.

(ii) The names of the variables to be printed are separated by commas. These instruct the machine to move the print head to the next tab stop between printing variables. (Tab stops are usually set 18 characters apart.) Had we wanted to join everything together without intervening gaps, we would have separated the variables with colons.

The second and third statements in our example use these techniques to print the strings "VAT" and "Total", and the values of the corresponding variables Vat and Charge below the item name and the discounted price on the customer's account. The fourth and fifth statements make similarly tabulated contributions to the reports of the credit and marketing managers.

When the machine has worked its way right through the list of customers, PRINTing on reports 1, 2 and 3 in cycle, we can order the spooler to ship those reports to the printer by saying

    PRINTER CLOSE

Or we can just have the program stop by including a STOP statement (see §8.6.3). In either case the reports will be printed one after the other without your taking any further action.

When you are writing and debugging a program it can be helpful to have output that is ultimately destined for the printer appear on the screen. In such a case there are three ways in which you can redirect all PRINTed output to your screen:

(i) You can issue the command "SP-ASSIGN H S" at TCL as explained in §5.1.1.

(ii) You can delete the PRINTER ON statement which initiates report construction.

(iii) You can add the statement PRINTER OFF to your program. A subsequent statement PRINTER ON will restart report construction.

Formatting output. To produce really impressive and readable reports on your machine you have to be able to specify exactly how you want certain numbers printed out. Should the machine round monetary amounts to the nearest penny? Should it put commas after the digit denominating thousands? Should it tabulate the data somehow? Pick BASIC provides a facility called a **format mask** with which you can instruct the machine in such matters.

It would take some time to give a full account of format masks, so our discussion will be confined to the most useful masks. A format mask is specified by following the name of the variable to be printed by a string of characters enclosed in quotation marks. For example

```
PRINT "Net cost of contract is",Cost "R2,"
```

Notice here the absence of a comma or a colon between "Cost" and the opening quotation mark of the format mask "R2,"—if there were either a comma or a colon before the quotation mark, Pick would print the contents of the double quotes rather than interpreting them as specifying a format mask.

What the format mask "R2," in our example says is "right justify the number, show exactly two places of decimals and insert a comma after the digits that enumerate thousands, millions, billions, etc." So the output might look like this:

```
Net cost of contract is        1,244,130.00
```

The letter R in our example specifies right justification of the number to be printed. (Numbers are usually right justified.) An L would have caused the number to be left justified. The digit 2 specifies two places of decimals—the format mask "R1," would have produced "1,244,130.0". The comma in our example format mask gives rise to the commas in the printed number. Leave the comma out of the mask if you don't want commas in your output.

You may find three other features of format masks useful:

(i) The symbol # followed by a number causes the value printed to be padded out to a string that is the given number of characters long. Depending on whether the justification is given as "L" or "R", the value will be placed at either the left or right end of this string, the rest of which is made up of space characters.[7] Thus in our example of how customer accounts might be printed, the mask "L#40" placed the value printed at the left end of a string 40 characters long. The format mask "R2,#15" would print a number to two decimal places, right justified on a field of fifteen characters.

(ii) Including a dollar sign in the format mask causes the machine to print a currency symbol[8] just to the left of a number. For example, you might use the format mask "R2,$#15" when printing large sums in a balance sheet.

(iii) Including an E in the format mask causes negative numbers such as losses (negative profits) to be enclosed in brackets.

Finally, we mention that Pick BASIC provides statements **HEADING** and **FOOTING** with which you can specify what you want to appear at the top and bottom of every page of your output. Unfortunately these statements only apply to report 0, that is, the report that is produced by statements which start "PRINT ON 0", or just "PRINT" which the machine understands to mean "PRINT ON 0".

---

[7] If you replace #with * the value will be padded with asterisks rather than spaces. This is useful when printing cheques, for example.

[8] i.e., a $ or £ or whatever, depending on how your machine has been set up.

8.2.3   Input from the keyboard

Essentially every program requires input from the keyboard. The standard statement for accomplishing this is INPUT. In its simplest form INPUT simply assigns a value to a variable. For example, you might have a piece of code like this:

```
CRT @(10,0):"Do you want to continue? (Y/N) ":
INPUT Answer
```

The resulting conversation with the machine would look like this:

```
Do you want to continue? (Y/N) ?Y
```

and the variable Answer would now be assigned the value "Y".

There are two respects in which this fragment of code is less than ideal. First, the machine printed two question marks, where we want only one. This arose because by default INPUT generates a question mark while it waits for your input. You may like this convention and rephrase your questions to the user accordingly. We prefer to turn off this question-mark-adding feature of INPUT at the outset by starting all our programs with

```
PROMPT ""
```

This replaces the prompt "?" with no prompt at all. If your job starts to get you down, you can subsequently change these PROMPT statements to

```
PROMPT "(Damn you!)"
```

and your colleagues will know soon enough how you feel about them.

The second respect in which our example of the use of INPUT is imperfect is that after typing Y the user had additionally to hit RETURN to complete the input. It is more efficient to arrange for such single-character inputs to be completed as soon as a key has been depressed. This you can do by adding a comma and a 1 at the end of the INPUT statement:

```
INPUT Answer,1
```

which means "read one character from the keyboard and assign it to the variable Answer". Now when your program reaches the INPUT statement the machine will assign to Answer the character generated by the first key depressed. If you are pedantic and wish to insist on a complete YES, you can write "INPUT Answer,3". The machine will then assign to Answer the string formed by the first three keys depressed.

In the examples just given, the cursor moves down a line (or tries to) immediately after reading Answer. If the cursor was at the bottom of the screen, everything on the screen will be moved up one line instead of the cursor moving down, and this may ruin a carefully formatted screen. So generally it is prudent to suppress the carriage return on inputting a variable by terminating each input statement with a colon. Thus you write

```
INPUT Answer:
```

or

```
    INPUT Answer,1:
```

according to taste.

In all the examples we have given, the characters typed in response to an INPUT request have been displayed on the screen as the keys were depressed. Sometimes, for example when a password is being entered, you don't want the screen to show which keys have been hit. Pick BASIC provides for this eventuality the statement

```
    ECHO OFF
```

Once you have issued this statement, responses to INPUT requests will be systematically suppressed until you cancel the order with the statement "ECHO ON". Be sure your program gets to an ECHO ON statement before it finishes or you will find that none of your subsequent TCL commands appear on the screen either!

INPUT provides many additional facilities, such as **input masks** and the INPUT @ statement. Input masks enable you to check that data input are of the required sort. For example, you can check that a valid date has been entered. The INPUT @ statement positions the cursor prior to input and enables you to specify a default value for the variable to be input. These facilities will save you the odd line of code each time you use them, but if you are not a professional programmer you will probably waste more time mastering them than you will save by their use.

Besides INPUT there is in most implementations of Pick BASIC another invaluable statement for reading the keyboard, the "IN" statement.[9] Its purpose is to report to your program *exactly* what key you depress on the keyboard. To understand how IN differs from INPUT consider the following code fragment:

```
    ECHO OFF
  1 IN Key
    Code=SEQ(Key); CRT "   IN reads code ":Code
    INPUT Key,1:
    Code=SEQ(Key); CRT "INPUT reads code ":Code
    GOTO 1
```

The second statement assigns to the variable Key the character associated with whatever key you depress. The third statement uses the 'intrinsic function' SEQ (see §8.5) to assign to Code the ASCII code for this character. For example, if you depress "A", Code is assigned the value 65 (see Appendix 2), while if you depress the space bar, Code is assigned the value 32. The fourth and fifth attributes of our code fragment try to repeat this operation with INPUT. So long as you depress the key of an honest-to-goodness character (sometimes called a "printable character") such as "A" or the space bar, everything goes fine. But now try depressing the backspace (or delete) key. IN reads this

---

[9] The "IN" statement is not absolutely standard Pick BASIC so it may not be available on your machine.

action correctly and `Code` is set to 8, the ASCII code of backspace. But you can depress backspace as often as you like and you will not get `INPUT` to report anything. `INPUT` fails to set `Key` to backspace because it is convinced that you are only depressing backspace to cancel something you started to enter incorrectly. Thus `INPUT` does not faithfully report what key you have depressed while `IN` does. Usually, this is exactly what you want. However, it is sometimes vital to have an input statement that works like `IN`—for example when writing a screen editor such as PickED (see Appendix 5).

8.3   Handling files

The Pick BASIC we have encountered thus far is nothing but a dialect of the BASIC which you will find on almost any computer. In this section on file handling we encounter features which are very special to Pick BASIC since they reflect the unusually rich structure of Pick files.

Before you can read from or write in a file, you have first to `OPEN` it—that is, instruct the computer to locate the file on disk and allocate an area of RAM into which bits of the file can be copied. Normally programs start by opening all the files they will require with statements such as

```
OPEN "","STAFF" TO People ELSE
      CRT "I can't find the STAFF file!"
      STOP
END
```

On executing this statement the machine tries to locate the file "STAFF". If found, the file is opened and must henceforward be referred to as "`People`" rather than "STAFF". If the file cannot be found the two attributes of code between "ELSE" and "END" will be executed. We shall explain `ELSE` ... `END` constructions like this in §8.4.1. For now just note that when you open a file an `ELSE` clause is mandatory.

The pair of quotation marks before ",`"STAFF"`" in our example are shorthand for "`"DATA"`", which indicates that you wish to open the data portion of the file (see §3.5). If you want to open the dictionary portion of `STAFF` you say

```
OPEN "DICT","STAFF" TO Dictionary ELSE NULL
```

This second example illustrates the use of the minimal `ELSE` clause: "else forget it". In practice you should put something more constructive than `NULL` after `ELSE`, but we don't want to get bogged down in such details here.

8.3.1   Dynamic arrays

Now that you have opened your file you can read an item from it like this

```
READ Employee FROM People,"BLOGGS-J" ELSE NULL
```

Again an ELSE clause is mandatory.

From §6.1.3 we know that there is an item "BLOGGS-J" in the STAFF file and that the System Editor displays its contents like this

```
001 Bloggs
002 Joe
003 M
004 21/04/50
005 14 Home Ave]Working]Surrey
006
007 (0347) 14576
```

When Pick BASIC READs this item from STAFF it copies its contents into the **dynamic array** "Employee". We can copy this information out of Employee and onto the screen with this fragment

```
FOR i=1 TO 7
    CRT Employee<i>
NEXT i
```

The first line written on the screen will be Bloggs, the second line Joe and so forth, since reading BLOGGS-J into Employee has the effect of the assignments Employee<1>=Bloggs, Employee<2>=Joe and so on down the item. This is really very remarkable since we have not previously mentioned the variable Employee. Almost magically on reading the item the variable into which we read the item becomes an array with exactly the structure of the item itself. Notice the use of pointed brackets around the element number in contrast to the round brackets used to enumerate an element of a dimensioned array (see §8.1.4).

The fifth attribute of BLOGGS-J is multi-valued. This is reflected in the structure of Employee. If, as in the last example, we refer simply to Employee<5>, the machine understands us to mean all values in the fifth attribute. But we can refer to, say, the third value thus:

```
CRT Employee<5,3>
```

This statement will elicit the response "Surrey". In a similar way, if any value is broken up into sub-values, we may point to a particular sub-value, say the second, by writing "Employee<5,3,2>".

Once we have read an item into a dynamic array, we can use each element of the array as a variable. For example we can correct a mistake in Bloggs' address by the assignment

```
Employee<5,2>="Woking"
```

Or, in view of the confusion we encountered in §6.2 as to exactly where Bloggs lives, it might be safer to write

```
Employee<5>=""
```

This last statement will have the effect of erasing all three values of the fifth attribute, leaving the attribute null (but still there; see §8.5.1 for how to eliminate an attribute altogether).

8.3.2   Writing an item back to a file

A typical Pick BASIC program reads an item from a file into a dynamic array[10] and then changes the array with assignments like those in the last section. However, since the array is stored in RAM rather than on the disk, nothing on the disk is changed when you modify the array. If you want your modification of a dynamic array to be permanently recorded on the disk, you must WRITE the array in a file. For example, we would write our array Employee back to the STAFF file thus

```
WRITE Employee ON People,"BLOGGS-J"
```

The format of this statement is very similar to a READ statement. The main difference is the absence of an ELSE statement.

8.3.3   The EXECUTE, READNEXT and DATA statements

You will often want to perform operations on every item in a file. For example, at the end of each month you might want the machine to update the tax, insurance and pay figures of each employee in his or her item on the STAFF file. Now the READ statement requires you to specify the ID of the employee; it doesn't allow you to read the item of "the first employee" or anything like that. The way we overcome this difficulty is to have ACCESS build us an alphabetical list of all items in the STAFF file and then take the IDs of employees one at a time from this list.

In §4.3.3 we saw that the TCL command that makes a list of the items in STAFF is

```
>SSELECT STAFF
```

We can achieve exactly the same result from within Pick BASIC with the statement

```
EXECUTE "SSELECT STAFF"
```

The computer understands this statement as meaning 'do now exactly what you would do if I had typed "SSELECT STAFF" at the TCL prompt'. Thus the EXECUTE statement just given builds a select-list of the IDs of items in STAFF (see §4.3.3). We use the READNEXT statement to draw on this list. Thus the fragment

```
   EXECUTE "SSELECT STAFF"
 1 READNEXT Person ELSE STOP
   READ Employee FROM People,Person ELSE NULL
   CRT Person,Employee<1>,Employee<3>
   GOTO 1
```

---

[10] Occasionally, you want to use a dynamic array that you have not read from a file. Unfortunately, if your program first mentions a variable "Employee", say, in a statement such as "Employee<3>="M"", Pick will issue an irritating error message when it executes the statement. But Pick won't complain if the first occurrence of Employee is in the statement "Employee=∅". A statement of this form, in which no attribute is specified, also serves to eliminate any attributes that a dynamic array may have acquired previously.

will write on the screen the ID, surname and sex of every employee in alphabetical order and then stop. It would be easy to change the code that follows the READ statement to do something more interesting.

When the EXECUTE statement in the last example is executed, you will see appear on the screen something like

```
[4Ø4] 13 items selected.
```

You can prevent this message being written on the screen by having it returned to a variable. If the program says

```
EXECUTE "SSELECT STAFF" CAPTURING Reply
```

the message "13 ITEMS SELECTED" will be captured in the variable "Reply" rather than written on the screen. (The error number "[4Ø4]" just gets lost, but see below.) This technique not only prevents the machine spoiling your carefully arranged screen with undesired output, but can be used to return information to the program. For example, you might want to start a sensitive program with

```
EXECUTE "WHO" CAPTURING Reply
```

As we saw in §4.1.1 the verb "WHO" tells you what line you are on and your user-name. That response will be captured into the variable "Reply", so after execution of the above attribute Reply will be assigned a string such as "18 SMITH". Hence the following code will prevent an unauthorized user from running your program:

```
EXECUTE "WHO" CAPTURING Reply
Line=Reply[1,2]
IF Line=Ø OR Line=1 THEN
    GOTO 1Ø
END ELSE
    CRT "You aren't authorized to run this program!"
    STOP
END
```

Now this program can only be run from the terminals connected to lines 0 and 1.

Sometimes the TCL command you issue through an EXECUTE statement will generate a numbered error message. For example, if we do[11]

```
EXECUTE 'SSELECT STAFF WITH SEX "NEUTER"'
```

we are likely to get the response

```
[4Ø1] No items present.
```

The error number "4Ø1" can be captured into the variable "Err" by modifying the above statement to

```
EXECUTE 'SSELECT STAFF WITH SEX "NEUTER"' RETURNING Err
```

---

[11] Notice a subtlety here: ACCESS requires double quotes around strings, so we now change our usual practice and demarcate the string passed to EXECUTE with single quotes. Within this string we can without confusion embed "NEUTER".

You could then handle the eventuality that nobody answers the given criteria
with a statement like

```
IF Err=401 THEN CRT "We've nobody like that on the staff."
```

The TCL command issued by an EXECUTE statement may require keyboard
input. The DATA statement allows you to supply this input from within your
Pick BASIC program. For example, you could delete the item "BLOGGS-J"
from the STAFF file in the following roundabout way:

```
DATA "FD"
DATA "Y"
EXECUTE "ED STAFF BLOGGS-J"
```

When the EXECUTE statement in this fragment is reached, the System Editor
is invoked (see §6.2). The Editor looks for a line of input from the keyboard
and is fed the argument of the first DATA statement executed—i.e., the string
"FD". The Editor responds to this request to delete the item currently being
edited by asking for confirmation from the keyboard. The Editor is now fed
the argument of the second DATA statement executed—"Y"—and so deletes
the item and exits to TCL, whence control returns to your Pick BASIC program. Note that any DATA statements required by an EXECUTE statement must
precede the relevant EXECUTE statement.

Any number of lines of keyboard input to a TCL command issued by an
EXECUTE statement can be stored by a series of DATA statements. The argu-
ments of these statements can be variables rather than strings. For example,
this fragment is functionally identical with the previous example:

```
Var1="FD"; Var2="Y"
DATA Var1; DATA Var2
EXECUTE "ED STAFF BLOGGS-J"
```

8.4   Control structures

Frequently, you will want to direct the machine to do one thing if something
is true, or another if it is false, or to do something to all the names in a list
until some condition is satisfied. Pick BASIC provides several devices for this
kind of work. In many cases there will be more than one way of encoding the
same logic, and a combination of taste and convenience will determine which
you use in a particular instance.

8.4.1   The IF-THEN-ELSE construction

The control structure that is closest to ordinary English goes like this:

```
IF Code=44 THEN
    Country="UK"
    ...
END ELSE
    Country="ABROAD"
    ...
END
```

If the variable "Code" has been assigned the value 44, the machine will execute the code starting from "Country="UK"", otherwise it will execute the code starting from "Country="ABROAD"". Notice the END before ELSE; this is mandatory and very easy to forget.[12]

You don't have to have an ELSE clause:

```
IF Code=44 THEN
        Country="UK"
END
CRT Country
```

is a lawful piece of code.

If you want to execute only one statement after THEN and ELSE, you can use a one-line version of IF-THEN-ELSE. For example you could write

```
IF Code=44 THEN Country="UK" ELSE Country="ABROAD"
CRT Country
```

8.4.2   The CASE and ON constructions

Suppose you are encoding a menu that allows a user to do a variety of things depending on which key he or she hits. You could use the IF-THEN construction for this job but it would be messy. Pick BASIC permits the following elegant solution of this problem:

```
1 CRT @(10,10):
INPUT Key,1:
BEGIN CASE
CASE Key="Q" OR Key="q"
    STOP
CASE Key=1
    GOSUB 100
CASE Key=2
    GOSUB 200
CASE Key=3
    GOSUB 300
CASE 1=1
    CRT CHAR(7)
    CRT @(10,23):"Sorry, you must hit 1-3 or Q to quit."
END CASE
GOTO 1
```

---

[12] It appears to be totally redundant and ripe for abolition!

The decision-making code all lies between the statements BEGIN CASE and END CASE. There is a CASE statement for each possibility, each CASE being followed by a condition, "Key=1" etc. The machine evaluates these in turn, starting at the top, until it finds one that is true. Then it executes the code that follows that CASE statement. So in our example, if the operator hits Q, the program will terminate, while if the operator hits 2, the machine will execute GOSUB 200, i.e. it will execute the subroutine labelled 200 (see §8.6). When this subroutine has been executed, control will pass to the statement after END CASE, that is, "GOTO 1". In our example the condition attached to the last CASE is certainly true; 1 *is* equal to 1. Hence if the key entered is none of the things associated with the other CASEs, the code following the last CASE will be executed. This ability to have a catch-all clause is one of the great strengths of the CASE construction.

With IF and CASE you will be able to direct the machine through any logical maze. But sometimes you will weary of writing all those BEGIN CASE, END CASE statements and want something snappier. So try this

```
1 INPUT @(10,10):Key,1:
  IF Key="Q" OR Key="q" THEN STOP
  ON Key GOSUB 100,200,300
  GOTO 1
```

This code isn't as powerful as our previous example, but it *is* snappier and it does much the same job; the subroutine 100 is executed if you hit 1, while the subroutine 200 is executed if you hit 2 etc. The GOSUB could be replaced by GOTO.

8.4.3   Repetition

We can work our way through a pile of identical tasks with the FOR-NEXT construction:

```
FOR i=1 TO 10
      Cost(i)=100*i/5+13
NEXT i
```

In this example i is assigned the values 1, 2... in turn and for each value the ith element of the array "Cost" is assigned the value $100*i/5+13$ (i.e. 33, 53...).

You can start and stop the repetition where you like, and you can move in steps of any size. For example we can write

```
Start=-40; Stop=30; Step=10
FOR i=Start TO Stop STEP Step
      Cost(i+41)=100*i/5+13
NEXT i
```

The variable "i" will now take the values $-40, -30, -20 \ldots$ until 30 is reached.

The FOR-NEXT construction is fine so long as you know how many times you want to repeat *before* the FOR statement is reached. But sometimes you want to do something until a condition is satisfied, and the right tool for this job is the LOOP construction. Here's an example:

```
CRT @(-1):"    Profitable Items":CHAR(13)
i=0
LOOP
     i=i+1
     Profit(i)=Price(i)-Cost(i)
UNTIL Profit(i)<0 DO
     CRT Stock(i),Profit(i)
REPEAT
i=i-1; CRT CHAR(13):"Number of profitable items: ":i
```

The LOOP construction breaks your code up into two sections. The section between LOOP and UNTIL is executed at least once, whereas the code between UNTIL and REPEAT is executed only if the condition given in the UNTIL statement is satisfied. If it is satisfied, and the code to REPEAT is executed, control then passes back to the statement following LOOP, and the code from there until UNTIL is executed once more. When the condition given in the UNTIL statement proves false, control passes to the statement following REPEAT and repetition ceases. In our example i is first increased from 0 to 1 and the profit on the first item is calculated. If this profit is greater than zero, it and the corresponding stock name are printed. i is then increased to 2, the profit on the second item calculated, and the cycle repeated until an unprofitable item is found. At that point i is decremented by one to the number of profitable items, this number is printed, and the cycle ceases.

8.4.4   Booleans

We have seen several examples of expressions like "IF Code=44 THEN" and "CASE Key=1". In these examples the behaviour of the program is controlled by the truth or falsehood of the conditions "Code=44" and "Key=1". From simple conditions like these we can construct more complex ones, such as

```
Code=44 AND Key=1
```

Any such condition is called a **Boolean** after George Boole (1815–1864), the father of symbolic logic. A knowledge of how to manipulate Booleans will enable you to write elegant programs to conquer the most complex of problems.

We can assign a Boolean to a variable thus[13]

```
Prop=(Code=44)
```

---

[13] The brackets around "Code=44" are very helpful to the eye but strictly speaking not called for by the computer.

When this statement is executed, the variable `Prop` is assigned the value 1 if the Boolean "Code=44" is true, and 0 if it is false.

The basic Booleans are formed with the six operators <, <=, =, >=, > and #. Here the symbols "<=" and ">=" stand for "less than or equal to" and "greater than or equal to". Thus the statement

```
Cheap=(Cost.increase<=0.2)
```

assigns "Cheap" the value 0 (false) only if `Cost.increase` is greater than 0.2. The "#" symbol means "not equal to". Thus we might program

```
Provincial=(Area.code#"01")
```

This example illustrates not only the use of "#", but the fact that we can use logical operators on strings such as `Area.code` as well as on numbers such as `Cost.increase`. Two strings are equal if they are identical and are not equal if they differ in any character. One string is less than another if it would come before the other in an alphabetical listing. Thus the statement

```
Prop=("string"<"strong")
```

assigns "Prop" the value 1 (true) since "string" would come before "strong" in an alphabetical list. A Boolean such as (`"string"<"strong"`) which involves alphabetical ordering, is called a **lexical Boolean**.

As far as Pick BASIC is concerned, capitals letters are quite different characters from their lower-case equivalents (see also §4.3.1). The difference between, for example, `A` and `a` profoundly affects lexical Booleans. For example, the Boolean (`"String"#"string"`) is true. The way Pick BASIC decides whether one string lexically precedes another is as follows.

The basic rule is exactly the same as that used to determine the positions of words in an ordinary dictionary. But the "alphabet" used by Pick BASIC is not the ordinary alphabet of 26 letters, but the sequence of 256 ASCII characters listed in Appendix 2. *All* capital letters precede *all* lower-case letters in this sequence. Hence these Booleans are both true: (`"String"<"string"`), (`"String"<"spring"`).

`NOT` is an operator that negates the Boolean to which it is applied. Thus

```
Prop.2=NOT(Prop.1)
```

causes `Prop.2` to be assigned the value 0 if `Prop.1` is true and 1 if `Prop.1` is false.

`NUM` can be used to discover whether a variable has been assigned a numeric rather than a string value. For example, the code

```
Cost=12
Profit="excessive"
Prop.1=NUM(Cost)
Prop.2=NUM(Profit)
```

will assign `Prop.1` the value 1 and `Prop.2` the value 0.

`ALPHA` tells us whether the value assigned to a variable is a string that contains only letters of the alphabet. Thus

```
Prop.1=ALPHA("excessive")
```

will assign `Prop.1` the value 1.

The logical operators "AND" and "OR" allow us to combine Booleans in the obvious way; the code

```
Area.code="Ø865"
Prop.1 = ("bad">"mad") AND (Area.code#"Ø1")
Prop.2 = ("bad">"mad") OR (Area.code#"Ø1")
Prop.3 = ALPHA(Area.code) OR ("bad"<"mad" AND NUM(Area.code))
```

would assign 0 (false) to `Prop.1`, and 1 (true) to `Prop.2` and to `Prop.3`.

8.5   Intrinsic functions

We have already encountered several of the **functions** that Pick BASIC makes available to you as a programmer. For example, `NUM`, `ALPHA` and `CHAR`. A function is a variable whose value depends on an **argument**—the thing you put in brackets after it. For example, `NUM(x)` is a function of the argument `x`, which takes the value 1 if `x` is a number and 0 otherwise. Appendix 3 contains a bewilderingly long list of such functions. Let's look at a few of the most useful of these functions ordered by function rather than alphabetically.

`ABS(x)` is simply `x` without its sign; so `ABS(x)` takes the value `x` if `x` is greater than or equal to zero and `ABS(x)` takes the value `-x` if `x` is less than zero.

`INT(x)` is the integer part of `x`. For example `n=INT(2.3)` assigns 2 to `n`.[14]

`CHAR(n)` is simply the nth ASCII character from Appendix 2.

`DATE()` returns today's date in internal Pick format. Most of our programs begin with

```
Today=DATE()
```

since we usually need today's date somewhere in the program.

`TIME()` returns the current time in Pick internal format, i.e., the number of seconds since midnight. For example, "`Time=TIME()`".

`TIMEDATE()` returns the current time and date in human format. Thus if at 6.30 pm on 20 June 1990 we execute the statement

```
Now=TIMEDATE()
```

the variable "`Now`" will be assigned the value "`18:30:00 20 JUN 1990`".

`ICONV(x,y)` converts dates and times from human format into internal Pick format (see §3.5.2). For example

---

[14] Strictly, `INT(x)` means "the greatest integer not larger than `x`". Thus `INT(-2.3)` takes the value -3, not -2.

```
Day=20; Month=6; Year=90
Hdate=Day:"-":Month:"-":Year
Date=ICONV(Hdate,"D")
Second=0; Minute=30; Hour=18
Htime=Hour:":":Minute:":":Second
Time=ICONV(Htime,"T")
```

would assign to the variable "Date" the internal Pick date of June 20th, 1990 and assign to Time the internal Pick time of 6.30 pm.

OCONV(x,y) converts times and dates from Pick format to human format. Thus if the variables "Date" and "Time" have been assigned as in the last example, doing

```
Hdate=OCONV(Date,"D")
Htime=OCONV(Time,"T")
```

will assign to Hdate the string "20 JUN 1990" and to Htime the string "18:30:00". A useful variation of the first of these statements is

```
Hdate=OCONV(Date,"D2")
```

When the second argument of OCONV is "D2" rather than "D", the computer gives you only the last two digits of the year. Thus in our second example Hdate is assigned the value "20 JUN 90".

DCOUNT(String,Char) returns one more than the number of times the character "Char" occurs in "String". DCOUNT lets you discover how many attributes there are in a dynamic array. For example,

```
Attributes=DCOUNT(Item,CHAR(254))
```

assigns to the variable "Attributes" the number of attributes in the dynamic array "Item" by counting attribute marks, CHAR(254) (see Appendix 2). Similarly, the statements

```
Values=DCOUNT(Item<4>,CHAR(253))
Sub.values=DCOUNT(Item<4,5>,CHAR(252))
```

respectively determine the number of values in Item's fourth attribute, and the number of sub-values in this attribute's fifth value.

INDEX(String,Bit,n) returns the position of the nth occurrence of the string "Bit" in the string "String". Thus the statement

```
x=INDEX("complicated","c",2)
```

assigns 7 to x since the seventh character in "complicated" is the second occurrence of the letter c.

```
x=INDEX("complicated","cat",1)
```

would also assign 7 to x since the first occurrence of "cat" in "complicated" starts at the seventh character. If the string being sought does not occur in the given string, INDEX returns the position 0. For example, after execution of

```
x=INDEX("complicated","cat",2)
```

x would be assigned the value 0.

FIELD(String,Mark,n) returns the piece of String which lies between the $(n-1)^{th}$ and n^{th} occurrences of the string Mark. In most applications the space character is assigned to Mark. Then doing

```
Word=FIELD(Sentence,Mark,n)
```

assigns the nth word in the string Sentence to Word. If Sentence consists of just one word, this is assigned to Word when 1 is assigned to n, and the null string is assigned to Word when n has any other value. Similarly, if Sentence contains several words, you extract the first word by assigning to n the value 1 and the last word by assigning to n the value m, where m is the number of words in Sentence.

COL1() and COL2(). After using FIELD these functions will return the columns of the Mark characters that delimit the string FIELD has just extracted. So

```
Word=FIELD("Cat sat on a mat"," ",2)
C1=COL1(); C2=COL2()
```

will assign "sat" to Word, 4 to C1 and 8 to C2.

LEN(String) returns the number of characters in String.

SEQ(String) returns the ASCII number of the first character of String. Thus

```
n=SEQ("Apple")
```

assigns 65 to n since this is the ASCII number of a capital A (see Appendix 2).

SPACE(n) returns a string consisting of n spaces.

STR(String,n) returns the string that consists of String repeated n times. Thus STR(" ",n) is identical with SPACE(n), and STR("no",2) returns "nono".

RND(n) returns a random integer in the range 0–n.

In addition to these relatively straightforward functions, we should discuss at somewhat greater length three functions concerned with the manipulation of dynamic arrays.

8.5.1   The INSERT & DELETE functions

Suppose the Daft Party comes to power and the Government announces legislation requiring employers to keep records of the colours their employee's eyes. Clearly, the new data should go into the file "STAFF" along with records of sex, age and so forth. It would be neat if the colour of each employee's eyes could be recorded on the fifth attribute of his or her item in STAFF, after the date of birth and before the home address. This program will enable you to enter the required data in an orderly way:

```
    PROMPT ""
    OPEN "","STAFF" TO People ELSE NULL
    EXECUTE "SSELECT STAFF"
  1 READNEXT Person ELSE STOP
    READ Employee FROM People,Person ELSE NULL
    CRT @(-4):"What colour are ":Person:"'s eyes? ":
    INPUT Colour:
    Employee=INSERT(Employee,5;Colour)
    WRITE Employee ON People,Person
    GOTO 1
```

After this program has been run, the addresses that were stored on the fifth
attribute of each item will have moved down to the sixth attribute, the post-
codes that were on the sixth attributes will have moved to the seventh, and
so on.

Fortunately, the Daft party don't remain in office long enough to enact
their colour-conscious legislation. So with a sigh you decide to delete all those
idiotic colours. All you have to do is to modify your old code by eliminating
two statements and changing a third, so that it reads

```
    PROMPT ""
    OPEN "","STAFF" TO People ELSE NULL
    EXECUTE "SSELECT STAFF"
  1 READNEXT Person ELSE STOP
    READ Employee FROM People,Person ELSE NULL
    Employee=DELETE(Employee,5)
    WRITE Employee ON People,Person
    GOTO 1
```

The statement containing DELETE eliminates the new fifth attributes, thus
restoring the file "STAFF" to its former state.

In this example, INSERT was used to add a new attribute. You can
also add a new value or sub-value. For example, the following statement
would have allowed you to add the colour data as a new second value of each
employee's third attribute, which now stores just their sex:

```
    Employee=INSERT(Employee,3,2;Colour)
```

If the Daft Party had stayed in power and subsequently announced a requirement that employers also record hair colour, the new data could then have
been added as a second sub-value alongside eye colour:

```
    Employee=INSERT(Employee,3,2,2;Hair.colour)
```

DELETE stands ready to undo either of these modifications. For example,
the statements

```
    Employee=DELETE(Employee,3,2,2)
    Employee=DELETE(Employee,3,2,1)
    Employee=DELETE(Employee,3,2)
```

would eliminate, respectively, data on the colour of hair, on the colour of eyes and of hair and eyes together.

Just two more things about INSERT and DELETE:

(i) Statements involving these functions can contain two different dynamic arrays. For example, if you executed the statement

```
Crazy=INSERT(Employee,5;Colour)
```

then the dynamic array "Employee" would remain unchanged, and the dynamic array "Crazy" would contain all the data in Employee plus the new colour data.

(ii) If an attribute, value or sub-value index in an INSERT statement is -1, then the new data are inserted *after* all existing data in the corresponding bit of the array. For example, the statement

```
Employee=INSERT(Employee,-1;Colour)
```

would add the value of Colour as a new last attribute of Employee.

8.5.2   The LOCATE function

The LOCATE function is provided to help you decide where you want to INSERT a bit of data. In its simplest form LOCATE simply inspects the attributes of a dynamic array looking for one that matches a given string. For example, executing

```
LOCATE("Joe",Employee;k) ELSE NULL
```

would assign to k the index of the attribute of the dynamic array "Employee" that has the value "Joe". If no attribute has the value "Joe", k is set to one more than the number of attributes searched and the statement that follows ELSE is executed. The ELSE clause is mandatory.

Frankly, in this form LOCATE isn't of much use. However, LOCATE *is* useful when you are trying to keep data in alphabetical or numerical order. For example, suppose that Committee is a dynamic array whose attributes contain the names of the members of a committee, and you want these ordered alphabetically. Then these are the statements to use when adding to Committee the name of a new member:

```
INPUT Name:
LOCATE(Name,Committee;k;"AL") ELSE NULL
Committee=INSERT(Committee,k;Name)
```

The "AL" in LOCATE's brackets stands for 'ascending order, left justified'. Normal alphabetical or numerical ordering is what is meant by ascending order. 'Left justification' means alphabetical rather than numerical ordering. So in our example the value assigned to k is that which will place Newman after Nemo and before Neymann. If you wanted to arrange the names of committee members in reverse alphabetical order, you would replace "AL" by "DL" for 'descending order, left justified'.

The statements

```
      INPUT Part.no:
      LOCATE(Part.no,Stock.list;k;"AR") ELSE NULL
      Stock.list=INSERT(Stock.list,k;Part.no)
```

would let you keep a list of numbers such as part numbers in numerical order. The "AR" stands for 'ascending order right justified'– right justification ensures that 90 comes before 100 even though 9 comes after 1. By replacing "AR" by "DR" you could keep a list of parts in descending numerical order.

In the examples we have given so far, LOCATE is used to order attributes within an item. But LOCATE can also be used to maintain order amongst the values of a single attribute, or amongst the sub-values of a single value. For example, if each part number were stored as a value of some attribute, say the third, of the array "Stock.list", then you would modify the last example by adding ",3" after the array-name "Stock.list":

```
      INPUT Part.no:
      LOCATE(Part.no,Stock.list,3;k;"AR") ELSE NULL
      Stock.list=INSERT(Stock.list,3,k;Part.no)
```

If the part numbers were to be stored as sub-values of the second value of the third attribute of Stock.list, the "3"s in the last example would be replaced by "3,2".

8.6 Subprograms

You will often need to use the same logic at several different points in a program. Fortunately you don't have to write this logic out more than once because Pick BASIC allows you to gather together a group of statements into a special unit, called a **subprogram**, which you can call upon at any time with a single statement. Identifying sections of code that can be rearranged into subprograms not only saves you time but makes your programs much easier to read and maintain since it helps you to separate tried and tested pieces of code from new, error-prone bits.

8.6.1 The GOSUB statement

Most of our programs contain a subprogram that looks something like this:

```
!                             Message printing
!
1000 IF Lines<0 THEN; CRT CHAR(7); Lines=-Lines; END
     IF Lines=2 THEN
           CRT @(0,21):@(-3):Text.1:
           CRT @(0,22):Text.2:
     END ELSE
           CRT @(0,22):@(-4):Text.1:
     END
     RETURN
```

Whenever the machine needs to say something that is a bit out of the main flow of the program, such as requesting supplementary information from the user or complaining that the user has entered something inappropriate, this **subroutine** is called by executing the statement

```
GOSUB 1000
```

However, before the statement "GOSUB 1000" is executed, the first line of the message the machine is to print is assigned to "Text.1" and any second line is assigned to "Text.2". Then "Lines" is set to the number of lines in the message, or minus that if the user has done something dumb. When these preparations are complete GOSUB 1000 is executed and control is transferred to the statement labelled 1000. The machine beeps if Lines is negative, prints the message at the bottom of the screen and leaves the cursor there waiting for the user to reply. When the RETURN statement is executed, control passes to the statement immediately following the GOSUB statement that activated the subroutine. The calling code might look like this

```
100 CRT @(10,3):"Date of arrival? (D/M/Y) ":
    INPUT Date:
    IF Date="Q" OR Date="q" THEN STOP
    K1=INDEX(Date,"/",2)
    IF K1=0 THEN
         Text.1="Invalid date!"; Lines=-1
         GOSUB 1000; GOTO 100
    END
    Day=FIELD(Date,"/",1); Month=FIELD(Date,"/",2)
    Year=FIELD(Date,"/",3)
    Pdate=ICONV(Day:"-":Month:"-":Year,"D")
    IF Pdate<=Today THEN
         Text.1="This date is already past!"
         Text.2="Are you sure that this is the correct date? (Y/N) "
         Lines=2; GOSUB 1000; INPUT Key:
         IF Key#"Y" AND Key#"y" THEN GOTO 100
    END
```

Here there are two calls to subroutine 1000. The first call is made if the user inputs an unintelligible date, the second if the date proves to be in the past. In the first case the machine beeps; in the second it asks you to confirm that the date is correct.

It is very important that control returns from a subroutine to the calling section by means of a RETURN statement. One is sometimes tempted to leave a subroutine by executing a GOTO statement, but though this may at first appear to work, it will eventually lead to disaster. Do it often enough and your program will fail, possibly bringing the whole system to a halt in the process.

8.6.2   The CALL statement

GOSUB works fine for transferring control to a small subroutine, but is not suitable for gluing together large sections of code or whole programs. One situation in which you might want something more powerful than GOSUB is the following. Imagine you are building a hotel-management system. You have constructed programs for maintaining staff records, room bookings and guests' charges. Now you want to make all of these programs available from a menu. So you write a new program that looks something like this

```
    OPEN "","STAFF" TO People ELSE NULL
    OPEN "","ROOM.FILE" TO Rooms ELSE NULL
    OPEN "","GUEST.FILE" TO Guests ELSE NULL
    PROMPT ""
  1 CRT @(-1):SPACE(35):"Main Menu"
    CRT @(10,3):"1) Staff records"
    CRT @(10,4):"2) Room enquiries"
    CRT @(10,5):"3) Guests' charges"
    CRT @(10,6):"4) Quit"
  2 CRT @(30,8):@(-4):"Enter your choice: ":
!
    INPUT Key,1:
    BEGIN CASE
    CASE Key=1
        CALL STAFF.REC(People)
    CASE Key=2
        CALL ROOM.REC(Rooms,Guests)
    CASE Key=3
        CALL GUEST.CHARGE(Rooms,Guests)
    CASE Key=4
        STOP
    CASE 1
        CRT CHAR(7); GOTO 2
    END CASE
    GOTO 1
```

This program starts by opening all the files that will be needed by your programs and setting the prompt. Then it displays a menu. As soon as the user selects a valid item from the menu, a CALL statement is executed. This starts up one of your existing programs. When this program is done it will return control to the statement that follows the original CALL statement, in this case the statement "GOTO 1". The user can then select again from the menu.

Once you have written this menu program, you next edit your old programs slightly to make them compatible with it. Consider for example the program that maintains the STAFF file. This currently opens the file "STAFF" to, say, the variable "Employees". To make this program compatible with the menu program you have to do the following:

1. Edit in a new first attribute which reads

```
SUBROUTINE STAFF.REC(Employees)
```

2. Delete the statements associated with opening `""STAFF" TO Employ-
ees"`.

3. Change every STOP statement to a RETURN statement.

The SUBROUTINE statement *must* be the very first attribute of the file;
you may not precede it with comment attributes.

When all your old programs have been similarly modified and compiled,
they must be CATALOGed (see the introduction to this chapter) under the
names given in the SUBROUTINE statements. Only then are you ready to run
your new menu program.

The fundamental difference between a GOSUB statement and a call to a
CATALOGed subroutine lies in the way variables are transferred between the
calling program and the subroutine. When you transfer control with GOSUB
all the variables that you have defined anywhere in the calling program are
available to the subroutine. So if a variable "Thing" is assigned the value
1066 in subroutine 200, the statement

```
Object=Thing
```

in subroutine 300 called a statement later will assign to Object the value 1066
as well. By contrast, if you assign the value 1066 to Thing and straight away
CALL a CATALOGed subroutine in which the statement Object=Thing is immediately executed, an error message will be printed and Object will be assigned
the value 0 *unless* Thing was an argument of the CALLed subroutine. Thus
Thing is not defined in the subroutine unless the latter is headed something
like

```
SUBROUTINE WORKHORSE(Thing,...)
```

In addition to simple variables such as Thing and file variables such
as People, you can also transfer dimensioned arrays or dynamic arrays to
a CALLed subroutine. Thus the calling program could pass an array called
"Pieces":

```
DIM Pieces(1Ø)
......
CALL WORKHORSE(Thing,MAT Pieces)
......
```

to a subroutine in which the array is called "Ofeight":

```
SUBROUTINE WORKHORSE(Object,MAT Ofeight)
DIM Ofeight(1Ø)
......
```

As this example shows, in the subroutine you need not call the variables by
their old names. However, you must correctly redimension any dimensioned
arrays and you must flag that the variable you are passing is a dimensioned
array by preceding its name with "MAT".

COMMON statements. COMMON statements provide an alternative, and in some ways more efficient, way of passing the values of variables to and from CALLed subroutines. COMMON statements should go near the beginning of your programs and look like this

```
COMMON Thing,Pieces(10),Object
```

Notice that both simple variables such as Object and Thing and dimensioned arrays such as Pieces can appear in a COMMON statement. Dynamic arrays by contrast may *not* appear in COMMON statements. Since the size of a dimensioned array is specified in the COMMON statement, an array which appears in a COMMON statement should *not* be additionally declared in a DIM statement.

The way a COMMON statement facilitates communication between a CALLed subprogram and the CALLing program is this. Suppose the calling program has the COMMON statement given above and suppose that the CALLed subroutine starts like this

```
SUBROUTINE WORKHORSE
COMMON Thing,Pieces(10),Object
...
```

Then any assignment such as "Thing=21" in the CALLing program will cause Thing to be subsequently assigned the value 21 in the CALLed program also. Conversely, if we make the assignment "Thing=21" in the CALLed program, then after we return to the CALLing program this assignment will still be in effect. Thus the given COMMON statements enable the variable Thing to be shared by both program units as if WORKHORSE were reached by a GOSUB statement rather than a CALL statement.

However, when we transfer control by a CALL statement rather than a GOSUB statement and use COMMON statements to transfer variables, the names of variables can change between CALLing and CALLed programs. For example, if we changed the first attributes of WORKHORSE to

```
SUBROUTINE WORKHORSE
COMMON It,Pieces(10),Object
...
```

then It would be assigned the value 21 whenever 21 had previously been assigned to Thing in the CALLing program.

Moreover, COMMON statements allow us, on passing between program units, to merge a simple variable into an array. For example, suppose WORKHORSE begins like this

```
SUBROUTINE WORKHORSE
COMMON Pieces(11),Object
...
```

Here the array Pieces has expanded to 11 elements and comes right at the beginning of the COMMON statement. Now assigning 21 to Thing in the CALLing program would in the CALLed subprogram have the effect of assigning 21 to Pieces(1) since in the CALLed subprogram the latter occupies the position in the COMMON statement that is occupied by Thing in the CALLing program. In other words, the correspondence between variables in two program units linked by COMMON statements is determined by their positions within their respective COMMON statements.

8.6.3   The STOP and CHAIN statements

Most programs end in a STOP statement. When this is executed the program finishes and the machine issues a TCL prompt while it awaits further instructions. Sometimes it is clear what the next TCL command should be. For example, you might want to ensure that the user is automatically logged off the machine once the execution of his or her program ceases. In that case you could replace each STOP statement with

    CHAIN "OFF"

This statement will do the trick because CHAIN passes control to whatever TCL command follows it, in this case the verb "OFF".

Any valid TCL command can be issued by CHAIN. For example, we could write

    CHAIN "RUN PROGRAMS POLISH-OFF"

and the machine's next action would be to run the Pick BASIC program "POLISH-OFF". Similarly,

    CHAIN 'SSELECT STAFF WITH SEX "NEUTER"'

is a valid statement. In this respect CHAIN is very like EXECUTE. The crucial difference is that when a program issues a TCL command with CHAIN, it does not recover control when the command has been carried out, whereas it does recover control if it issues the command with EXECUTE; after a CHAINed command the machine returns to TCL.

With CHAIN, as with EXECUTE, one or more DATA statements can be used to store information which the command you are about to issue will seek from the keyboard. Thus the following is lawful:

    DATA "FD"; DATA "Y"
    CHAIN "ED STAFF 'BLOGGS-J'"

The item "BLOGGS-J" in STAFF will be deleted and then the machine will issue a TCL prompt.

In the special case in which the CHAIN statement is being used to transfer control between two Pick BASIC programs, there is provision for transferring the values of variables declared in DIM and COMMON statements between the expiring program and the program that is to assume control. You instruct the machine to transfer the values of these variables by appending "(I)" to the name of the program the machine is to CHAIN to. Thus the expiring program we might read

```
DIM Var(1),Array.1(1Ø),Array.2(23)
COMMON Single,Lots(2Ø)
......
CHAIN "POLISH-OFF (I)"
```

while in the program that is to take over we have

```
DIM Thing(1),Matrix(33)
COMMON Single,Lots(2Ø)
......
```

When the new program takes over, the single element of Thing will be assigned the same value as Var(1) and the first ten elements of Matrix will be assigned the values of the elements of Array.1. Elements 11-33 of Matrix will be assigned the values of the elements of Array.2. The variable "Single" and the array "Lots" will have the same values in the new program as in the old.

8.7   File locking

Before leaving the subject of Pick BASIC we must discuss the vexed topic of 'file locking'. The problem is the following. One user, let's say George the warehouseman, reads the item "WIDGET" in the file "STOCK" preparatory to recording that he has just dispatched 100 widgets to the Consolidated Gadget Corp. Unfortunately, before he can record this movement, the 'phone rings and many minutes go by while he discusses with his girlfriend their plans for the weekend. Meanwhile Sandra in marketing, working at top speed, changes the price of widgets as recorded in the item "WIDGET" of the file "STOCK". Eventually George puts down the 'phone and finishes recording his shipment of widgets. But the copy of the item "WIDGET" he has loaded into his program is now out of date—it was read from the disk before Sandra recorded the increased price of widgets and so shows the old price rather than the new. George doesn't know this, so he calmly finishes recording his shipment unaware that he is about to bankrupt his employer and lose his job; when he hits RETURN to record the shipment, his copy of the item "WIDGET" is written on the disk, and Sandra's price increase is lost. So the Consolidated Gadget Corp. gets billed for those 100 widgets, but the old uneconomic price remains in force for a month before anybody finds out, and George's outfit goes into bankruptcy.

Pick has two answers to this horror story. From the fact that there are *two* answers you know that neither is entirely satisfactory.

The READU statement.   George's program READ the item "WIDGET". Had it READUed the item, the mischief could have been avoided. The READU statement works just like the READ statement (§8.3.1) except that it **locks** the item. Locking an item prevents any other user either (i) reading the item with a READU statement, or (ii) writing over it. So if Sandra's program had attempted to READU the item "WIDGET" while George was on the 'phone,

Pick would have told it to wait because the requested item was locked. Pick would also have caused George's terminal to beep to let him know that he was holding someone up and should finish recording his shipment, pronto. The item would have been automatically unlocked when George's program wrote it with a WRITE statement.[15]

Items that are locked can still be read with a READ statement. Hence a possible strategy for avoiding clashes such as that of George and Sandra is the following:

(i) Ensure that *every* program that might conceivably write an item to disk reads it by means of a READU statement rather than a READ statement.

(ii) Programs that simply seek information and cannot write an item should merely READ the item.

There are two problems with this strategy:

(i) A program may lock an item with READU and then fail to unlock it by subsequently executing a WRITE statement. This might happen, for example, when a user aborts an update operation, perhaps because it was started in error. Pick BASIC has a statement "RELEASE" that will unlock *all* locks set by a program. If you use READU anywhere, you should ensure that a RELEASE statement is executed whenever an update is aborted. If this is not done, forgotten locks will eventually bring your system to a halt. In such a case you can get things going again by using the TCL command "CLEAR-BASIC-LOCKS" to unlock all locked items, but prevention is surely better than cure.

(ii) In older versions of Pick, READU doesn't just lock an individual item but a whole group (see §3.2.1). Hence users may be needlessly held up by a lock which is designed to protect an item they don't actually wish to read.

The WRITEV statement.   In view of the difficulties with record locking just discussed, it is worth considering an alternative strategy for eliminating the conflict between George and Sandra which is based on the WRITEV statement. WRITEV writes just one attribute rather than the entire item. In George's program the format would be

```
WRITEV Quantity ON Stockfile,"WIDGET",5
```

Here Quantity is the name of the variable which contains the number of widgets in hand, which George has just reduced by 100, Stockfile is the variable to which the file "STOCK" was opened and 5 is the number of the attribute in which quantities in stock are held. Sandra's program would contain a statement like

```
WRITEV Price ON Stockfile,"WIDGET",3
```

---

[15] For the unlikely event that you wanted the lock to remain in place after the item was written, Pick provides the WRITEU statement, which works like WRITE except that it leaves the item locked.

Now George and Sandra would not get in each other's way since they would each only write the particular attributes for which they, and they alone, were responsible. Consequently they could both READ the same item, no locks would need to be imposed and no seizure would threaten. This is surely the best solution to the problem.

Unfortunately not all occurrences of update conflicts are as simple as that of George and Sandra, so you may need to use READU at some point. But beware!

8.8   The BASIC Debugger

Computer programs almost never work first time. All too frequently they get stuck in some rut, endlessly repeating the same instructions. At this point it is good to have some way of attracting your computer's attention short of pulling out the plug. You send an emergency halt signal by hitting the BREAK key or typing Ctrl-C (see §4.1). If the machine was running a Pick BASIC program this action will produce the following response:

```
>RUN PROGRAMS BOTCHED
*I175
*
```

The 175 is the number of the attribute of the program "BOTCHED" that the machine was executing when you hit the break key. The asterisk tells you that you are now speaking to the **BASIC debugger**.

The three most useful commands one can issue to the debugger are:

GO: this causes execution of your program to resume where it left off;
END: this terminates the program and returns the machine to TCL;
OFF: this terminates program execution and logs you off the machine.

From time to time users of perfectly good software can accidentally hit BREAK and bring their program to a halt, which is irritating for all concerned. So once you are *absolutely* sure that you've got the last bug out of your program, it is not a bad idea to disable the break key. You do this by executing the statement

    BREAK OFF

in your program (see also §7.8.4). Before the program terminates it should restore the potency of the break key by executing

    BREAK ON

9 The PROC language

Pick provides another sort of programming language in addition to Pick BASIC. This language is called PROC, which is short for "procedure". Programs written in PROC are themselves also called PROCs. In essence a PROC is just a string of TCL commands stored in a file in the order in which you would like Pick to obey them. Unfortunately, this is not the whole story, because you usually want your stored lists of TCL commands to be slightly flexible rather than doing *exactly* the same thing time after time. Allowing for this flexibility turns out to be difficult, and PROC is a rather unwieldy programming tool. Often a task that can be accomplished by a PROC could be handled more elegantly by a Pick BASIC program—a principle which we will illustrate below.

So is it really worth bothering to learn another language when there are so many more entertaining things to do? There are two reasons why it may be worth learning a little about PROCs: (i) your machine is just full of the wretched things, and (ii) some things can only be done with the aid of a PROC. Much of your machine's software is written in PROC because until recently it was not possible to encode most TCL commands in Pick BASIC; for this job you need the **EXECUTE** statement, which is a recent arrival on the scene. So over the years mountains of PROCs have been accumulated and generations of programmers have learnt to scramble nimbly over them. Consequently, you are as likely to be obliged to read a PROC as a historian is an inscription in Latin; even if PROC were to become a dead language, it would remain for some time a language with an important literature.

Our aim in this chapter is therefore two-fold:

(i) To show you how to do those few things which are best accomplished with a PROC.

(ii) To make you sufficiently familiar with PROC to be able to decipher any PROC in your system and then to change or replace it.

Alongside many of our examples we show you how the same effect can be achieved from within Pick BASIC. To understand these examples you will need to be familiar with at least the contents of §8.1 and preferably with §§8.2–8.6 as well.

9.1   Elementary PROC grammar and the POB

Every PROC is an item either in your master dictionary or in an ordinary file reserved for PROCs, called "PROCLIB", perhaps. Let us imagine for the moment that all your PROCs are in your MD—in §9.4.1 we discuss the advantages of gathering them into a library such as PROCLIB.

Consider now the following elementary PROC:

File: MD	Item: QUI

```
PQ
HWHO
P
```

The first attribute of every PROC must be PQ. These letters tell the machine it is dealing with a PROC. The second attribute in our example starts with the letter H in honour of Herman Hollerith (1860–1929), one of founders of IBM. "Hollerith" is archaic computerese for "string" (see §8.2). So the H at the beginning of the second line of our PROC introduces the string "WHO". When the machine reads "HWHO" it puts "WHO" into a thing called the **primary output buffer** (POB). The machine has two "output buffers" in which to put things. These buffers are like note pads on which the computer can compile lists. By default everything goes into the POB.

The third attribute of our example contains only the letter P for "Pass". This tells the machine to pass to the TCL interpreter everything it currently has stored in the POB, in this case just WHO, and the interpreter then executes the command. Thus once we have edited our example into an item in the MD, say the item "QUI", we can get exactly the same effect by typing "QUI" at the TCL prompt as we would by typing "WHO"; on seeing "QUI" the machine locates the item in your MD with that ID, puts "WHO" in the POB and then passes this command to the TCL interpreter for execution.

We could achieve the same effect as is achieved by our PROC "QUI" by CATALOGing as "QUI" the one-line BASIC program

```
CHAIN "WHO"
```

Logon PROCs.   Every time you log onto your Pick computer the machine runs a PROC that can be used to tailor the machine to your personal requirements. This PROC, which we shall call the **logon PROC**, is filed in your MD in the item whose ID matches your user name. Thus if your user name is SMITH, you can inspect your logon PROC by typing (see §6.2)

```
>ED MD SMITH
```

Often a particular user will run just one program. For example, the pay clerk might only run the program called "PAY" that calculates pay, insurance, taxes and so forth. Suppose the pay clerk's user name is JENNY. Then it would be a good idea to make the PROC "JENNY" read

```
HRUN PROGRAMS PAY
P
```

Then JENNY's program will start up automatically whenever she logs on, since her logon PROC passes to the TCL interpreter the command "RUN PROGRAMS PAY".

Summary

- The H command causes the string that follows the H to be transferred to the POB.
- The P command passes the contents of the POB to the TCL interpreter for execution.
- Each user has a logon PROC in his or her MD which determines what the machine does when that user logs on.

9.2   The PIB

9.2.1   The T, IP, GO & X commands and parameters

Our first example of a PROC wasn't very interesting since it didn't allow us to input anything from the keyboard. But consider the following PROC, called "HOTEL":

File: MD	Item: HOTEL

```
PQ
10 T (-1),(10,3),"1) Staff records"
T (10,4),"2) Room enquiries"
T (10,5),"3) Guests' charges"
T (10,6),"4) Quit"
T (20,8),(-4),"Enter your choice "
IP
GO A1
1 HSTAFF.REC
P
GO 10
2 HROOM.REC
P
GO 10
3 HGUEST.CHARGE
P
GO 10
4 XHave a horrible day.
```

This is the PROC you would have written before the EXECUTE statement became available, to integrate into a single menu the hotel management programs described in §8.6.2. After the statutory PQ, comes an attribute starting with T for "Terminal". The T command may be followed either by a simple string or by the same screen-formatting codes as the @-codes introduced in §8.2.1. These codes should be in brackets but without any preceding @ sign. In our example the code (-1) for "clear screen" is followed by (1∅,3) for "position the cursor at column 10, row 3". Then follows a string in quotes which is to be displayed on the screen. As this example shows, a single T command may introduce several strings or @-codes separated by commas. Our PROC "HOTEL" starts with a set of five T commands which together write on the screen something like this

```
1) Staff records
2) Room enquiries
3) Guests' charges
4) Quit
```

Enter your choice

After the T commands there comes an IP command. IP inputs a string from the keyboard into a thing called the **primary input buffer (PIB)**. There are two input buffers, but we shall have occasion to use only the default, primary one. From the moment a PROC is activated there is always something in the PIB; initially the PIB contains the line you typed at TCL to start up the PROC. In this case you type just "HOTEL", so the PIB will contain the string "HOTEL". The command IP overwrites this with whatever you enter at the keyboard. The menu printed out by all those T commands invites you to enter a number 1–4. So let us suppose you reply with "3". Then the PIB will contain just the string "3".

The contents of the PIB are divided into **parameters**; the end of one parameter and the beginning of the next is marked by a space. The first parameter is referred to as "A1" and the second as "A2" and so on.

The command "GO A1" that follows the IP command tells the machine to go to the attribute of your PROC which begins with the label that matches the first (and only) parameter in the PIB, in our case "3". This attribute says "HGUEST.CHARGE". So, obedient to the introductory H, the machine copies the string "GUEST.CHARGE" into the POB and moves to the next command, which is a P. The machine now passes to the TCL interpreter the contents of the POB, i.e. "GUEST.CHARGE".

Assuming a BASIC program "GUEST.CHARGE" has been CATALOGed, Pick now runs it. When the program terminates at a STOP statement, the computer returns to the PROC and reads the attribute after the "P", which says "GO 1∅". So the machine goes to the attribute labelled "10", which happens to be the second attribute. The menu is again displayed on the screen and the user is again invited to enter a number.

Thus the PROC "HOTEL" allows you to run your programs again and again in any order until a "4" is entered. Entering a "4" sends the machine to the attribute that starts with X for "eXit". At this point the machine exits from the PROC, returns to TCL and prints the offensive message "Have a horrible day." that follows the X. The message is optional—an X all on its own will tell the machine to return to TCL silently.

Summary

- The T command prints what follows it on the terminal. The text T is to print may contain formatting codes similar to BASIC's @-codes.
- The PIB is a series of strings, called parameters, which are separated by spaces.
- The parameters of the PIB are called A1, A2, . . .
- The IP command inputs a string from the keyboard into the PIB. By default the string becomes A1, overwriting the previous A1.
- The GO command transfers control to the attribute that starts with the given label; "GO 3" transfers control to the attribute labelled 3.
- The X command causes the machine to exit from the PROC to TCL.

9.2.2   The A command

Now let's look at a PROC that starts with more than one parameter in the PIB. The following PROC, "C" will save you much tedious typing when compiling Pick BASIC programs

File: MD	Item: C

```
PQ
HCOMPILE PROGRAMS
A2
P
```

If you put this PROC into the item "C" of your MD, you can subsequently compile the program "PROG" in the file "PROGRAMS" by typing simply "C PROG". On seeing "C" the machine locates this PROC. The second attribute of the PROC places "COMPILE PROGRAMS" in the PIB. The third attribute "A2" appends to this string a space, followed by the second parameter in the PIB. In our example this is the word "PROG" since the PIB consists of the string "C PROG". The terminating P then passes to the TCL interpreter the command

COMPILE PROGRAMS PROG

Thus this PROC effectively condenses "COMPILE PROGRAMS" into "C".

As another example, suppose you need to find all your clients whose telephone numbers start with a certain area code. It's easy to do this with an ACCESS command, but the following PROC makes it easier still:

```
          ┌──────────┬──────────────────┐
          │ File: MD │ Item: PROSPECTS  │
          └──────────┴──────────────────┘
PQ
HSORT CUSTOMERS WITH AREA.CODE
A"2
HNAME PHONE
A3
P
```

We'll call this PROC "PROSPECTS". You use it like this:

```
>PROSPECTS Ø1 ADDRESS
```

After you type this line, the PIB will contain three parameters: "PROSPECTS", "Ø1" and "ADDRESS". The machine first copies the string "SORT CUSTOMERS WITH AREA.CODE" into the POB. Then the A"2 copies the second parameter, "Ø1", from the PIB to the POB. The double quote " after the A and before the 2 tells the machine to enclose the copied parameter in quotes—so what is actually added to the POB is the string ""Ø1"". Had we typed "A'2", the string placed in the POB would have been "'Ø1'", and so on.

The attribute "HNAME PHONE" simply appends NAME PHONE to the POB.

The penultimate attribute, A3, appends the third parameter of the PIB, in our case "ADDRESS", to the POB. If you had omitted to specify a third parameter by typing simply "'PROSPECTS Ø1", the A3 command would have added nothing to the POB.

When the terminating P passes the contents of the POB to the TCL interpreter, the effect is identical to that achieved by typing

```
>SORT CUSTOMERS WITH AREA.CODE "Ø1" NAME PHONE ADDRESS
```

Summary

- An attribute beginning with A causes a parameter to be copied from the PIB to the POB. "A1" copies the first parameter, "A2" the second parameter and so on.
- If a punctuation character is inserted between the A and the digit, then the copy of the parameter in the POB is surrounded by that character.

9.2.3   The B, D, F, O, IF & S commands

As a second example of the use of a PROC to take parameters from the command line, consider the following useful PROC "CLEAN":

```
          ┌──────────┬──────────────┐
          │ File: MD │ Item: CLEAN  │
          └──────────┴──────────────┘
PQ
HCLEAR-FILE DATA
A2
OYou have asked me to erase all data in the file +
D2
O.
OAre you sure you want me to do this? (Y/N) +
IP
IF A3 # Y XAborted
P
```

This PROC would let you clear out the data section of the file "PROGRAMS" by typing "CLEAN PROGRAMS". Since this is rather a drastic step to take, CLEAN, unlike the underlying Pick utility CLEAR-FILE, will give you a chance for second thoughts by asking for confirmation.

The way CLEAN works is this. The second and third attributes assemble in the POB the fatal line "CLEAR-FILE DATA PROGRAMS". Then an attribute starting with "O" for Output writes on the screen the message "You have asked me to erase all data in the file ". The O command works very much like the T command, which we could equally have used here, except that the text to be displayed should not be enclosed in quotation marks. However, an O command, unlike a T command, usually causes the cursor to drop down to a new line after printing the text that follows the O. In our example this is undesirable, so we have added plus signs at the end of two of the O attributes; these tell the cursor to wait at the end of the line it has just printed, allowing us to add to it later.

The attribute "D2" in CLEAN displays on the screen the second parameter in the PIB, i.e. the name of the file to be cleared. The following two O commands complete the message on the screen, which is

```
You have asked me to erase all data in the file PROGRAMS.
Are you sure you want me to do this? (Y/N)
```

Now the IP command inputs a further parameter to the PIB. The new parameter goes to the end of the PIB and becomes A3. CLEAN's penultimate attribute ensures that unless A3 is a "Y", the machine eXits to TCL printing the message "Aborted". If A3 is the letter Y, the fatal line is Passed to the TCL interpreter and the file is cleared.

The IF command works in a way very similar to BASIC's IF statement (§8.4.1). It understands the following relations: >,], =, [, < and #. Three of these are less than self-explanatory. In this context the symbols "]" and "[" mean "greater than or equal to" and "less than or equal to" respectively. So an attribute

```
IF A1]1Ø X
```

would cause the machine to exit to TCL if the parameter A1 were greater than or equal to 10.

As in Pick BASIC "#" means "not equal to". Thus "IF 1Ø#9" means "if 10 is not equal to 9". However, in PROCs # also performs the function of BASIC's NOT. Thus

```
IF #A1 = Y GO 1Ø
```

would cause the machine to go to the attribute labelled 10 if the first parameter in the PIB were *not* the letter Y.

There is one other form of the IF command: "IF A3 GO 1Ø" instructs the computer to go to the attribute labelled 1Ø if the PIB contains a third parameter, no matter what it is. Similarly "IF #A3 GO 1Ø" instructs the

computer to go to the attribute labelled 1Ø if there is *no* third parameter in
the PIB.

In the PROC "HOTEL" of §9.2.1, characters read from the keyboard by
the IP command overwrite the existing value of the parameter A1. So why in
CLEAN does the parameter read by an IP command become A3? The answer to
this question involves the **PIB pointer**. The PIB is equipped with a pointer,
which can be moved by any one of several commands, and which determines
where a parameter input by the IP command will be placed. When a PROC
starts up, the pointer is at the beginning of the PIB. Hence if, as in HOTEL,
a parameter is input to the PIB before the pointer has been moved, the new
parameter becomes A1. In CLEAN, by contrast, the PIB's pointer is at the end
of the PIB when the IP command is executed, so the parameter added by IP
goes into the PIB after the existing parameters, A1 and A2 and thus becomes
A3. It is the command "A2" which is responsible for moving the pointer from
the beginning to the end of the PIB; an A command moves the pointer to after
the parameter copied to the POB by that command. Thus if we execute "IP"
just after executing "A1", the new parameter becomes A2, while if we do "IP"
after "A2", the new parameter becomes A3.

While copying a parameter with the A command moves the PIB pointer,
merely referring to, say, "A2" does not. Thus in HOTEL the pointer is not
moved by the command "GO A1", and a statement of the form "IF A3 GO
1Ø" does not move the pointer either.

The A command moves the PIB pointer as a side-effect of its main function,
but PROC has several commands which *only* move the PIB's pointer. These
are:

(i) The B command which moves the pointer Back one parameter.

(ii) The F command which moves the pointer Forward one parameter.

(iii) The Sn command which Sets the pointer to the nth parameter. If n is
less than or equal to one, Sn will set the pointer to the beginning of the
PIB, while if n is greater than the number of parameters in the PIB, Sn
will set the pointer to the end of the PIB.

One of the hardest things about writing PROCs is keeping clear in one's
head what is happening in the PIB. Fortunately the command "DØ" can be
used to display the whole PIB. Thus if your PROC contains the sequence

```
DØ
D1
D
```

then when the machine reaches "DØ" it will write out the entire PIB as a single
line, while on encountering "D1" it will write just the first parameter. The
letter D all on its own causes the machine to display on the screen just the
parameter to which the PIB pointer is currently pointing. (It is worth noting
that the A command admits a similar variation; an attribute containing just
the letter A will copy to the POB the parameter to which the PIB pointer is

pointing, and "IF A # Y X" will cause the machine to return to TCL if the current parameter is not the letter Y.)

As a further example of the use of the IF and A commands, consider again the PROC "PROSPECTS" described at the start of §9.2.2. Suppose you want to ensure that whenever the third parameter is omitted, this is done intentionally rather than by accident. Then you would modify PROSPECTS like this:

File: MD	Item: PROSPECTS

```
PQ
IF A3 GO 10
S3
ODo you want to any additional attribute to be output+
IP?
10 HSORT CUSTOMERS WITH AREA.CODE
A"2
HNAME PHONE
A3
P
```

The second attribute of this example sends the machine to the attribute labelled 10 if a third parameter *was* specified. In the next attribute the S command is used to set the PIB's pointer to the third position. This ensures that the parameter input two attributes later by the IP command will become A3 rather than overwriting the old A1. Notice that this IP command is followed by a question mark. When IP is followed by a punctuation character in this way, this character is used as the prompt character in place of the default prompt character, a colon. Thus in our example the machine writes

> Do you want any additional attribute to be output?

and waits for your response. From the attribute labelled 10 onwards this PROC is identical with our original PROC "PROSPECTS".

Summary

- The O command, like the T command, outputs to the screen the text that follows it. It differs from the T command in three respects: (i) you don't need to put quotes around the string to be printed; (ii) @-codes don't work with it, and (iii) by default it causes the cursor to drop to the start of a new line after printing the given text. A new line is not started if the text finishes with a plus sign.
- The D command displays on the screen either a single parameter or the entire PIB.
- The IF command causes another command to be executed if a specified condition is satisfied.
- The S command sets the PIB's pointer to a given position. Thus executing "S2" before an IP command causes the parameter input to become A2 and so forth.

- The B command moves the PIB pointer back one parameter and the F command moves the pointer forward one parameter.

9.2.4 Passing the command line to a BASIC program

Now let's see how we use a Pick BASIC program rather than the PROC "PROSPECTS" to convert "PROSPECTS Ø1 ADDRESS" into the command

```
SORT CUSTOMERS WITH PHONE "Ø1" NAME PHONE ADDRESS
```

Unfortunately, Pick BASIC doesn't provide a way of transferring to the program the contents of the line which you typed at TCL to start the program— "PROSPECTS Ø1 ADDRESS" in this case. But one *can* achieve the same effect by starting the program from within a simple PROC. The following PROC "PROSPECTS" does this:

| File: MD | Item: PROSPECTS |

```
PQ
HRUN PROGRAMS BP
P
```

When we type at the TCL prompt "PROSPECTS Ø1 ADDRESS" this PROC passes to the TCL interpreter the command "RUN PROGRAMS BP", thus starting the following BASIC program BP:

```
DIM Parm(8)
CALL PARM.FIND(MAT Parm,Nparm)
Text='SORT CUSTOMERS WITH AREA.CODE "'
EXECUTE Text:Parm(2):'" NAME PHONE ':Parm(3)
STOP
```

Here we have CALLed the BASIC program "PARM.FIND" of Appendix 4 to transfer the second and third parameters from the calling PROC's PIB to the BASIC variables Parm(2) and Parm(3). In our example the PIB of the calling PROC is "PROSPECTS Ø1 ADDRESS", so PARM.FIND assigns "Ø1" to Parm(2) and "ADDRESS" to Parm(3). These variables are then concatenated with the rest of the desired SORT command to form the argument of the EXECUTE statement. Thus by combining a BASIC program with a simple PROC one can do the job of the PROC that started this sub-section. The required combination of a PROC and a BASIC program is rather cumbersome, but is automatically set up if you use the utility "CATALOGUE" of Appendix 4 to catalogue your BASIC programs rather than using the standard Pick utility "CATALOG"; doing "CATALOGUE PROGRAMS MYPROG" creates in your MD under the ID "MYPROG" the PROC

| File: MD | Item: MYPROG |

```
PQ
HRUN PROGRAMS MYPROG
P
```

Then, when subsequently you type "MYPROG" at the TCL prompt, the machine locates this PROC in your MD, and your BASIC program is called by the PROC rather than directly from TCL.

9.3   The SOB

Suppose you want to execute from within a PROC a TCL command that requires keyboard input in addition to whatever parameters follow the verb.
For example, suppose you often have to move items from one file into another
and tire of using the standard TCL verb COPY which requires you to enter your
requirements on two lines (see §4.2.7). You dream at night of a PROC "FIRE"
that will enable you to type simply

```
>FIRE BLOGGS-J
```

and the item BLOGGS-J in the file "STAFF" will be magically copied to the
file "FIRED" and then deleted from STAFF. The following PROC is the PROC of
your dreams:

File: MD	Item: FIRE

```
PQ
HCOPY STAFF
A2
H(D)
STON
H(FIRED<
P
```

FIRE works as follows. When you enter "FIRE BLOGGS-J" attributes 2 to 4
assemble in the POB the command "COPY STAFF BLOGGS-J (D)". Then comes
the command "STON", which stands for 'stack on'. Once this command has
been executed everything that formerly would have flowed into the POB goes
into the **secondary output buffer** (**SOB**). Anything sent to the SOB rests
there quietly until a command initiated by the contents of the POB needs
keyboard input. The contents of the SOB are then fed to the TCL command
that is demanding input. So in this example, the attribute "H(FIRED<" places
"(FIRED" followed by a carriage return into the SOB; in this context "<" is
interpreted as a carriage return. When the attribute "P" is reached and the
contents of the POB, namely "COPY STAFF BLOGGS-J (D)", is passed to the
TCL interpreter, COPY demands keyboard input. On being fed "(FIRED" COPY
copies BLOGGS-J to the file "FIRED" and deletes him from the file "STAFF".

The command "STON" is cancelled by "STOFF", which directs everything
sent to an output buffer into the POB again rather than the SOB. We illustrate
this with the following rather complex example, a PROC "KEYS" which can be
used to give users keys to the update and retrieval locks on files. In §7.8.2 we
explained how the keys that a user possesses are determined by the contents
of attributes 5 and 6 of his or her user-defining item in the file "SYSTEM". The
PROC "KEYS" is so constructed that after entering

```
>KEYS BINNEY A B
```

the item with ID "BINNEY" in the system dictionary will have attributes 5 and 6 equal to "A" and "B" respectively. Our PROC achieves this by using the System Editor (§6.2) to edit the given strings into BINNEY's attributes 5 and 6. Here it is:

File: MD	Item: KEYS

```
PQ
C Place desired read and write keys on attributes 5
C and 6 of item A2 in SYSTEM.
C Turn stack on and stash into SOB responses Editor
C will require.
STON
C First delete attributes 5 and 6
H5<
HDE2<
C Go to top of item and then to attribute 4
HF<
H4<
C Now insert A3 and A4 after existing attribute 4
HI<
A3
H<
A4
H<
C Enter a blank line to finish insertion
H<
C File item
HFI<
STOFF
HED SYSTEM
A2
PH
```

Since this is rather a long PROC we have added comment attributes to explain what is going on; attributes starting with "C" are ignored by the machine. After the comment attributes 2–5 comes the attribute "STON" which turns on the stack so that we can store in the SOB the keyboard input that will be required by the Editor when we finally invoke it: "5" to move to attribute 5, "DE2" to delete the two attributes 5 and 6, "F" to go to the top of the item again, "4" to go to attribute 4, "I" to start insertion. The attributes that stash this stuff into the SOB all start with an H and finish with the character < to indicate a carriage return. The attribute "A3" then copies into the SOB the third parameter. In our example in which the PROC was started by the command "KEYS BINNEY A B", the third parameter is the letter A. Then there comes an attribute "H<" to generate a carriage return after the parameter A3. (This carriage return has to be put on an attribute by itself; "A3<" will not work.) Two more attributes copy into the SOB the fourth parameter—"B" in our example—followed by a carriage return. Then the third attribute "H<" copies into the SOB a blank line which, when it is fed to the Editor, will stop insertion. The next attribute "HFI<" will tell the Editor to file the item.

Now that we have assembled in the SOB all the keyboard input that will be required by the System Editor, we are ready to set the Editor going by passing to the TCL interpreter the command "ED SYSTEM USERNAME", where "USERNAME" is the username of the person we wish to assign keys, in our example BINNEY. However, before we can assemble this command in the POB ready for dispatch to the TCL interpreter, we have to turn off the stack with the command "STOFF". So STOFF comes three attributes from the bottom of KEYS and is followed by the attributes "HED SYSTEM" and "A2". In our example these attributes assemble in the POB the command "ED SYSTEM BINNEY".

Our final step is to pass this command to the TCL interpreter. We could do this by saying just "P", but this would be messy since the Editor would then write all kinds of stuff on the screen which we would rather not see. So we issue a variant of the P command, "PH" which does the same job as plain P except that it suppresses (i.e., hides) any output generated by the command it passes. So when the machine reads PH it starts the System Editor and suppresses everything it would normally have displayed on the screen. The edit is completed in a moment since the Editor finds all the input it requires in the SOB and does not have to wait for a human to respond to its prompts. At the end of the edit the desired strings will be on attributes 5 and 6 of the indicated item in the System dictionary.

This is a job that can be more easily accomplished in Pick BASIC; Appendix 4 lists a program, "KEYS", that does this job and more in as many lines.

Summary

- The SOB (secondary output buffer) is used to store input which will be required by a program or TCL command that your PROC is about to start up. After the STON command has been issued, everything that the A, or H commands would normally have placed in the POB goes instead to the SOB.

- The STOFF command cancels this redirection.

- When placing parameters in the SOB, you must explicitly add any carriage returns you require by putting "<" characters at the end of your H commands.

- You can add comments on what a PROC is doing by putting them on attributes that start with a "C".

- The PH command passes the contents of the POB to the TCL interpreter but suppresses any output the passed command would ordinarily have displayed on the screen.

9.4   Calling PROCs, PROC libraries and sub-PROCs

PROC has equivalents of Pick BASIC's "CALL" and "CHAIN" statements (see §§8.6.2 and 8.6.3). For example, suppose you have in your MD a PROC called "FIXIT" and a PROC called "CLEVER" which looks like this:

```
 File: MD │ Item: CLEVER
```

```
PQ
T (-1),(10,3),"I delegate all my work to FIXIT"
[MD FIXIT]
T (10,13),"You see what I mean?"
```

Then, when at the TCL prompt you type "CLEVER", the screen will be cleared and CLEVER's first message will be displayed starting at column 10 of line 3. Then control will be transferred to FIXIT. When the machine encounters an X command in FIXIT it will return to CLEVER and write the second message above. Thus enclosing the name of a PROC in square brackets is equivalent to CALLing a CATALOGed subroutine in BASIC.

Now consider

```
 File: MD │ Item: LAZY
```

```
PQ
T (-1),(10,3),"I delegate all my work to FIXIT"
(MD FIXIT)
T (10,13),"You see what I mean?"
```

This differs from the previous example only in that "MD FIXIT" is now surrounded by round rather than by square brackets. This has the effect of transferring control to FIXIT without any possibility of return; when the machine encounters an X command in FIXIT, it will exit to TCL rather than returning to CLEVER, so CLEVER's second message will never be displayed. Thus enclosing the name of a PROC in round brackets is equivalent to CHAINing another program in BASIC.

9.4.1   PROC libraries

Every time you enter a command at the TCL prompt the machine searches through your MD to see if it can find the command you entered. It is important that this search can be quickly accomplished. However, it won't be if your MD overflows its allotted disk space and the disk heads have to jump all over the place when searching for an item (see §3.2.1). So it is important to keep the entries in your MD short and snappy, and it is not a good idea to store long PROCs in the MD. Rather you should have an ordinary Pick file "PROCLIB" devoted to PROCs. Then if you write an elaborate PROC called "STREAMLINE", say, you should make it an item in this file and in order to have the machine execute this PROC whenever you type "STREAMLINE COMPANY" at TCL, you create the following item "STREAMLINE" in your MD:

```
File: MD │ Item: STREAMLINE
```

```
PQ
(PROCLIB)
```

On seeing "STREAMLINE" the machine locates this entry in your MD. The round brackets tell it to transfer control to another PROC. However, the brackets contain only one word, where the brackets in the example "CLEVER" above contained two. The machine assumes the single word given is the name of the file containing the target PROC and that it should look for the item "STREAMLINE" in that file. Hence in this context "(PROCLIB)" is functionally equivalent to "(PROCLIB STREAMLINE)". The PROC "STREAMLINE" in PROCLIB then takes control and gets going on its elaborate task.

When the PROC in the file "PROCLIB" gets control, the PIB still contains "STREAMLINE COMPANY" just as it did when the PROC "STREAMLINE" in your MD was executed. Thus the name, "COMPANY", of the object on which you wish STREAMLINE to operate, is communicated to the version of STREAMLINE in the file "PROCLIB".

9.4.2   Sub-PROCs

The following demonstrates PROC's equivalent of BASIC's "GOSUB" statement:

```
File: MD │ Item: SILLY
```

```
PQ
1 0A demonstration of the use of sub-PROCs
0Enter 1 to continue, 0 to quit: +
IP
IF A1 = 0 X
[] 10
0This is written on return from the sub-PROC
GO 1
10 0This is written by the sub-PROC
X
```

The second and third attributes display a message on the screen. Then IP inputs a parameter from the keyboard to the PIB and this parameter is tested to see whether you want to quit. If you don't enter 0, the attribute starting with "[]" directs control to the attribute labelled 10. The machine has now entered a **sub-PROC**. The sub-PROC consists of an instruction to write a message and an X. On encountering the X the machine does not exit to TCL as it would if it were not currently in a sub-PROC, but simply goes back to the attribute following the empty square brackets "[]" that sent it into the sub-PROC. Thus from within a sub-PROC an X behaves like BASIC's "RETURN" rather than like "STOP" as it does elsewhere.

Summary

- PROC has analogues of BASIC's "CALL", "CHAIN" and "GOSUB" statements.
- When the machine reaches the name of a PROC enclosed in brackets, control is transferred to that PROC.

- The transfer of control is temporary if the brackets are square (equivalent to BASIC's "CALL"), and permanent if they are round (equivalent to BASIC's "CHAIN").
- If the brackets contain only the name of a file, Pick assumes that the CALLed or CHAINed PROC is to be found in that file under the same item ID as the currently executing PROC.
- A label preceded by empty square brackets is PROC's analogue of BASIC's "GOSUB" statement. An X command then becomes the analogue of BASIC's "RETURN" statement.

9.5   Other commands

In Table 9.1 (overleaf) we give a complete list of PROC commands. Many of the commands which we have not discussed in this chapter are merely variants of commands which we have discussed. To understand the rôles of the others you will need to consult your Pick manual. With any luck you'll never have to bother with these commands. But you should at least be aware of their existence so that you will recognize any of them that you encounter in PROCs.

Table 9.1.   Complete list of PROC commands

Command	Function	See
A	Copies parameter from input to output buffer.	§9.2.2
B	Moves input buffer pointer back one parameter.	§9.2.3
C	Introduces comment attribute.	§9.3
D	Displays parameter on screen.	§9.2.3
F	Moves input buffer pointer forward one parameter.	§9.2.3
GO	Transfers control to attribute with given label.	§9.2.1
H	Places given string in output buffer.	§9.1
IF	Transfers control if given condition satisfied.	§9.2.3
IH	Places given string in input buffer.	–
IP	Inputs string and puts it in current input buffer.	§9.2.1
IS	Inputs string and puts it in secondary input buffer.	–
IT	Clears input buffer and then inserts tape label.	–
O	Displays given string on screen.	§9.2.3
P	Passes contents of POB to TCL interpreter.	§9.1
PH	As P except suppresses command's output to screen.	§9.3
PP	As P except displays command before execution.	–
PW	As PP except waits for confirmation before execution.	–
PX	As P except exits to TCL after execution.	–
RI	Clears input buffers.	–
RO	Clears output buffers.	–
S	Sets position of current input buffer pointer.	§9.2.3
SP	Makes the PIB the active input buffer.	–
SS	Makes the secondary input buffer active.	–
STON	Redirects output to SOB.	§9.3
STOFF	Redirects output to POB.	§9.3
T	Displays strings (including @-codes) on screen.	§9.2.1
TB	Causes terminal to beep.	–
TC	Clears screen.	–
U	Exits to specified subroutine.	–
X	Exits to TCL.	§9.2.1
+	Adds a number to a parameter in an input buffer.	–
–	As + except subtracts rather than adds.	–

Appendices

Appendix 1   Port characteristics

Every Pick computer is equipped with one or more sockets, or ports, into which one can plug a cable that runs to a peripheral such as a terminal or a printer (see §1.2). Unfortunately, it is normally not enough merely to plug a peripheral into a port to get the peripheral running correctly. One has also to ensure that the port is of the right kind and set its 'characteristics' to those demanded by the peripheral. In this appendix we explain about the different kinds of port and about port characteristics.

The job of a port is to send characters (or bytes) to a peripheral. In the computer each byte is represented by a sequence of zeros and ones rather as plain English words may be represented by letters of the alphabet. But whereas English has many tens of thousands of words and these may be expressed as sequences of letters drawn from the 26-letter Roman alphabet, there are only 256 possible bytes and these may conveniently be expressed as sequences of **bits** drawn from the two-letter 'alphabet' that consists of just zero and one. For example a computer spells the byte that represents the character @ as the sequence of bits 01000000, while it spells A 01000001, and so on.

Conceptually the simplest way of transmitting such sets of bits down a cable is this. We construct a cable that has one wire for each of the byte's eight bits. Then the computer can send a byte by applying a voltage to just those wires that correspond to 1 when the byte is spelled out in bits. For example, to send an @ sign the computer would only apply a voltage to the second wire from the left, while it would send an A by applying voltages both to this wire and to the wire on the extreme right.

Most computers have at least one port that is constructed on the plan just described. Such a port is called a **parallel port**[1] since the bits that make

---

[1] Sometimes also called a Centronics interface.

up each character are sent in parallel down separate wires. Parallel ports are only used to connect printers to computers, never for terminals or modems.

Although only eight wires are needed to transmit data, the cable coming out of a parallel port contains a least thirteen wires. One of the extra wires is used by the computer to send the printer an initialization signal, something like "wake up, move your print head to the left edge of the paper and pay attention". Three other spare wires are used by the printer to send signals back to the computer. After correctly receiving each character the printer briefly raises a voltage on one wire to say "yes sir, got that". If the printer is having difficulty keeping up with the pace of the computer's dictation, it raises a voltage on another wire to say "hang on a moment, please". A third spare wire is used by the printer to signal that it is out of paper. At least one other wire is needed to provide a reference, or 'ground' voltage.

The nice thing about a parallel port is that there is nothing to set; any parallel printer should communicate successfully with any computer as soon as you plug its lead into the computer's parallel port. (Would that this could be said of communication via other types of port!) However, while a parallel port is conceptually very simple, it is physically rather cumbersome because it requires a twelve-wire cable. It is also inflexible in that it can transmit data only from the computer to a peripheral, not the other way around. Hence it cannot connect a terminal or a modem to the computer. So we now discuss an alternative strategy for sending bytes down a wire.

Data transmission through a parallel port is a bit like naval ships communicating by hoisting flags; all units of the message can be seen simultaneously. When radio transmitters were introduced in the early years of this century, navies went over to communicating in Morse code; the message was translated into a series of dots and dashes and then these were broadcast one after the other. When a computer sends data out of a **serial port** it sends the zeros and ones that make up the bytes it needs to communicate, one after another just if it were transmitting in a Morse code based on zeros and ones rather than dots and dashes.

In detail, the way communication through a serial port works is this. The computer and the peripheral are each allocated a wire whose voltage they control. When either partner wants to send a byte, it raises and lowers the voltage of its wire according to the bit pattern that represents the byte. So to send the character @, represented by 01000000, the computer (working, like an Arab, from right to left) would keep the voltage low for six time units, then raise it for a time unit and then hold it down for a further time unit. At the other end of the cable the peripheral would reconstruct the byte by monitoring these voltage variations. The key thing here is that both partners must be clear about the meaning of "one time unit". That is, they must both be told at the outset how long it takes to send or receive a bit of data, or, equivalently, how many bits can be sent per second. Terminals usually communicate with computers at 9600 bits per second, or 9600 **baud** in the jargon of the trade. Modems usually communicate with one another at either 1200 baud or 2400 baud. The lowest commonly used baud rate is 300, and the highest you are likely to encounter is 19200. The commonest single cause of trouble with serial communication is disagreement between communicating partners as to the correct baud rate to use.

Unfortunately, getting both partners to use the same baud rate isn't enough to establish smooth communication through a serial port. It is also necessary to ensure that the partners are using the same 'parity' and the same numbers of 'data bits' and 'stop bits'.

Data bits.   The most commonly used bytes, including those associated with all the keys on a normal terminal, have a zero for their left-most bit.[2] So to save time it is common to take it as understood that the left-most bit of every byte is a zero and to send only the remaining seven bits. When this understanding is in force, one says that the equipment is set to '7 data bits', in contrast to the normal setting of '8 data bits'.

Stop bits.   Just as in ordinary text one word is divided from another by a space, so in serial communication each byte is separated from the next by one **start bit** and one or more **stop bits**. (What is crucial for communication is the fall in voltage between the stop bit of one character and start bit of the next character, since the partners use the instant of this voltage change to synchronize the clocks with which they mark off each data bit.) Most equipment is set to terminate each byte with one stop bit, but it is not uncommon to use two stop bits instead.

Parity.   Stray electrical signals can creep into long cables in a variety of ways, so the receiving device may not read exactly the series of bits that was originally sent. Since erroneous data can frequently do terrible damage, it is important to be able to detect such malfunctions quickly. A simple check on the validity of every byte received is to count the number of ones in it as it is sent, and then again when it is received, and to ensure that these two numbers are either both odd or both even. In this scheme the transmitting device follows each byte by an additional bit, called the **parity bit**, that might be zero when the byte contains an even number of ones, and one otherwise. We would then say that the device had 'parity set even'. Alternatively, the parity bit could be a zero when the byte contained an odd number of ones, and one otherwise, and in this case one would say that the 'parity was set odd'. The devices are said to be communicating with 'no parity' when they are saving time by dispensing with checks on the number of zeros and ones, and not transmitting parity bits at all.

---

[2] This bit is often called the 'most significant bit'.

In summary, to establish serial communication between two devices you have to ensure that the following are set to the same values on each machine:

  (i) the baud rate;
 (ii) the number of data bits;
(iii) the number of stop bits;
 (iv) the parity.

If you don't know how some device is set up, first try the settings (9600, 8, 1, n), meaning 9600 baud, 8 data bits, 1 stop bit and no parity.

Appendix 2   The ASCII characters

0 Ctrl-@	44 ,	88 X
1 Ctrl-A	45 -	89 Y
2 Ctrl-B	46 .	90 Z
3 Ctrl-C	47 /	91 [
4 Ctrl-D	48 Ø	92 \
5 Ctrl-E	49 1	93]
6 Ctrl-F	50 2	94 ^
7 Ctrl-G (bell)	51 3	95 _
8 Ctrl-H (backspace)	52 4	96 `
9 Ctrl-I (tab)	53 5	97 a
10 Ctrl-J (line feed)	54 6	98 b
11 Ctrl-K	55 7	99 c
12 Ctrl-L (form feed)	56 8	100 d
13 Ctrl-M (enter)	57 9	101 e
14 Ctrl-N	58 :	102 f
15 Ctrl-O	59 ;	103 g
16 Ctrl-P (delete)	60 <	104 h
17 Ctrl-Q	61 =	105 i
18 Ctrl-R	62 >	106 j
19 Ctrl-S	63 ?	107 k
20 Ctrl-T	64 @	108 l
21 Ctrl-U	65 A	109 m
22 Ctrl-V	66 B	110 n
23 Ctrl-W	67 C	111 o
24 Ctrl-X	68 D	112 p
25 Ctrl-Y	69 E	113 q
26 Ctrl-Z	70 F	114 r
27 Ctrl-[(escape)	71 G	115 s
28 Ctrl-\	72 H	116 t
29 Ctrl-]	73 I	117 u
30 Ctrl-^	74 J	118 v
31 Ctrl-_	75 K	119 w
32 (space)	76 L	120 x
33 !	77 M	121 y
34 "	78 N	122 z
35 #	79 O	123 {
36 $	80 P	124	
37 %	81 Q	125 }
38 &	82 R	126 ~
39 '	83 S	127 (delete)
40 (	84 T	
41)	85 U	252 (sub-value mark)
42 *	86 V	253 (value mark)
43 +	87 W	254 (attribute mark)

Appendix 3 Pick BASIC statements and functions

Table A3.1 Pick BASIC statements

Statement	Purpose	See
ABORT	As STOP but also abandon any calling PROC	–
BEGIN CASE	Start of the CASE construction	§8.4.2
BREAK ON/OFF	Enable or disable BREAK key	§8.8
CALL	Call a CATALOGed subroutine	§8.6.2
CASE	Introduce a possibility in the CASE control structure	§8.4.2
CHAIN	Pass control to a TCL command	§8.6.3
CLEAR	Assign value 0 to all variables in the program	–
CLEARFILE	Clear out the data portion of a specified file	–
COMMON	Declare which variables will be shared between subprograms with COMMON statements	§8.6.2
CRT	Display on the screen	§8.2.1
DATA	Store responses that will be required by an EXECUTEd or CHAINed process	§8.3.3
DELETE	Delete a specified item from a given file	–
DIM	Declare a dimensioned array	§8.1.4
ECHO ON/OFF	Control whether characters entered on the keyboard will appear on the screen	§8.2.3
ENTER	Transfer control to a CATALOGed program	–
END	End a control structure such as IF-THEN-ELSE	§8.4.1
EXECUTE	Pass a command to the TCL interpreter	§8.3.3
EQUATE	Give a variable an alias, for example "EQUATE This TO That" makes "This" and "That" alternative names for the same variable	–
FOOTING	Specifies line to appear at the bottom of every page of a report written with the statement "PRINT ON 0"	§8.2.2–
FOR	Start of FOR-NEXT control structure	§8.4.3
GOSUB	Transfer control to subroutine in same item	§8.6.1
GOTO	Transfer control to labelled statement	§8.2.3
HEADING	Specifies the line to appear at the top of every page of a report written with the statement "PRINT ON 0"	§8.2.2
IF	Start of IF-THEN-ELSE control structure	§8.4.1
IN	Assign to a variable the character that *exactly* corresponds to the key hit	§8.2.3
INPUT	Read the value of a variable from keyboard	§8.2.3
INPUTERR	Display message at bottom of the screen before reading the value of a variable from keyboard	–
INPUTTRAP	GOTO a labelled statement or execute a GOSUB statement if specified characters are read from keyboard	–
INPUTNULL	Specifies a character to be interpreted as the null string on subsequent INPUTs	–

Table A3.1   Pick BASIC statements (continued)

Statement	Purpose	See
LOCATE	Find a string in a dynamic array	§8.5.2
LOCK	Set a semaphore ('execution lock')	–
LOOP	Start of a LOOP-UNTIL/WHILE-REPEAT control structure	§8.4.3
MAT	(i) Declare a dimensioned array in a CALL statement; (ii) assign values to all elements of a dimensioned array, e.g., "MAT Y=∅" assigns ∅ to all elements of the array Y	§8.6.2
MATREAD	Read value of a dimensioned array from a file	–
MATREADU	Read value of a dimensioned array from a file and lock the item read	–
MATWRITE	Write value of a dimensioned array to a file and clear any lock	–
MATWRITEU	Write value of a dimensioned array to a file but do not clear lock	–
NEXT	End of FOR-NEXT control structure	§8.4.3
NULL	Dummy statement, does nothing	§8.3
ON	Starts ON-GOTO/GOSUB control structure	§8.4.2
OPEN	Open a file	§8.3
PAGE	Start a new page on report ∅ and optionally set page number	–
PRECISION	Declares number of decimal places with which a variable is to be stored	–
PRINT	Print variable(s) on screen or printer	§8.2.2
PRINTER ON/OFF	Direct output from PRINT statements to printer or screen	§8.2.2
PRINTER CLOSE	Send reports to spooler	§8.2.2
PROCREAD	Read command line which started the PROC from which the program was started	§9.2.4
PROCWRITE	Write value of a variable in the PIB of a calling PROC	–
PROMPT	Set the character with which machine prompts for input	§8.2.3
READ	Read an item in a file into a dynamic array	§8.3.1
READNEXT	Get the next item ID from an active select list	§8.3.3
READT	Read next record from magnetic tape or floppy disk	–
READU	Read an item in a file into a dynamic array and set lock	§8.7
READV	Read an attribute in a file into a dimensioned array	–
READVU	Read an attribute in a file into a dimensioned array and set lock	–
RELEASE	Unlock a specified item in a given file. If no file is specified, all locks set by the program are cleared	–
REM	Introduces a comment statement	§8.1.2

Table A3.1 Pick BASIC statements (continued)

Statement	Purpose	See
REPEAT	End of a LOOP-UNTIL/WHILE-REPEAT control structure	§8.4.3
RETURN	Transfer control from a subroutine back to calling segment	§8.6.1
REWIND	Rewind tape	–
RQM	Pause for a specified number of seconds or until a specified time	–
SELECT	(i) As TCL verb "SELECT" but no selection criteria may be specified; (ii) form a select list of the attributes in a dynamic array	–
SLEEP	Same as RQM	–
STOP	Finish execution and return control to TCL or calling PROC	§8.6.3
SUBROUTINE	First statement in a CATALOGed subroutine	§8.6.2
UNLOCK	Clear one or all semaphores ('execution locks') set by LOCK	–
UNTIL	Part of FOR-UNTIL or LOOP-UNTIL control structures	§8.4
WEOF	Write end of file mark on magnetic tape or floppy	–
WHILE	Part of FOR-WHILE or LOOP-WHILE control structures	–
WRITE	Write dynamic array on item in a file and clear any lock	§8.3.2
WRITET	Write the value of a variable on magnetic tape to form a single data block	–
WRITEU	Write a dynamic array on an item in a file but do not clear lock	§8.7
WRITEV	Write the value of a variable on an attribute in an item of a file and clear any lock	§8.7
WRITEVU	Write the value of a variable on an attribute in an item of a file but do not clear lock	–

Table A3.2 Pick BASIC intrinsic functions

Function	Purpose	See
@()	Generates code to position cursor on screen	§8.2.1
ABS()	Returns absolute value of a variable	§8.5
ALPHA()	Returns 1 if its argument contains only letters of the alphabet	§8.4.4
ASCII()	Returns the character which occupies the position in the ASCII table that its argument does in the EBCDIC table	–
CHAR()	Returns the character which occupies the position in the table of ASCII characters which is specified by its argument	§8.2.2
COL1()	Returns the position of the character just before the start of the string last found with FIELD	§8.5
COL2()	Returns the position of the character just after the end of the string last found with FIELD	§8.5
COS()	Returns cosine of an argument given in degrees	–
COUNT()	Counts the number of occurrences of one string in another	–
DATE()	Returns current date in Pick internal format	§8.5
DCOUNT()	Returns one plus number COUNT would return	§8.5
DELETE()	Removes an attribute, value or sub-value from a dynamic array	§8.5.1
EBCDIC()	Returns the character which occupies the position in the EBCDIC table that its argument does in the ASCII table	–
EXP()	Returns $e = 2.718\ldots$ raised to the power of its argument	–
EXTRACT()	Returns the value of a specified piece of a dynamic array	–
FIELD()	Searches a string for a sub-string that is bounded by given delimiters	§8.5
ICONV()	Converts a human-readable date or time to Pick internal format	§8.5
INDEX()	Finds a sub-string within a given string	§8.5
INSERT()	Adds a new piece with specified value to a dynamic array and moves old pieces down to make room	§8.5.1
INT()	Returns the integer part of a number	§8.5
LEN()	Returns the number of characters in a string	§8.5
LN()	Returns the natural logarithm of its argument	–
MOD()	Finds the remainder when one number is divided by another	–
NOT()	Changes true Booleans into false and *vice versa*	§8.4.4
NUM()	Returns 1 if its argument has a numeric value, 0 otherwise	§8.4.4
OCONV()	Converts a date or time in Pick internal format into human-readable form	§8.5
PWR()	Raises one number to the power of another	–
REM()	As MOD	–
REPLACE()	Changes the value of a piece of a dynamic array	–

Table A3.2 Pick BASIC intrinsic functions (continued)

Function	Purpose	See
RND()	Returns a random integer between 0 and one less than the value of its argument	–
SEQ()	Returns the position of its argument's first character in the ASCII table—see Appendix 2	§8.2.2
SIN()	Returns the sine of an argument given in degrees	–
SPACE()	Returns a string consisting of a given number of space characters	§8.5
SQRT()	Returns the square root of its argument	–
STR()	Returns a string consisting of a specified number of occurrences of a given string	§8.5
TAN()	Returns the tangent of an argument given in degrees	–
TIME()	Returns current time in Pick internal format	§8.5
TIMEDATE()	Returns current time and date in human-readable form	§8.5
TRIM()	Removes redundant space characters from its argument	–

Appendix 4   Useful BASIC programs

A4.1   Extracting parameters from a command line

```
    SUBROUTINE PARM.FIND(MAT Parm,Nparm)
!
! Returns in Parm(8) the Nparm parameters in the PIB of the Proc that
! started the calling program
!
    DIM Parm(8);!                     Extracts up to 8 parameters
    PROCREAD Line ELSE
        CRT "Error in PARM.FIND: you haven't started me from a PROC!"
        Nparm=0; RETURN
    END
    k=1
    FOR i=1 TO 8 UNTIL k=0
        Parm(i)=FIELD(Line," ",i)
        k=INDEX(Line," ",i)
    NEXT i
    Nparm=i-1
    RETURN
```

A4.2   Cataloguing a BASIC program

Put the following program into the item "CATALOGUE" of your program file
and run it one time by issuing the command "RUN FILENAME CATALOGUE",
where "FILENAME" is the name of the file. (Ignore the error message about
not being started from a PROC that will be generated at this stage.) Then
when you subsequently type at the TCL prompt "CATALOGUE FILENAME PROG"
a PROC "PROG" will be created in your MD which RUNs the program "PROG".
Once PROG has been CATALOGUEd in this way, whenever you enter PROG at the
TCL prompt, your program will be started from a PROC, so you will be able
to use the PROCREAD statement to extract parameters from the command line.
(See the program "PARM.FIND" above.)

```
    DIM Parm(8)
    OPEN 'MD' TO Dict ELSE
        CRT "I can't open your MD."; STOP
    END
    MAT Parm=0; Nparm=0
    CALL PARM.FIND(MAT Parm,Nparm)
    BEGIN CASE
    CASE Nparm=0
        Parm(3)="CATALOGUE"; Parm(2)="PROGRAMS"
    CASE Nparm=1
        CRT "You must specify at least one argument."; STOP
    CASE Nparm=2
        Parm(3)=Parm(2); Parm(2)="PROGRAMS"
    END CASE
    READ Entry FROM Dict,Parm(3) THEN
        IF Entry<1>[1,1]="D" THEN
            CRT "Error! You have a file called ":Parm(3)
            CRT CHAR(7):"Aborted."; STOP
        END
```

```
     END
     Entry=0; Entry<1>="PQ"
     Entry<2>="HRUN ":Parm(2):" ":Parm(3)
     Entry<3>="P"
     WRITE Entry ON Dict,Parm(3)
     STOP
```

A4.3   Creating a dictionary entry

```
!  Program NEW.WORD
!
!  Menu-driven program to create attribute-defining entries in Pick dictionaries.
!  Start the program by entering NEW.WORD and answer the computer's questions.
!
     DIM Title(6),Order(6),Reply(6)
     Title(1)="Attr No"; Title(2)="Heading"; Title(3)="Conversion"
     Title(4)="Correlative"; Title(5)="Justification"; Title(6)="Width"
     Order(1)=2; Order(2)=3; Order(3)=7; Order(4)=8; Order(5)=9; Order(6)=10
!
     PROMPT ""
     CRT @(-1):"            CREATING A DICTIONARY ENTRY"
10   CRT @(-3):@(10,3):"Name of file with data? ":
     INPUT Fname:
     IF Fname="Q" OR Fname="q" THEN STOP
     OPEN 'DICT',Fname TO Dict ELSE
          CRT CHAR(7):@(10,5):"I can't find 'DICT' of ":Fname:"."
          CRT @(10,6):"Please enter a new name or Q to Quit. ":
          GOTO 10
     END
20   Entry=0
     Entry<1>="A"
     Text="What name should I file this under in the dictionary? "
     CRT @(10,5):@(-3):Text:
     INPUT ID:
     CRT @(10,6):"Number of attribute to be described? ":
     INPUT Reply(1):
     CRT @(10,7):"What heading should I use on reports? [":ID:"] ":
     INPUT Reply(2):
     IF Reply(2)="" THEN Reply(2)=ID
     Wide=LEN(Reply(2))+1
     CRT @(10,8):"Is there some conversion I should do on output? (e.g. D) ":
     INPUT Reply(3):
     CRT @(10,9):"If you want to draw on data from other attributes or files,"
     CRT @(10,10):"Enter your correlative here: ":
     INPUT Reply(4)
     LOOP
          CRT @(10,11):"Right, Left, Text, or U (one-line) justification? ":
          INPUT Reply(5)
          Err=(Reply(5)#"R" AND Reply(5)#"L" AND Reply(5)#"T" AND Reply(5)#"U")
     UNTIL NOT(Err) DO
          CRT CHAR(7):@(10,12):"Sorry, but I must have one of R, L, T, or U."
     REPEAT
     Text="Width of space reserved for this word on reports? [":Wide:"] "
     CRT @(10,13):Text:
     INPUT Reply(6):
     IF Reply(6)="" THEN Reply(6)=Wide
!
```

```
LOOP
      CRT @(10,6):@(-3):@(10,7):"My instructions are"
      FOR i=1 TO 6
            CRT @(15,7+i):i,Title(i),Reply(i)
      NEXT i
      CRT @(10,14):"Enter the number of anything you wish to change, ":
      CRT "or 0 to file ":
      INPUT Key,1:
UNTIL Key=0  DO
      CRT @(10,15):Title(Key):" ":
      INPUT Reply(Key)
REPEAT
FOR i=1 TO 6
      Entry<Order(i)>=Reply(i)
NEXT i
WRITE Entry ON Dict,ID
CRT @(10,17):ID:" written on dictionary of ":Fname
CRT @(10,18):"Do you want to make another dictionary entry? (Y/N) ":
INPUT Key,1:
IF Key="Y" OR Key="y" THEN GOTO 20
STOP
```

A4.4 Creating a user

This program will create a new synonym user. You have to be logged on as
SYSPROG to use it. COMPILE and CATALOG the program. Then simply type
"CREATE-USER" at TCL and answer the computer's questions.

```
! Program CREATE-USER
!
! Creates a new user
!
      CRT "USER NAME":
      INPUT Username
      CRT "L/RET CODE(S)":
      INPUT Lret
      CRT "L/UPD CODE(S)":
      INPUT Lupd
      CRT "PASSWORD":
      ECHO OFF
      INPUT Password
      ECHO ON
      CRT "PRIVILEGES":
      INPUT Privileges
      IF Privileges="" THEN Privileges="SYS0"
      CRT "MASTER DICTIONARY":
      INPUT Md
!
      OPEN "","SYSTEM" TO System THEN
            READ Useritem FROM System,Username THEN
                  CRT "A user already exists with that user name"
            END ELSE
                  Useritem=0
                  Useritem<1>="Q"
                  Useritem<2>=Md
                  Useritem<6>=Privileges
                  Useritem<7>="L"
```

```
!               WRITE Useritem ON System,Username
!
               DATA "4"; DATA "I"
               DATA Lret; DATA Lupd
               DATA ""; DATA "FI"
               EXECUTE "ED SYSTEM ":Username CAPTURING Garbage
!
               DATA Username
               DATA Password
               EXECUTE "PASSWORD" CAPTURING Garbage
               CRT "User '":Username:"' created.  MD is ":Md
      END
   END ELSE
      CRT "Unable to open SYSTEM"
   END
   STOP
```

A4.5 Assigning keys to a user

If at the TCL prompt you enter KEYS BINNEY ABC B this program KEYS will
give the user BINNEY the three retrieval keys A, B and C and the single update
key B.

```
! Program KEYS
!
!                           First get parameters from command line
   DIM Parm(8)
   PROMPT ""; MAT Parm=""; Nparm=0
   CALL PARM.FIND(MAT Parm,Nparm)
   User=Parm(2); Retrieval=Parm(3); Update=Parm(4)
!
!                           Adjust attributes 5 and 6
!
   OPEN "","SYSTEM" TO SysDict THEN
      READ Account FROM SysDict,User THEN
         IF Account<5>#"" OR Account<6>#"" THEN
            CRT "This account now has keys: ":
            CRT Account<5>:", ":Account<6>
         END ELSE
            CRT "This account currently has no keys."
         END
         CRT "You want this account to have keys: ":
         CRT Retieval:", ":Update:" ? (y/n) ":
         INPUT Key,1
         IF Key="y" OR Key="Y" THEN
            DATA "5"; DATA "DE2"; DATA "F"
            DATA "4"; DATA "I"
            DATA Retrieval; DATA Update
            DATA ""; DATA "FI"
            EXECUTE "ED SYSTEM ":User CAPTURING Garbage
            CRT "Keys assigned."
         END ELSE
            CRT "Aborted."
         END
      END ELSE
         PRINT "Can't find account entry for user ":User
      END
```

```
    END ELSE
          CRT "Can't open system dictionary."
    END
    STOP
```

A4.6   Discovering what characters your keys produce

Sometimes you need to know what character (or sequence of characters) is
sent to the computer by each of your terminal's keys. The following little
program will enable you to discover this information without poring for hours
over the (probably unintelligible) manual for your terminal. Just start up the
program, hit a key and note down the number(s) displayed on the screen—
this is the ASCII code(s) of the character(s) produced by the key you hit. You
exit from the program by doing Ctrl-X.

```
! Program READ.KEYS
!
! Prints ASCII codes of character sequence generated by any key.
! Exit program with Ctrl-X
!
    ECHO OFF
    LOOP
          Old=TIME()
          IN Key
          New=TIME()
    UNTIL Key=CHAR(24) DO
          IF (New-Old)>0.2 THEN
                CRT; CRT "The key you just hit produces these characters:"
          END
          i=SEQ(Key)
          CRT SPACE(10):"ASCII code :",i
    REPEAT
    ECHO ON
    STOP
```

A4.7   Resizing a file

In §7.5.2 we explain why it is sometimes necessary to resize a file. The following program makes it easy to modify a file's file-defining item so that the
next time the file is restored from a backup it will go onto the disk with a
new mod and sep (see §7.5.2). You must be logged on as SYSPROG. Then type
"RESIZE" at TCL and answer the machine's questions.

```
! Program RESIZE
!
! Changes attribute 13 of a file-defining item to resize file at next restore.
!
    PROMPT ""
  1 CRT "Name of file you want me to resize? (Q to quit) ":
    INPUT File
    IF File = "q" OR File = "Q" THEN STOP
    CRT "Account name of MD in which file is defined? (Q to quit) ":
    INPUT Account
```

```
IF Account = "q" OR Account = "Q" THEN STOP
OPEN "",Account TO Dictionary ELSE; CRT "I cannot open MD"; STOP; END
READ Defining FROM Dictionary,File ELSE
     CRT "I cannot find a file-defining item ":File
     GOTO 1
END
CRT "The mod and sep of this file are currently ":
CRT Defining<3>:" and ":Defining<4>
CRT "What should the new mod be? [":Defining<3>:"] ":
INPUT Mod
IF Mod="" THEN Mod=Defining<3>
CRT "What should the new sep be? [":Defining<4>:"] ":
INPUT Sep
IF Sep="" THEN Sep=Defining<4>
CRT "After the file has been restored its mod and sep will be ":
CRT Mod:" and ":Sep
Defining<13>="(":Mod:",":Sep:")"
WRITE Defining ON Dictionary,File
STOP
```

Appendix 5   The PickED screen editor

A5.1   Installing PickED

Operating systems are usually sold with a line editor but no screen editor. One reason for this is the following. A convenient screen editor will invariably employ keys other than the ordinary typewriter keys (the letter keys, keys for return, shift and punctuation marks). As explained in §7.10, the same non-typewriter key on two different terminals will generally generate two different ASCII codes. Hence before you can use a screen editor on a new terminal type you must first "customize" the editor by telling it what ASCII codes are generated by various non-typewriter keys.

As listed in this appendix and shipped on floppy disks, PickED is customized for terminals conforming to DEC VT52 standard (see §7.10 and Table 7.3). Far and away the easiest way to get PickED running is to ensure that your terminal is conforming to the VT52 standard. Then all you have to do is

1. copy the source code into a program file;
2. COMPILE and CATALOGUE the code using the "CATALOGUE" program of Appendix 4.

PickED can then be run by typing at the TCL prompt one of the following:

```
>PICKED FILENAME ITEMNAME
>PICKED ITEMNAME
>PICKED
```

If you are dead-set on using a terminal that is not of type VT52, you'll have to edit PickED's source code—see the section entitled "Customizing PickED" below.

The VT52 standard is rather an old-fashioned one, but a great many machines can conform to it. In particular, any IBM-compatible PC running Kermit conforms to this standard with minor modifications and we here explain how to use PickED on such a machine. If you use a true VT52 terminal you will need to reinterpret our instructions as follows:

1: for 'function keys F1–F10' read 'keys 1, 2, . . . , 0 on the numeric keypad;
2: for HOME key read 'key PF1' above the numeric keypad;
3: for END key read 'key PF2' above the numeric keypad;
4: for 'Ctrl-left-arrow' read 'key PF3' above the numeric keypad;
5: for 'Ctrl-right-arrow' read 'key PF4' above the numeric keypad.

A5.2   How to use PickED

When PickED starts up, it first inspects the command line to see whether you have specified the name of a file and the ID of the item in that file which you wish to edit first. If you omit only to name a file, PickED will assume that you wish to edit items in the default file, "PROGRAMS". If you fail to name either a file or an item, you will be asked for the name of the file whose items you wish to edit. Just hit RETURN if you wish to edit items in the file "PROGRAMS".[3] Otherwise enter the name of your chosen file. Next you will be asked for the ID of an item. If PickED cannot find the item you specify, it asks you to confirm that you wish to create a new item. The cursor will now move to the top left corner of the screen with the first 23 attributes of the item displayed below, one attribute per line.

The cursor can be moved with the arrow keys, and text entered with the character keys. The number of the attribute the cursor is on is given at the bottom right corner of the screen. You can move 16 attributes down by hitting the END key and 16 attributes up by hitting the HOME key. Hitting the right-arrow key while holding down the CTRL key moves the cursor one word right, and similarly for the combination Ctrl-left-arrow key. You can get to the beginning of the line with the key combination Ctrl-A and to the end of the line with the combination Ctrl-E.

There are other important CTRL-key combinations:

Push to TCL (Ctrl-P). Doing Ctrl-P will cause your item to disappear from the screen and the usual TCL prompt to appear. In computerese you have 'pushed' to TCL. Actually PickED is still running, but is passing everything you type to the TCL interpreter. So you can, for example, compile and run the program you have just been editing. You return to your editing by typing either "exit" or "EXIT" at the TCL prompt.

You can get back earlier commands (up to 16) by depressing either the up- or down-arrow keys. Each time you use up-arrow you move one command further back into history. Down-arrow reverses the effect of up-arrow. Just hit RETURN when you see the command you want and the TCL interpreter will execute it. Alternatively, you can enter a new command at any stage.

Update-item (Ctrl-U). Before you push to TCL to compile and run your program, you should first write it on the disk. You do this by doing Ctrl-U. PickED will give you a chance to change the ID under which the item you are editing should be filed. Just hit RETURN to file under the ID you originally gave PickED. You can continue editing after writing in the file in this way.

If you decide you don't want to write the item you are working on in the file, you can cancel the whole operation by doing Ctrl-G when PickED is asking you under what ID you wish to file the item. Ctrl-G usually aborts whatever operation you have started if you done when PickED is waiting for input at the bottom of the screen.

Find-item (Ctrl-F). When you are bored with editing an item, you can switch to a new item by doing Ctrl-F. PickED will first ask whether you wish to write the current item on the disk. Then it will ask for the ID of another

---

[3] You can alter the default file name by editing the statement "EQU Default.file TO "PROGRAMS"" at the end of the starred section at the head of PickED's listing.

item. You can go back to where you were before you did Ctrl-F by doing Ctrl-G in reply to either of these requests for input.

Exit (Ctrl-Z).   You quit PickED by doing Ctrl-Z. PickED will ask whether you wish to write on the disk the item you are editing and will then exit to TCL. Ctrl-G aborts this operation too.

Function keys, and cut (Ctrl-W) and yank (Ctrl-Y).   The ten function keys serve to tell PickED to do some definite job.

F1: Delete to end of attribute. Hitting the function key "F1" will erase the contents of the attribute the cursor is sitting on from the cursor to the end of the attribute. If the attribute is null, F1 will eliminate it altogether. You can get what you have just erased back by doing Ctrl-Y ("yank").

F2: Set mark. Hitting F2 causes the words "Mark set" to appear at the bottom of the screen. The significance of this is that PickED has placed an invisible marker at the current position of the cursor. When you move the cursor this mark stays put. Then you can delete the text between the current cursor position and the invisible mark by doing Ctrl-W ("cut"). You get what you have deleted back by doing Ctrl-Y.

F3: Delete from start of word to cursor. Hitting F3 erases from the position of the cursor to the next space to the left of the cursor. Thus if the cursor is sitting on a space just after a word, F3 will erase that word. What you have just deleted in this way can be restored by the key-combination Ctrl-Y.

F4: Delete to end of word. Hitting F4 deletes from the cursor to the next space to the *right* of the cursor. Again Ctrl-Y will undo the effect of hitting F4.

F5: Backward search. When you hit F5 PickED asks for a string. Enter a string and PickED will search backwards through the item starting from the previous attribute looking for the string you have entered. If it finds the string in some attribute, it moves the cursor to that attribute.

F6: Forward search. The F6 key works much the same way as F5, except that PickED searches forwards for the string you enter.

F7: Go to top of item. Hitting F7 moves the cursor to the first attribute of the item.

F8: Go to end of item. Hitting F8 moves the cursor to the last attribute of the item.

F9: Go to attribute. When you hit F9 PickED will ask at the bottom of the screen for an attribute number. When you enter a number, PickED will move the cursor to that attribute. You can get to the beginning of the item by entering 1.

F10: Delete current character. The F10 key deletes the character on which the cursor sits.

You can transfer material between items as follows. Use the F2 key and the cursor to mark off the material you want to move. Then use `Ctrl-W` to cut[4] this material (and immediately restore it with `Ctrl-Y` if you want to have the material in both items). Now your material is in PickED's "kill buffer". Do `Ctrl-F` to bring the second item onto the screen. Move the cursor to the place you wish to insert the transferred material, do `Ctrl-Y` and *presto*, the material appears in the new item.

A5.3   How PickED works

PickED's source code is listed below. The program starts by defining the characters generated by special keys such as the function and arrow keys. The settings given are for the VT52 terminal standard. Then the program initializes the variables that record how your work is stored. There are three levels of storage:

(i) the entire item being edited is stored in the dynamic array `Item`, which has `Tfile` attributes;

(ii) in the interests of speed of access `Item`'s attributes from `Row0` to `Row1` inclusive are additionally stored in a dimensioned array `Work`;

(iii) `Work`'s elements from `Top` to `Bottom` are displayed on the screen.

One should think of the array `Work` as a window, up to 75 attributes long, which slides up and down the material of `Item`, while the screen is a window `Nscreen` attributes long which slides up and down `Work`. This arrangement minimizes the number of occasions on which all `Item`'s material has to be rearranged. Subroutine 1200 copies material from `Item` to `Work` while subroutine 1400 copies material from `Work` back into `Item`. Subroutine 1100 moves the window formed by the screen up and down `Work`.

When you give an item ID, PickED loads that item into `Item` and the first part of `Item` into `Work`. Subroutine 800 then displays a screen-full of `Work`. That done the program starts executing the main loop, which runs between the two lines of plus signs in the listing. After displaying the number of the attribute on which the cursor sits, the machine waits for a key to be input. Once a key has been read, the machine first asks whether it is a special key, such as `Ctrl`-right-arrow, a carriage return, a function key or whatever. If the key read proves not to be a special key, the corresponding character is simply added to the attribute on which the cursor sits at the current cursor position. Otherwise the cursor is moved or some subroutine is invoked to move right one word, move down a line or whatever.

A complication arises from the fact that the cursor and function keys generate more than one ASCII character every time you hit the key. On a VT52 terminal the first character generated by any of these keys is ASCII 27, which in the program is assigned to the variable `Esc.key`. So PickED first asks whether the first character read (called `Key.a`) equals `Esc.key`. If it is,

---

[4] Alternatively, the material may be cut with F1, F3 or F4.

a second character is read into the variable Key.b. If this proves to be equal to the variable Func.key, then you have hit a function key and the machine must determine which function key you hit by reading a third character into Key.c. What happens next depends on whether Key.c proves to be equal to the variable F1, or F2 etc.

On a VT52 terminal the arrow keys and the HOME and END keys generate two characters each. The first character is always the character assigned to Esc.key. So if the character first read (Key.a) equals Esc.key but the next character read, Key.b proves not to be equal to the variable Func.key, the machine looks to see if Key.b is equal to Right.key or Left.key etc, and moves the cursor appropriately.

When the machine has decided what to do with the key you hit, it does it and returns to the attribute labelled 20 just below the first line of plus signs, reads another character into Key.a and the whole process repeats itself.

A5.4   Customizing PickED

The object of this subsection is explain how to adapt PickED to run on a terminal that does not conform to DEC's VT52 standard.

Your first step should be to determine what ASCII character(s) each of your terminal's keys generates. You may be able to discover this information from an appropriate manual. Failing this, use the Pick BASIC program "READ.KEYS" listed in Appendix 4. You need to know the codes of ten 'function keys', the four 'arrow keys' that move the cursor, the HOME key and the END key. As regards the arrow keys, be sure to determine not only the codes generated by hitting just each arrow key, but also the codes generated by hitting the left- and right-arrow keys while holding down the CTRL key.

The next stage is simple if your function keys each generate three characters, of the form Esc.key:Func.key:Key.c. In this case you need simply to

1. change the numbers 27 and 63 in the starred section at the start of PickED's listing to the ASCII codes on your machine of Esc.key and Func.key respectively, and
2. change the assignments F1="q" etc. in the same section so that F1 is assigned whatever value Key.c takes when you hit F1, and so on for all the function keys.

Similarly, life is simple if your arrow keys generate two characters each of the form Esc.key:Key.b, since then you have only to change the assignments in PickED's starred section of the variables Left.key, Right.key, etc., to the values taken by Key.b on your machine.

If your function keys generate more or less than 3 characters, or your arrow keys generate other than two characters each, you will have to make some less trivial modifications to PickED's logic.

If you don't like the way jobs have been assigned to the different function keys, it is easy to redistribute the jobs; all you need to do is change, say, F1 to F2 in the statement

```
    CASE Key.c=F1;!                          F1: Delete to end line
```

and hitting F2 rather than F1 will delete to the end of the line. Similar considerations apply to redistributions of jobs amongst the `Ctrl`-keys.

A5.5   PickED's source-code

```
!    Important variables:
!
!    Nscreen              Number of lines used for text on screen
!    Item<>               Dynamic array for item being edited
!    Tfile                End of item being edited is in Item<Tfile>
!    Tlength              Total number of attributes in item if saved now
!    Work(3*Nscreen+3)    Dimensioned array for text on and near screen
!    Tlines               Last used line of Work is Work(Tlines)
!    Row0, Row1           Attribute numbers of first and last lines read into Work
!    Top, Bot             Work(Top), Work(Bot) first and last lines on screen
!    Work.no              Cursor on line stored in Work(Work.no)=Cline
!    L.Cline              L.Cline=LEN(Cline)
!    Colm, Row            Cursor on Colm th column and Row th line down
!    File, Fname          File "File" opened to Fname
!    ID                   Name of item in file being edited
!    Save$                Last string killed and ready to be yanked
!    Save<>               Last block of text killed and ready to be yanked
!    Modify               Modify=0 if Item<> is up-to-date, otherwise 1
!
      DIM Parm(6),Work(75),Cmnd(16)
!*********************** VT52 key settings ***********************
      EQU Esc.key TO CHAR(27), Abort.key TO CHAR(7)
      EQU Home.key TO "H", End.key TO "K"
      EQU PF1 TO "P", PF2 TO "Q", PF3 TO "R", PF4 TO "S"
      EQU Up.key TO "A", Down.key TO "B"
      EQU Left.key TO "D", Right.key TO "C"
      EQU Ctrl.left TO CHAR(240), Ctrl.right TO CHAR(241)
      EQU Erase TO CHAR(8), Del TO CHAR(127)
      EQU Func.key TO "?"
      EQU F1 TO "q", F2 TO "r", F3 TO "s", F4 TO "t", F5 TO "u"
      EQU F6 TO "v", F7 TO "w", F8 TO "x", F9 TO "y", F10 TO "p"
      EQU Default.file TO "PROGRAMS"
!*****************************************************************
      PROMPT ""; ECHO OFF
      CRT @(-1):@(24,10):"        PickED Screen Editor"
      CRT @(24,12):"(C) 1990, J.J.Binney & M.E.J.Newman"
!
!                              Initialize file vars
      Tfile=1; Tlines=1; Row0=1; Row1=1; Nscreen=23
      Top=1; Bot=1; Modify=0; Search=""
      Bot=1; Saved.word=""; Save=0; Nsave=0; Work.no=1
      Ncomm=0; Tcomm=0; Maxcomm=16
      FOR i=1 TO 75; Work(i)=""; NEXT i
!
!                              Read any filename/ID from command line
```

```
        Nparm=0; k=1
        PROCREAD Line THEN
              LOOP
                    Nparm=Nparm+1; Parm(Nparm)=FIELD(Line," ",Nparm)
              UNTIL k=0 DO
                    k=INDEX(Line," ",Nparm)
              REPEAT
              IF Nparm<4 THEN File=Default.file
              IF Nparm=4 THEN; File=Parm(2); ID=Parm(3); END
              IF Nparm=3 THEN ID=Parm(2)
        END ELSE
              Nparm=1
        END
10      IF Nparm<2 THEN
              CRT @(0,Nscreen):@(-4):" File? [":Default.file:"] ":
              Nlett=180; GOSUB 1800; File=Key
              IF File="" THEN File=Default.file
        END
        OPEN '',File TO Fname ELSE
              CRT @(30,Nscreen):"Can't open ":File
              Nparm=1; GOTO 10
        END
        GOSUB 700
!
! +++++++++++++++++++++++++ Start of main loop +++++++++++++++++++++++++
!
20      Old.no=Line.no; Line.no=Row0-1+Work.no
        Cline=Work(Work.no); L.Cline=LEN(Cline)
        Tlength=Row0-1+Tlines+Tfile-Row1
        IF Old.no#Line.no THEN
              CRT @(75,Nscreen):@(-4):Line.no:
        END
        CRT @(Colm-1,Row-1):
        IN Key.a
        IF Key.a=CHAR(28) THEN Key.a=CHAR(252);!        Sub-value mark
        IF Key.a=CHAR(29) THEN Key.a=CHAR(253);!        Value mark
        BEGIN CASE
        CASE Key.a=Ctrl.left;!                          Left a word
              GOSUB 900; Colm=Sp
              CRT @(Colm-1,Row-1):
        CASE Key.a=Ctrl.right;!                         Right a word
              GOSUB 950; Colm=Colm+Sp
              CRT @(Colm-1,Row-1):
        CASE Key.a=CHAR(13);!                           Input a CR
              GOSUB 100; Modify=1
        CASE Key.a=Erase;!                              Input a delete
              GOSUB 200
              IF Tlines<=Nscreen AND Row1<Tfile THEN GOSUB 1100
        CASE Key.a=CHAR(1);!                            Beginning line (Ctrl A)
              Colm=1
        CASE Key.a=CHAR(5);!                            End of line (Ctrl E)
              Colm=L.Cline+1
        CASE Key.a=CHAR(6);!                            Find-item (C-F)
              GOSUB 700
        CASE Key.a=CHAR(11);!                           Kill line (C-K)
              GOSUB 300
        CASE Key.a=CHAR(16);!                           Push (C-P)
              GOSUB 1700; GOSUB 800
```

```
    CASE Key.a=CHAR(21);!                            Update-item (C-U)
        GOSUB 600
    CASE Key.a=CHAR(23);!                            Cut (Ctrl W)
        GOSUB 1500
    CASE Key.a=CHAR(25) AND Saved.word="";!          Yank (Ctrl Y)
        GOSUB 1600
    CASE Key.a=CHAR(25);!                            Yank word (Ctrl Y)
        Old.Colm=Colm; K=LEN(Cline)
        L.Saved.word=LEN(Saved.word); Modify=1
        BEGIN CASE
        CASE L.Cline+L.Saved.word<=80;!                      (All on a line)
            Cline=Cline[1,Colm-1]:Saved.word:Cline[Colm,280]
        CASE Colm+L.Saved.word<=80;!                         (On 2 lines)
            GOSUB 100; Colm=280; GOSUB 400; Colm=Old.Colm
            Cline=Cline[1,Colm-1]:Saved.word
        CASE 1;!                                             (On 3 lines)
            GOSUB 100; GOSUB 100; GOSUB 400
            Cline=Saved.word
        END CASE
        Work(Work.no)=Cline; L.Cline=LEN(Cline)
        CRT @(0,Row-1):@(-4):Cline:@(Colm-1,Row-1):
    CASE Key.a=CHAR(26);!                            Exit (C-Z)
        CRT @(0,Nscreen):@(-4):" Write to file? ":
        Nlett=1; GOSUB 1800; IF Scrap=1 THEN GOTO 20
        IF Key="Y" OR Key="y" THEN GOSUB 600
        IF Scrap=1 THEN GOTO 20
        RQM; CRT @(0,Nscreen):@(-4):@(0,Bot):
        ECHO ON
        STOP
    CASE Key.a=Del;!                                 Del key
        GOSUB 250
    CASE Key.a=Esc.key
        IN Key.b
        BEGIN CASE
        CASE Key.b=Func.key;!                   Input a func key
            CRT @(30,Nscreen):@(-4):

            IN Key.c
            BEGIN CASE
            CASE Key.c=F1;!                         F1: Delete to end line
                GOSUB 300
            CASE Key.c=F2;!                         F2: Set mark
                Mark.line=Line.no
                Mark.colm=Colm
                CRT @(30,Nscreen):"Mark set     ":
            CASE Key.c=F3;!                         F3: Delete left word
                Modify=1; GOSUB 900
                IF Sp>1 THEN
                    Saved.word=Cline[Sp,Colm-Sp]
                    Cline=Cline[1,Sp-1]:Cline[Colm,280]
                END ELSE
                    Saved.word=Cline[1,Colm]
                    Cline=Cline[Colm,280]
                END
                Work(Work.no)=Cline
                L.Cline=LEN(Cline); Colm=Sp
                CRT @(0,Row-1):@(-4):Cline:
            CASE Key.c=F4;!                         F4: Delete right word
```

```
                    Modify=1
                    Sp=INDEX(Cline[Colm+1,28Ø]," ",1)
                    IF Sp>Ø THEN
                            Saved.word=Cline[Colm,Sp]
                            Cline=Cline[1,Colm-1]:Cline[Colm+Sp,28Ø]
                    END ELSE
                            Saved.word=Cline[Colm,28Ø]
                            Cline=Cline[1,Colm-1]
                    END
                    Work(Work.no)=Cline
                    L.Cline=LEN(Cline)
                    CRT @(Ø,Row-1):@(-4):Cline:
            CASE Key.c=F5 OR Key.c=F6;!          F5 or F6: Search
                    CRT @(3Ø,Nscreen):@(-4):
                    IF Key.c=F6 THEN
                            L1=Line.no+1; L2=Tlength; Pas=1
                            CRT "Forward-find string: [":Search:"] ":
                    END ELSE
                            L1=Line.no-1; L2=1; Pas=-1
                            CRT "Backward-find string: [":Search:"] ":
                    END
                    Nlett=18Ø; GOSUB 18ØØ; IF Scrap=1 THEN GOTO 2Ø
                    IF Key#"" THEN Search=Key
                    GOSUB 14ØØ;!                      (Write to Item)
                    Col=Ø
                    FOR Lno=L1 TO L2 STEP Pas UNTIL Col>Ø
                            Col=INDEX(Item<Lno>,Search,1)
                    NEXT i
                    IF Col=Ø THEN
                            CRT CHAR(7):@(3Ø,Nscreen):@(-4):
                            CRT "Failing search for: ":Search:
                    END ELSE
                            Line.no=Lno-Pas; Colm=Col; GOSUB 12ØØ
                    END
            CASE Key.c=F7;!                   F7: Goto top
                    Diff=2-(RowØ+Work.no); GOSUB 1ØØØ
            CASE Key.c=F8;!                   F8: Goto end
                    Diff=1ØØØØ; GOSUB 1ØØØ
            CASE Key.c=F9;!                   F9: Goto attribute
                    CRT @(3Ø,Nscreen):
                    CRT "Goto attribute? ":
                    Nlett=18Ø; GOSUB 18ØØ; IF Scrap=1 THEN GOTO 2Ø
                    Diff=Key-(RowØ+Work.no-1); GOSUB 1ØØØ
            CASE Key.c=F1Ø;!                  F1Ø: Del current character
                    GOSUB 25Ø
            END CASE
                                    Input a move key

    CASE Key.b=Left.key AND Colm>1;!                   Left
            Colm=Colm-1
    CASE Key.b=Left.key AND Colm<=1
            IF Work.no>1 THEN
                    Colm=28Ø; GOSUB 4ØØ
            END
    CASE Key.b=Right.key AND Colm<=L.Cline;!     Right
            Colm=Colm+1
    CASE Key.b=Right.key AND Colm>L.Cline
            IF Work.no<Tlines THEN Colm=1
```

```
                GOSUB 500
          CASE Key.b=Up.key;!                          Up
                GOSUB 400
          CASE Key.b=Down.key;!                        Down
                GOSUB 500
          CASE Key.b=Home.key OR Key.b=PF1;!           Page up
                Diff=-16;GOSUB 1000
          CASE Key.b=End.key OR Key.b=PF2;!            Page down
                Diff=16;GOSUB 1000
          CASE Key.b=PF3;!                             Left a word
                GOSUB 900; Colm=Sp
                CRT @(Colm-1,Row-1):
          CASE Key.b=PF4;!                             Right a word
                GOSUB 950; Colm=Colm+Sp
                CRT @(Colm-1,Row-1):
          END CASE
     CASE SEQ(Key.a)<32;!                   Unauthorized control character
          CRT CHAR(7):
     CASE 1;!                               Adding something
          Modify=1
          IF Colm=L.Cline+1 THEN;!               put on end
                Cline=Cline:Key.a
          END ELSE;!                             add to middle
                Cline=Cline[1,Colm-1]:Key.a:Cline[Colm,280]
          END
          Colm=Colm+1
          L.Cline=L.Cline+1
          IF L.Cline>75 THEN CRT CHAR(7):
          CRT @(Colm-2,Row-1):Cline[Colm-1,280]:
          Work(Work.no)=Cline
     END CASE
     GOTO 20
!
! ++++++++++++++++++++++ End of main loop +++++++++++++++++++++++++
!
100  NULL;!                                   On a carriage return
     Work(Work.no)=Cline[1,Colm-1]
!                                             Move later lines down
     IF Work.no<Tlines THEN
          FOR i=1 TO Tlines-Work.no
                Work(Tlines-i+2)=Work(Tlines-i+1)
          NEXT i
     END
     Tlines=Tlines+1
     Work.no=Work.no+1; Line.no=Line.no+1
!                                             New line balance of old
     IF Colm<L.Cline+1 THEN
          Cline=Cline[Colm,280]
     END ELSE
          Cline=""
     END
     Work(Work.no)=Cline
     CRT @(Colm-1,Row-1):@(-4):
     L.Cline=L.Cline-Colm+1
     Colm=1; Row=Row+1
     IF Row>Nscreen-3 OR Tlines>=3*Nscreen THEN
          GOSUB 1100
     END ELSE
```

```
                Bot=Bot+1; IF Bot-Top+1>Nscreen THEN Bot=Bot-1
                RowP=Row-1
                CRT @(Ø,RowP):
                FOR i=Work.no TO Bot
                      CRT @(Ø,RowP):Work(i):@(-4):
                      RowP=RowP+1
                NEXT i
        END
        RETURN
200   NULL;!                                  Last input a delete
      IF Colm>1 THEN
            Modify=1; Colm=Colm-1
            IF Colm>1 THEN
                  Cline=Cline[1,Colm-1]:Cline[Colm+1,28Ø]
            END ELSE
                  Cline=Cline[2,28Ø]
            END
            Work(Work.no)=Cline
            CRT @(Colm-1,Row-1):Cline[Colm,28Ø]:" ":
      END ELSE;!                              Move up to prev line
            IF Work.no>1 THEN
                  Modify=1; Work.no=Work.no-1; Row=Row-1
                  Tlines=Tlines-1
                  IF Bot>Tlines THEN Bot=Tlines
                  Colm=LEN(Work(Work.no))+1
                  Work(Work.no)=Work(Work.no):Cline
                  Cline=Work(Work.no)
                  L.Cline=LEN(Cline)
                  RowP=Row
                  CRT @(Ø,RowP-1):@(-3):
                  IF Work.no<Tlines THEN
                        FOR i=Work.no+1 TO Tlines
                              Work(i)=Work(i+1)
                        NEXT i
                        FOR i=Work.no TO Bot
                              CRT @(Ø,RowP-1):Work(i):
                              RowP=RowP+1
                        NEXT i
                  END ELSE
                        CRT @(Ø,Row-1):Cline:
                  END
            END
            IF Row<3 AND (Top>1 OR RowØ>1) THEN GOSUB 11ØØ
      END
      RETURN
250   NULL;!                                  Delete character cursor is on
      IF Colm<L.Cline+1 THEN
            Modify=1
            IF Colm<L.Cline THEN
                  Cline=Cline[1,Colm-1]:Cline[Colm+1,28Ø]
            END ELSE
                  Cline=Cline[1,Colm-1]
            END
            Work(Work.no)=Cline
            CRT @(Colm-1,Row-1):Cline[Colm,28Ø]:" ":
      END
      RETURN
300   NULL;!                                  Kill line
```

```
        IF Cline="" THEN
             GOSUB 200; Colm=1; GOSUB 500
        END ELSE
             Modify=1; Saved.word=Cline[Colm,280]
             Work(Work.no)=Cline[1,Colm-1]
             CRT @(Colm-1,Row-1):@(-4):
        END
        RETURN
400     NULL;!                                          Up
        IF Work.no=1 AND Top=1 AND Row0=1 THEN RETURN
        Work.no=Work.no-1
        Cline=Work(Work.no)
        L.Cline=LEN(Cline)
        Row=Row-1
        IF Colm>L.Cline+1 THEN Colm=L.Cline+1
        IF Row<3 AND (Top>1 OR Row0>1) THEN GOSUB 1100
        RETURN
500     NULL;!                                          Down
        IF Work.no=Tlines AND Row1=Tfile THEN RETURN
        Work.no=Work.no+1
        Cline=Work(Work.no)
        L.Cline=LEN(Cline)
        Row=Row+1
        IF Colm>L.Cline+1 THEN Colm=L.Cline+1
        IF Row1=Tfile AND Bot=Tlines THEN RETURN
        IF Row>Nscreen-3 THEN GOSUB 1100
        RETURN
600     NULL;!                                          Update-item
        CRT @(0,Nscreen):@(-4):@(1,Nscreen):"Item? [":ID:"] ":
        Nlett=1; GOSUB 1800; IF Scrap=1 THEN RETURN
        IF Key#"" THEN ID=Key
        CRT "  Writing ":ID:" ....":
        GOSUB 1400
        WRITE Item ON Fname,ID
        CRT @(0,Nscreen):@(-4):@(1,Nscreen):ID:" written":
        RETURN
700     NULL;!                                          Find-item
        IF Work(Work.no)#"" OR Tlines#1 THEN
             CRT @(0,Nscreen):@(-4):" Write to file? ":
             Nlett=1; GOSUB 1800; IF Scrap=1 THEN RETURN
             IF Key="Y" OR Key="y" THEN GOSUB 600
             IF Scrap=1 THEN RETURN
        END
  730   IF Nparm=1 THEN
             CRT @(0,Nscreen):@(-4):" Item to read? ":
             Nlett=180; GOSUB 1800; IF Scrap=1 THEN RETURN
             ID=Key
        END
        Nparm=1; Item=0; Top=1; Colm=1; Row=1; Row0=1
        Line.no=1; Work.no=1; Mark.line=1; Mark.colm=1
        READ Item FROM Fname,ID THEN
             Tfile=DCOUNT(Item,CHAR(254)); GOSUB 1200
        END ELSE
             CRT @(60,Nscreen):@(-4):@(60,Nscreen):"New item? ":
             Nlett=1; GOSUB 1800
             IF Key="N" OR Key="n" THEN GOTO 730
             Work(1)=""
             Tlines=1;Tfile=1
```

```
              Row1=1;Bot=1
              CRT @(Ø,Ø):@(-3):
      END
      CRT @(Ø,Nscreen):"Editing ":File:" ":ID:@(-4):@(Ø,Ø):
      RETURN
800   NULL;!                                        Display Work
      CRT @(Ø,Ø):@(-3):
      RowP=Ø
      FOR i=Top TO Bot
              CRT @(Ø,RowP):Work(i):
              RowP=RowP+1
      NEXT i
      CRT @(Colm-1,Row-1):
      Cline=Work(Work.no)
      CRT @(Ø,Nscreen):"Editing ":File:" ":ID:@(-4):@(Ø,Ø):
      RETURN
900   NULL;!                                  Find space to left of cursor
      Sp=1
      Nspace=1
      LOOP
              Sp1=INDEX(Cline," ",Nspace)
              IF Sp1=Ø THEN Sp1=28Ø
      UNTIL Colm<=Sp1 DO
              Sp=Sp1
              Nspace=Nspace+1
      REPEAT
      RETURN
  950 NULL;!                                 Find space to right of cursor
      Sp=INDEX(Cline[Colm+1,28Ø]," ",1)
      IF Sp=Ø THEN Sp=LEN(Cline[Colm,28Ø])
      RETURN
1000  NULL;!                                 Home or end key or goto line
      Work.no=Work.no+Diff
      IF Work.no+RowØ-1<1 THEN Work.no=2-RowØ
      IF Work.no+RowØ-1>Tlength THEN Work.no=Tlength-RowØ+1
      GOSUB 1100
      RETURN
1100  NULL;!                                 Centre Line.no within screen
      Old.Top=Top
      Top=Work.no-11
      Shift=Top-Old.Top
      IF Top<1 OR Top>2*Nscreen THEN
              Move=Shift
              IF Move<Ø AND Move>-Nscreen THEN Move=Move-Nscreen
              IF Move>Ø AND Move<Nscreen THEN Move=Move+Nscreen
              GOSUB 13ØØ;!                   (Shift window in file)
              Top=Work.no-11
              IF Top<1 THEN Top=1
      END
      Bot=Top+Nscreen-1
      IF Bot>Tlines AND Tlines>=Nscreen THEN
              Shift=Bot-Tlines
              Top=Top-Shift; Bot=Bot-Shift
      END
      IF Bot>Tlines THEN Bot=Tlines
      Row=Work.no-Top+1
      K=LEN(Work(Work.no)); IF Colm>K THEN Colm=K+1
      GOSUB 8ØØ
```

```
      RETURN
1200 NULL;!                                        Copy from Item to Work
!                                                  s.t. cursor on Line.no
     Row0=Line.no-11; IF Row0<1 THEN Row0=1
     Row1=Row0+INT(5*Nscreen/2)-1; IF Row1>Tfile THEN Row1=Tfile
     Tlines=Row1-Row0+1
     Row=Line.no-Row0+1
     Top=1; Work.no=Row
     Bot=Nscreen; IF Bot-Top+1>Tlines THEN Bot=Tlines
     FOR i=Row0 TO Row1
          Work(i-Row0+1)=Item<i>
     NEXT i
     Modify=0; GOSUB 800
     RETURN
1300 NULL;!                                        Move window Move lines down file
     IF Modify=1 THEN GOSUB 1400;!                 (Go write window to Item)
     BEGIN CASE
     CASE Move>0;!                                 (Move down file)
          IF Tfile-Row1<Move THEN Move=Tfile-Row1
     CASE Move<0
          IF Move<1-Row0 THEN Move=1-Row0
     END CASE
     Work.no=Work.no-Move
     Row0=Row0+Move
     Row1=Row0+INT(5*Nscreen/2)
     IF Row1>Tfile THEN Row1=Tfile
     Tlines=Row1-Row0+1
     IF Work.no>Tlines THEN Work.no=Tlines
     FOR i=1 TO Tlines
          Work(i)=Item<Row0+i-1>
     NEXT i
     RETURN
1400 NULL;!                                        Copy Work into Item.
     BEGIN CASE;!                                  1) Move residual of file
!                                                     either down or up
     CASE Tlines>Row1-Row0+1 AND Tfile>Row1;!      (a) Lines added but not eof
          Extra=Tlines-(Row1-Row0+1)
          FOR i=1 TO Extra
               Item=INSERT(Item,Row0;" ")
          NEXT i
          Tfile=Tfile+Extra
     CASE Tlines<Row1-Row0+1 AND Tfile>Row1;!      (b) Subtract lines but not eof
          Extra=(Row1-Row0+1)-Tlines
          FOR i=1 TO Extra
               Item=DELETE(Item,Row0)
          NEXT i
          Tfile=Tfile-Extra
     CASE Tfile<=Row1;!                            (c) Nothing after Work
          Take=Tfile-(Row0+Tlines-1)
          IF Take>0 THEN
               FOR i=Tfile TO Tfile-Take+1 STEP -1
                    Item=DELETE(Item,i)
               NEXT i
          END
          Tfile=Row0+Tlines-1
     END CASE
     FOR i=1 TO Tlines;!                           2) Copy from Work to Item
          Item<Row0+i-1>=Work(i)
```

```
        NEXT i
        Row1=Row∅+Tlines-1; Modify=∅
        RETURN
15∅∅ NULL;!                                        Cut
        Saved.word=""
        IF Mark.line<=Line.no THEN
              L1=Mark.line; L2=Line.no; C1=Mark.colm; C2=Colm
        END ELSE
              L2=Mark.line; L1=Line.no; C2=Mark.colm; C1=Colm
        END
        BEGIN CASE
        CASE L1=L2 AND C1#C2
              IF Colm<Mark.colm THEN
                    C1=Colm; C2=Mark.colm
              END ELSE
                    C2=Colm; C1=Mark.colm
              END
              Save<1>=Cline[C1,C2-C1]; Nsave=1
              Cline=Cline[1,C1-1]:Cline[C2,28∅]
              Work(Work.no)=Cline; L.Cline=LEN(Cline)
              Modify=1; Colm=C1; GOSUB 8∅∅
        CASE L1=L2-1
              IF L1#Line.no THEN;!                 (Ensure cursor is at start
                    Colm=C1; GOSUB 4∅∅;!            of section to be cut)
              END
              Save<1>=Cline[Colm,28∅]
              Work(Work.no)=Cline[1,Colm-1]
              GOSUB 5∅∅; Colm=C2;!                  (Move down to end section to cut)
              Save<2>=Cline[1,C2-1]; Nsave=2
              Cline=Cline[C2,28∅]
              Colm=1; GOSUB 2∅∅;!                   (Merge lines with a delete)
        CASE L1<L2-1
              Work(Work.no)=Cline; GOSUB 14∅∅;!     (Update Item)
              IF L2>Tfile THEN L2=Tfile
              Save<1>=Item<L1>[C1,28∅]
              Save<L2-L1+1>=Item<L2>[1,C2-1]
              Item<L1>=Item<L1>[1,C1-1]:Item<L2>[C2,28∅]
              FOR i=2 TO L2-L1
                    Save<i>=Item<L1+i-1>
              NEXT i
              Nsave=L2-L1+1; Cut=L2-L1; Tfile=Tfile-Cut
              FOR i=1 TO Cut
                    Item=DELETE(Item,L1+1)
              NEXT i
              Line.no=L1; Colm=C1; GOSUB 12∅∅
        END CASE
        RETURN
16∅∅ NULL;!                                        Paste
        BEGIN CASE
        CASE Nsave=1
              Cline=Cline[1,Colm-1]:Save<1>:Cline[Colm,28∅]
              L.Cline=LEN(Cline); Work(Work.no)=Cline
              CRT @(∅,Row-1):Cline:@(Colm-1,Row-1):
        CASE Nsave=2
              GOSUB 1∅∅;!                           (Carriage return)
              Work(Work.no)=Save<2>:Work(Work.no)
              Work.no=Work.no-1; Row=Row-1
              Colm=LEN(Work(Work.no))+1
```

```
                Work(Work.no)=Work(Work.no):Save<1>
                GOSUB 800
        CASE Nsave>2
                GOSUB 100
                Line.no=Row0-1+Work.no
                Old.colm=LEN(Work(Work.no-1))+1
                Work(Work.no-1)=Work(Work.no-1):Save<1>
                Work(Work.no)=Save<Nsave>:Work(Work.no)
                GOSUB 1400;!                           (Update Item)
                FOR i=1 TO Nsave-2
                        Item=INSERT(Item,Line.no;Save<Nsave-i>)
                NEXT i
                Tfile=Tfile+Nsave-2
                Line.no=Line.no-1; Colm=Old.colm
                GOSUB 1200
        END CASE
        RETURN
1700 NULL;!                                         Push to TCL
        CRT @(-1):@(0,Nscreen):@(-4):@(30):"PickED TCL Interface":@(0,0):
        LOOP
                CRT ">":
                Nlett=180; GOSUB 1800; Command=Key
                IF Scrap=2 AND Tcomm>0 THEN GOSUB 1750
        UNTIL Command="EXIT" OR Command="exit" DO
                Ncomm=Ncomm+1; IF Ncomm>Maxcomm THEN Ncomm=1
                IF Tcomm<Ncomm THEN Tcomm=Ncomm
                Cmnd(Ncomm)=Command; CRT; ECHO ON
                EXECUTE Command; ECHO OFF
        REPEAT
        RETURN
 1750 NULL
 1755 IF Key.b=Down.key THEN; Pas=1
                END ELSE; Pas=-1; END
        Ncomm=Ncomm+Pas
        IF Ncomm<1 THEN Ncomm=Tcomm
        IF Ncomm>Tcomm THEN Ncomm=1
        CRT @(0):@(-4):">[":Cmnd(Ncomm):"]":
        Nlett=180; GOSUB 1800; Command=Key
        IF Scrap=2 THEN GOTO 1755
        IF Command="" THEN Command=Cmnd(Ncomm)
        RETURN
 1800 NULL;!                                         Input a variable
        Scrap=0; Key=""
        LOOP
                IN Key.a
        UNTIL (Key.a=CHAR(13) OR Key.a=Abort.key OR Key.a=Esc.key) DO
                BEGIN CASE
                CASE Key.a=Erase AND Key#""
                        CRT @(-9):@(-4):
                        Key=Key[1,LEN(Key)-1]
                CASE Key.a#Erase
                        Key=Key:Key.a; CRT Key.a:
                        IF LEN(Key)>Nlett THEN CRT CHAR(7):
                END CASE
        REPEAT
        BEGIN CASE
        CASE Key.a=Abort.key
                Scrap=1; CRT CHAR(7):
```

```
CASE Key.a=Esc.key
     Scrap=2;  IN Key.b
END CASE
RETURN
```

Appendix 6   Obtaining software on floppies

The source code of PickED and of the programs of Appendix 4 can be obtained
in machine readable form by sending (i) a formatted floppy disk, (ii) a cheque
for £5.95 and (iii) a copy of the form below to

>   McGraw-Hill Book Company (UK) Ltd.,
>   Shoppenhangers Road,
>   Maidenhead, Berks SL6 2QL,
>   England.

Neither the publisher nor the authors can engage in correspondence about
this software, which is not warranted to be free of errors. You are welcome
to use, copy and adapt these programs in any way you please, excepting that
PickED may not be reproduced without the copyright notice with which it is
supplied, nor may it be sold.

Name   . . . .

Address   . . . .

             . . . .

             . . . .

             . . . .

The format of the enclosed floppy disk is:			
Size	DOS	Pick	Apple Mac
$5\frac{1}{4}''$ 360 Kb			N.A.
$5\frac{1}{4}''$ 1.2 Mb			N.A.
$3\frac{1}{2}''$ 720 Kb		N.A.	
$3\frac{1}{2}''$ 1.4 Mb		N.A.	

A copy of Kermit will be included in the software supplied on DOS and Apple
Macintosh floppies.

Index

Boldface numbers indicate the pages it will
usually be most profitable to consult first.